FOR LOVE
NOT MONEY

FOR LOVE NOT MONEY

THE SIMON POIDEVIN STORY

an ABC BOOK

AS TOLD TO JIM WEBSTER

Published by ABC Enterprises for the
AUSTRALIAN BROADCASTING CORPORATION
GPO Box 9994 Sydney NSW 2001

Copyright © Simon Poidevin, Jim Webster, 1990

First published 1990 in hardback
Reprinted September 1990
This paperback edition first published April 1991
Reprinted and updated April 1992

This book is copyright. Apart from any fair dealing for the purposes of private study, research, criticism, or review, as permitted under the Copyright Act, no part of this publication may be reproduced, stored in a retrieval system, or transmitted, in any form or by any means, without prior written permission. Inquiries should be addressed to the Australian Broadcasting Corporation

National Library of Australia
Cataloguing-in-Publication entry
Poidevin, Simon, 1958– .
   For love not money: the Simon Poidevin story.
   ISBN 0 7333 0148 7.
   1. Poidevin, Simon, 1958– . 2. Rugby Union
   football—Australia—Biography. I. Webster,
   Jim. II. Title.
796.333092

Edited by Evan Johnstone
Designed by Felicity Meyer
Cover design by Geoffrey Morrison
Set in 11/12 pt Cheltenham Book by Caxtons Pty Ltd, Adelaide
Printed and bound in Australia by Griffin Press Ltd, Adelaide
5-5-1995 (3.5-3-3500 HB)

The authors gratefully acknowledge News Ltd,
The Sydney Morning Herald and *The Goulburn Post*
(Leon Oberg), for the provision of photographs.

CONTENTS

Australia Scales Everest	9
Goulburn, Family, City Lights	15
Sydney, Crittle and the Dream Comes True	28
Cut Down to Size	41
Adventures in the Land of the Long White Cloud	56
Pumas, Frogs and Pain	69
The Beginning of the Jones Era	84
The Calm Before the Storm—Fiji and New Zealand	92
The Grand Slam Begins	105
Victors Then Vanquished	117
The Pinnacle	126
World Cup Despair	140
South Africa, Argentina and the Empire Slides	154
Controversy, Controversy, Controversy	165
Never Say Die	179
The Most Difficult Question	194
Changing Times	205
Australia Comes of Age	210

FOREWORD

I am honoured to be asked to write the Foreword to Simon Poidevin's book *For Love Not Money*.

Although I didn't have the pleasure of playing Rugby during the same era as Simon I did have the pleasure of being coach of a Combined Southern Hemisphere team, of which he was a member, to celebrate the IRB Centennial. During this time I got to know and respect him personally.

When I was involved as a New Zealand selector and coach of the All Blacks, Simon was always an automatic selection for Australian teams. I know from comments made by a number of prominent All Blacks that, apart from respecting Simon as a great player on the field, he was the Australian whom they most respected, liked and related to off the field as a determined, exceptionally talented player who just got on with the game.

This book is essential reading for both Rugby enthusiasts and people who enjoy human interest stories. I didn't really know Simon's early background so I have found his account of his early sporting days in the country interesting and absorbing, particularly because I also grew up with sport on a farm of a similar size to Simon's parents. I am sure Simon is grateful for the parental support he received in making those early sporting activities available. In country towns, where there are not large numbers from which to select teams, you tend to become a 'jack-of-all-trades' by trying out many different sports and team positions. All this helps you later in your career to become more sympathetic and understanding to others and also more grateful for their help.

I'm sure that readers will be enthralled by the incidents involving the Australian team that were not documented by the media — the highs, the lows, the difficult periods and the celebrations. All International teams go through the same exhilarations and frustrations and I am sure this is what makes us all so close socially, once we forget that the player whose company we are enjoying is from that other country which our coach and supporters demand that we crush in our next encounter!

When Simon eventually retires I'm sure that, like me, he will find it very easy to relate to all the other members of the most exclusive club in the world, the ex-International Club. I can assure you that it makes all the effort and training, thrills and disappointments worthwhile.

Simon, you deserve it — you've worked for it!

BRIAN LOCHORE

To my parents Ann and Paul

AUSTRALIA SCALES EVEREST

*T*he emotion came quickly. We'd only just trooped off Murrayfield and into our dressing-room on that sullen, overcast afternoon. In between tugging off their sodden jerseys and the rest of their gear the Wallabies were shouting, pumping each other's hands, slapping backs, ripping the tops off Fosters cans and smiling for all they were worth. Jonesy, with a monstrous grin on his face, was stomping around in his Wellington boots in the darkly-lit room, quoting from Shakespeare or Churchill or somebody else to the Aussie media boys who'd followed us in.

We'd just comprehensively whipped Scotland, thus enabling us to successfully complete the 1984 Grand Slam of the British Isles; the only Australian team in history to do it, and among the precious few international Rugby sides ever to defeat England, Ireland, Wales and Scotland on the same tour. Hence the unbridled jubilation.

It's extremely difficult at times like that to fully appreciate what you've done. A bit like winning a gold medal at the Olympics I guess. The full realisation doesn't sink in for weeks, even months, afterwards. In the meantime, though, we were really doing our utmost to savour the immediate and overwhelming feeling of success, achievement and pride in what we'd done.

It wasn't simply having won the Grand Slam, but also the manner in which we'd done it. We scored exactly a century of points in the four Test victories, the most ever by a touring team in Britain. Our twelve tries was also a record. The 37-12 hiding of Scotland that afternoon was Australia's highest Test score against a major Rugby nation and also the biggest winning margin. Michael Lynagh's 21 points against the Scots equalled the record number of points for an Australian against an international Rugby Board country, and his total of 42 points for the Test series was also a record. Finally, Mark Ella's tries in each of the Tests was also the first such feat ever performed by anyone in a touring team. In the end, there were hardly any records left to be broken.

While all this sank in, some of the boys continued to sit there elated and exhausted, but most stripped off, jumped under the piping hot showers and began singing 'I still call Australia home' at the tops of their voices, horribly off-key. And our Argentinean prop Enrique (Topo) Rodriguez was declaring to all and sundry in his very best English: 'Un-bee-lievable, mate; bloody un-bee-lievable ...'.

While there were all these outward signs of emotion, and almost of hysteria, inwardly I wasn't feeling that way at all. Deep down I was numb. I'd been around a fair while and had suffered more than my share of Test defeats. So I was more in a state of disbelief. I just couldn't conceive that we'd finally achieved what we'd set out to do those many weeks before. All those training sessions ... Jonesy yelling and driving us on, often in the bitter cold and wet, those countless rucks and mauls, repeating the same moves over and over again, and so many scrums and lineouts that you'd nod off to sleep thinking about them and wake up the same way.

An enormous responsibility had also been blown away. The horrible fear of losing that last international and being denied the Grand Slam—something which haunted each and every one of us as the wins accumulated—had at last gone forever. Earlier that day in his talk to the team, Jonesy had used the analogy that Martina Navratilova had only just lost her first major tennis event after winning umpteen matches on the trot. He likened the Wallabies to her. Did we similarly want to falter after coming so very, very far? We'd beaten England, Ireland and Wales. Only the Scots to go. Were we going to let the Scots stop us now at the most crucial moment of all?

In his most erudite and stirring way, Jonesy had put that question to us and laid the challenge firmly at our feet. Now in this packed and noisy dressing-room, as the Murrayfield grandstands emptied the last of their 65 000 spectactors, it was finally over. And thankfully we hadn't let down ourselves or Jonesy.

After things finally settled down, we all dressed and boarded the bus for the ride back to the North British Hotel where our first duty was to dump our bags and head for the traditional happy hour which the Wallabies always have after each tour game: a time when the players and team officials get together behind closed doors for a natter about the game, maybe have a song or two and sometimes a bit of skylarking. Generally it's light-hearted (just how light-hearted being determined by the score that afternoon) and we were obviously all looking forward to this particular happy hour.

I arrived early at the team-room and spotted our big second-rower Steve (Swill) Williams. Swill was just sitting by himself sipping an orange juice, which definitely wasn't his normal drink. When I asked why, he muttered: 'I don't know. I just feel totally drained and want to take it easy for a while.' So I left him to it. Then the bulk of the players began filing in. When the doors closed, there were just the 31 players, the manager Dr Charles (Chilla) Wilson, Jonesy, his assistant Alex Evans, the medical officer Dr Syd Sugerman and Graham Short our baggage man.

Normally on those occasions, Jonesy gets up and says his piece about the game and where we went right or wrong. His speeches were always clipped and emphatic. But this time there was an entirely different tenor to what he had to say, and it showed in his voice. He spoke quietly and with far deeper emotion than I've ever heard from him. It had been a week he'd never forget. He'd been crippled the whole week with a back injury, but had struggled along with that enormous disability and had finally had everything he'd ever dreamed of in Rugby come true.

When he finished you could hear a pin drop. Then he mentioned that our skipper Andrew Slack might like to save his comments for the official dinner that evening and sat down. But Slacky wouldn't have a bar of that. Suddenly, he was on his feet. He's a pretty emotional sort of person, and as he also tried to get across to the rest of us what winning the Grand Slam meant to him, he had to stop. The words were there, but there was a lump in his throat stopping them coming out. Again, the room was suddenly full of silence.

Then, simultaneously it seemed, we all heard the sniffle and looked around to see Topo Rodriguez, our mighty prop, someone feared and respected by every Rugby forward in the world, quietly crying. The tears were trickling down his cheeks and into the tips of his shiny black moustache.

Topo's emotion was infectious. No sooner had we seen him crying than almost everyone else in the team started shedding tears too, some more than others. It went on for some minutes.

Nobody outside that room will ever know or fully understand why that extraordinary outpouring of emotion happened. Many will scarcely believe it: a team of international footballers weeping! Others will paint us as a bunch of nancies. I often wonder what the reaction might have been if the masses of joyful Aussies who were choking all the bars and pubs and watering holes in Edinburgh at that very moment (some had obviously made it, judging from the noise, to the corridor outside our meeting-room) had suddenly walked in. Fairly perplexed I'd suggest. All I can say is that had you been through what all the people in that room had been through, worked as hard and wanted something as badly as we had, then you'd understand.

At the end of every happy hour, the team always stood and sang the national anthem. It always gave us a sense of pride, and reminded us that we were playing for Australia. Well, I don't think I've ever sung Advance Australia Fair with as much pride as I did on that occasion, knowing we'd not only done so much for ourselves but also for everybody back home who would get such a fantastic lift out of this Grand Slam.

Had my Rugby career ended then and there I'd have had much to be thankful for. But I'm a pretty lucky Australian. I lived to fight more wars and one more great and succcessful battle.

Two years later I found myself in the midst of another jubilant

FOR LOVE NOT MONEY

dressing-room on the other side of the world, sharing another great victory with many of those same teammates and the same coach.

We'd just beaten the New Zealand All Blacks at Eden Park in Auckland by 22-9 to win the series against them by two Tests to one and regain possession of the Bledisloe Cup.

I'd been in Test teams which had previously beaten the All Blacks, and was part of the team which took the Bledisloe Cup from them back home in 1980. But this was the first and only time in my long career that we'd ever beaten them in a series in New Zealand. On their own dung-heap; right in their own backyard!

A fortnight before we'd been beaten in the second Test by 13-12 after winning the first by the same score, and in the eerie silence of that dressing-room at Carisbrook Park in Dunedin every player had vowed that we'd not lose the third and deciding Test. Defeat would not be considered.

Now we'd succeeded and, take it from me, there's no sweeter smell of success in all of Rugby than beating the All Blacks in a series on New Zealand soil. They're an arrogant team and have every right to be, because they're so damned successful. But this arrogance, and the competitiveness of both nations at any sport, has festered into an absolute blind hatred between our national Rugby teams. I stress that it's between the teams, because there's a great deal of underlying respect and, in some cases, even friendship among the players. But put the teams on opposite ends of a Rugby paddock and it's like two bull mastiffs going at each other to the death.

The New Zealand crowds also stir up a lot of the hatred from the Australians. They're fanatical and terribly parochial. While that's understandable, and the support they give their team is something our crowds could learn from, they're also very unfair in that they're reluctant to acknowledge the outstanding qualities or play of rival teams the same way that crowds do at the major British grounds or even in France. That really gets to us and makes us want to humble their precious All Blacks in front of them more than ever.

I remember that very day before we ran out onto Eden Park. The walls of the dressing-rooms have louvre windows between the players and the public outside. The locals know that, and the rude and barbed jibes that drifted through as we prepared for that deciding Test worked better than a blow-torch to the stomach in getting us stirred up for the conflict. As I recall, there wasn't much noise coming from outside those windows about 4.45 that afternoon.

Then again, we probably wouldn't have heard it. The dressing-room was packed with people, there were television lights and photographic flashes, Jonesy was running around shouting hoarsely (who ever thought he'd go hoarse!) that this was '... bigger than Quo Vadis', we had our arms around each other, singing and congratulating ourselves, and every now and then you'd be passed the massive Bledisloe Cup, take a swig of champers from it, and pass it on.

Here we were deep in enemy territory, and we were the champions. We were absolutely racked with exhaustion, but it's remarkable what that euphoria did for all those aches and pains.

I spared a thought for Andrew Slack, as he'd achieved another great victory as captain. Slacky had been around a few years longer than me and to be still playing centre for Australia as well as he was, and leading us so well, was a fantastic achievement. He was always vastly underestimated and this further success should have finally changed a lot of people's opinions of him.

Another I thought of was Jeff Miller, who'd played such gutsy football in the second and third Tests. What a little dynamo he'd proved to be. And Mark Hartill, who'd been brought in from nowhere to fill the shoes of Andy McIntyre. He'd been under intense pressure in the three Tests but had never buckled. And Steve Cutler and Bill Campbell, who had dominated the lineouts so much during the series. Many thought a team couldn't afford to carry beanstalks like these two in the pack. But we had, and they'd done a fantastic job for us in securing possession.

Amidst all the dressing-room din, in walked Brian Lochore, the All Black coach. This was akin to Rommel suddenly appearing in the doorway of Monty's headquarters at El Alamein. But Brian's big in humility as well as size. The noise quietened at his presence. Then, choosing his words carefully, he warmly congratulated Australia on the way they had played. Lochore had been my coach during the International Rugby Board centenary matches earlier that year in Britain, and I had come to know and respect him as a great coach and a fantastic person.

As Brian spoke, I could see the great sadness in his eyes and I felt very sorry for him, for it was only the fourth time this century the All Blacks had lost a series at home and he was going to have to bear the brunt of that humiliation.

Often I'm asked to compare the two occasions—winning the Grand Slam and taking that series from the All Blacks.

A tour of the British Isles is certainly the most interesting a Rugby player can make, moving as you do through four different countries, experiencing the history and contrasting cultures, and playing on such famous grounds as Twickenham and Cardiff Arms Park. For those reasons alone, such a tour is very absorbing, a great experience in itself. To have won the Grand Slam made it even more memorable and highly emotional.

In contrast, a tour of New Zealand is where the commitment to the game of Rugby is more intense and the basic principles of winning and losing are honed more sharply than anywhere else on earth. Therefore, winning a series there is really the ultimate in terms of pure footballing satisfaction. I remember Greg Growden from *The Sydney Morning Herald* asking me that afternoon in the Eden Park dressing-room what winning that 1986 series meant. I replied: 'Now I can live life in peace.' It meant that much to me.

l to r: Chris Roache, Ross Reynolds and Steve Cutler look on in disbelief as I line up Alan Jones

GOULBURN, FAMILY, CITY LIGHTS

*I*n that Eden Park dressing-room, with all the Rugby success I'd ever dreamed of behind me, I couldn't help but think briefly of where it all started. And I guess I was luckier than most, because heredity and how I spent my early childhood had much to do with what I achieved.

Generations of my family on both sides came from Goulburn, about 200 kilometres south-west of Sydney on the beautiful southern tablelands of NSW, and Australia's oldest inland city. Sport was a way of life in country centres in the early days with everyone playing social and club cricket and tennis, and going to race meetings, football matches and sports days. These activities bound the whole community together.

Mum's father, Les Hannan, was by all accounts quite a dashing Rugby centre three-quarter in the early 1900s and, in no small way, had an influence on the beginnings of Rugby League in Australia. A Goulburn lad, he was playing at the time of Dally Messenger, one of the best Australian footballers of all time, and was selected for the 1908 Wallaby tour of the United Kingdom but unfortunately broke a leg before the team departed.

In those days, Rugby authorities flatly refused any claims for compensation for injuries and lost wages, and it was injuries like those to my grandfather which prompted the well-known Sydney entrepreneur James J Giltinan to organise a breakaway movement from the code. He gathered together a group of sporting and business personalities who met in 1907 in a room above the sport store owned by the cricket legend Victor Trumper. Giltinan had heard of this new game that had started up in England and, as a result of that meeting, Rugby League was begun in Australia with Messenger being lured across in August of that year to foster the infant code.

None of this benefited my grandfather very much. He still didn't get any help with his medical fees, and eventually went off to the First World War in the 1st Light Horse where, because he was so nimble on his feet and able to duck and weave quickly, some cluey sergeant delegating jobs decided the only place for Les Hannan was picking his way between the falling shells as a stretcher bearer! Les's grandson, Guy Hannan, carried on the family tradition by playing during the 1980s for NSW Country.

Dad's side of the family had more than its share of sport as well, because his cousin, Dr Leslie Oswald Poidevin (known to most as LOS Poidevin), was a tremendous batsman, hitting 151 not out for New South Wales against McLaren's MCC side, and in the 1918–19 season becoming the first Australian to score a hundred centuries at all levels of cricket. Later he was one of the co-founders of the inter-club cricket competition in Sydney known as the Poidevin-Gray Shield which every youngster worth his salt must pass through before graduating to Sheffield Shield and Test status.

Besides his cricketing achievements, LOS Poidevin was also a tennis player of some renown. While studying medicine in Britain, he won the Swiss championship and also played in the Davis Cup. In 1906, he represented Australasia with the Kiwi, Anthony Wilding, when they were beaten by the United States at Newport, Wales. He dashed back to Lancashire after one day's play in the tennis to score a century for the County. The sporting prowess of LOS Poidevin certainly filtered through to his son, Dr Leslie Poidevin, who won the singles tennis championship at Sydney University six years in a row from 1932 to 1937. He also competed in the Australian championships in 1935.

So there was more than a fair share of sporting blood coursing through my veins when I arrived on the scene fairly hurriedly on October 31, 1958. Mum reached Goulburn Base Hospital with only seconds to spare, and my urgency to get moving was a forerunner of my whole approach to life. I also wasn't too small and delicate, and when our next-door neighbour, Mrs Harry Bell, had her first look at me she told mum: 'You haven't had a baby, Ann, you've had a footballer!' I was the middle offspring of Paul and Ann Poidevin's five children. Ahead are Andrew and Jane and behind are Joanne and young Lucy, who turned up rather unexpectedly after mum had an eight-year break from childbearing.

On the farm at Goulburn, 1967. Dad, centre, back row

Incidentally, the Gallic surname comes from Pierre Le Poidevin, a French sailor who had been imprisoned by the English in the 1820s, eventually settled in Australia and took an Irish wife. The Irish ancestry in that union undoubtedly accounts for my quick temper. On the other side, while my French is lousy, I definitely gained a love for a drop of good wine.

Neither mum nor dad were champion sports people in their own right, although mum and her brothers were excellent runners, and at Sydney University she was always in the cricket and basketball teams. She was also an accomplished horsewoman and still runs a dozen horses.

Dad also won a boxing tournament in Queensland when he was in the Army during the Second World War and, with his physique, he'd have taken pretty good care of himself. He doesn't say too much about things like that. In fact, he's not one for chatter about most things in life. By nature, dad's a very quiet sort of person until he gets to know someone and then he'll open up.

Besides his quietness, the other notable feature about dad that was apparent to me from a very early age was his enormous physical power. Nothing ever seemed too heavy for him, and I like to think that he passed some of that strength down the line.

My family owns 'Braemar', a 360-hectare property a few kilometres out of Goulburn, where we raise fat lambs and some cattle. The rambling old home needs a fair bit of work, because dad and mum still run the place by themselves. The only help they have is when the kids are home for holidays. While I always look forward to hopping on the freeway out of Sydney and whizzing home whenever I can, it never seems often enough. Mum's cooking sure beats mine and there's nothing more enjoyable than helping dad around the paddocks or in the yards, although keeping up with him is still no mean feat.

Where we are, out on Mummell Road, has become quite a haven for Rugby internationals in recent years. Jim Roxburgh, the Wallaby who was my English teacher at St Patrick's College in Goulburn, lived along the road, as did two other Wallabies, John Klem and Barry McDonald. We've also had some of Jimmy Hindmarsh's cattle on agistment there in recent times. And 'Lynton', the adjoining property to ours, has been bought by yet another former Wallaby, Alan Cardy! I'm not sure if wallabies gather in schools, flocks or herds, but whatever it is there's one of them out on Mummell Road and I don't have to go too far when I'm home to swap a few Rugby yarns.

Growing up on a farm is great fun, as any kid brought up on one will testify. I had my chores, as we all did, but once they were done we'd have the times of our lives, running wild around the paddocks, riding our horses, climbing trees or exploring all the nooks and crannies that you find around a property. I was pretty active when it came to all these pastimes and had some pretty spectacular adventures as a kid. I've come off horses lots of times and often been kicked by them. I fell off a truck on my head once, and was bitten a few times when I annoyed or got in the way of some of dad's sheep dogs. The one thing we really had to be careful of around our property was snakes. They were fairly prevalent in summer, and once I got the fright of my life when I was firing an air gun down by the creek. After shooting what I thought was a frog, I leant down, hoisted it out of the water with my hand, and found to my horror it was a highly venomous tiger snake. I didn't hang onto it too long I can assure you!

We didn't have much money in those days. Our prime aim always was to hang onto our land and not sell it off like so many other family farmers in the district. Because of low sheep prices and some of the droughts we had on the tablelands it became a tough job for mum and dad raising five kids and then wanting to give them a private Catholic education.

But somehow they managed it, and I feel we've all done well enough in our careers to justify their sacrifices. I only hope they think so. Andy was bright enough to win a scholarship to Chevalier College at Bowral where, apart from his scholastic achievements, he was Chevalier's outstanding sportsman and represented NSW schoolboys at Rugby. He went on to play for the Australian National University, ACT U/23s at breakaway and later we even played together for the University of NSW. Incidentally, he's the only fellow I know who ever switched from playing prop-forward to wing, which he did because of a bad back. Jane and Joanne also gained degrees and excelled at various sports.

While the family might have battled financially, there was always a very warm atmosphere at home and the door was always open to a steady stream of friends and relatives.

My first school was Our Lady of Mercy preparatory school in Goulburn where I was introduced to football. The school had two under-6 Rugby League teams, but I couldn't find a spot in either of them. Paul Feeney, who became a well-known motor-bike rider, asked his father Jeff if he'd coach a third team. Jeff agreed, and that team of rejects was to win virtually every game for the next three years. Other than me, the team had some pretty useful young footballers in Paul Feeney and two brothers, Bruce and Gavin Miller. But more of them later.

For my primary education I went to another of the town's schools, St Patrick's Primary, where Rugby League was the only football code. My first team at St Pat's was the under-10s, and my first season was marked by the fact that in one match I was sent off! A nine-year-old being sent off, mind you. I got into a bit of a tiff with an opponent from South Goulburn Public School and got my marching orders for the first time in my life. I've been in the odd bit of rough stuff since then, but I don't know that I've ever been quite as upset about any incident on the field as I was about that. Mum and dad weren't too happy either and must have wondered what sort of wild man they were rearing.

Rugby League clash, Goulburn v Canberra Under-10s, 1967

I remember being driven to my matches in those early days by dad in our well-worn Holden utility. He'd drop me off and then just melt into the background. He was never one to give any vocal advice from the touchline. In fact, he wouldn't even stand on the touchline. He'd stay in the old ute, parked way back from the playing field and just quietly take it all in. That was his nature, and I think I was very fortunate that I didn't have any pressure at all from him or mum, either then or at any time during my sporting career. They always stayed right out of sight and let me do it my way, which meant that I didn't feel any need to achieve any sporting goals for their sake. Many parents I see these days running up and down touchlines behaving like lunatics could well take a lesson from their behaviour.

Even then I was starting to show a fair bit of promise. On one occasion our team went to Canberra for a school tournament and we were very much looked upon as the kids from the country without much hope. One of our matches was against Holy Cross College at Ryde, which has become a veritable home for future Rugby League stars, and all their players looked like giants to me. During the game the guy who looked the biggest of them all was really giving me a hard time and making me angry and so, although I wasn't that big, I picked him up and dumped him smack on his head. A bit too hard, it seems because he didn't get up. The game was stopped while they tried to bring him around, which they eventually did.

As you might gather, I was a tough little rooster. Another time I was playing in a knockout competition in Yass based on weight, not age, and because I was heavy-boned I found myself playing against kids several years older than me. I spent the whole competition running around tackling these older kids as hard as I could but in the final game of the tournament we were flogged. I was broken-hearted at having lost but, as we were walking off, one of the other coaches walked over to me, put his arm around my shoulders, and told me matter-of-factly: 'One day, son, you'll play for Australia.' I often wonder if he knows that I did.

I mentioned earlier that in those days of schoolboy Rugby League I came across Bruce and Gavin Miller. The elder brother Bruce was very strong for his age and a really good player. The boys' father was fanatical about the game and held very high hopes of Bruce one day playing League for Australia. But Bruce died at a very early age in mysterious circumstances. He was returning home from a football game and had to walk across a river flat just outside town and was apparently bitten by something—a snake or spider.

Unfortunately he couldn't be saved, and the whole town went into mourning over Bruce's death, not only because he was so young but because he genuinely was a highly talented footballer with a very big future.

Their father's expectations then switched to Gavin and he became the apple of his eye. Justifiably so. He was a tremendous player in his own right, and many times in those early years I found myself either playing with or against Gavin Miller before our paths finally diverged. I soon switched to Rugby Union, but he stayed with League and went on to become the well-known international forward with Cronulla-Sutherland.

I changed football codes when I moved into the senior school at St Pat's, where Rugby and discipline were just about as important as Shakespeare and logarithms. I can't imagine any school keeping its pupils more in line than the Christian Brothers did with us, and two of the brothers, Bro Marzorini and Bro Powell, set standards of discipline and excellence that other schools would shrink from. Not that it did any harm. I reckon that Australia as a whole would be a much better place if schools laid down the law like they did at St Pat's and taught kids to work hard and do their homework, or else be punished.

While I did well at schoolwork, I know I'd have done even better had I devoted all my time to study, but I believe that my development as a person was very much enhanced by my involvement with sport, especially Rugby.

The amateur code was the only one played at St Pat's, and so keen was the school on Rugby that to make the 1st XV was the ambition of every kid who ever passed through the school's entrance. The driving force being the school's Rugby was Bro Powell. Because of his authoritarian manner and technical skills, St Pat's had one of the toughest and most disciplined school teams you could imagine. My earliest ambition was to one day make Bro Powell's 1st XV.

But first I had to do a long apprenticeship, and at times it seemed that I'd never get there. I was immediately drafted into the 13As. As well as beginning my Rugby career at breakaway, where I've always played, I was also the team's goalkicker in those days. I've kept telling coaches ever since that I was a decent goalkicker as a kid but for some unknown reason none of them has ever taken any notice of me.

Changing codes was an easy transition for me. I hardly noticed any difference at all and it obviously didn't affect my football too much because I merrily went through the 13As, 14As, 15As and 16As without ever looking like I'd be dropped. The closer I got to making the 1st XV the more I realised just how much those players in the firsts were idolised. They were absolute gods. And the more I watched them up on that pedestal the more I wanted to make it too.

I'd even search for extra matches so I could improve my Rugby. It was nothing for me to finish one game and go around looking to see if any other teams in my age division were short and wanted me. One day I actually played three games in one morning, which I thought was terrific. Other people thought I was crackers. But I could take it. I spent so much time working on the farm in those days that I didn't have an ounce of fat on me and could keep going, either tossing sheep or tackling rival backs, all day long.

I wasn't a bad all-round athlete. I was always one of the fastest kids at the school over 100 metres and threw the discus and javelin fairly well too. One regret was that I couldn't ever swim very well, but there wasn't the opportunity to develop. If ever we went swimming in the local Wollondilly River there was always the danger that one of those tiger snakes would come slithering across the surface, which was a pretty common occurrence and didn't exactly encourage you to stay in too long. But my lack of swimming ability was later worked on when mum took us all for swimming lessons, and subsequently we had great fun on beach holidays at Currawong and Bateman's Bay.

But Rugby and horse-riding were my major sporting loves and in

1975, my penultimate year at school, I was finally called up by Bro Powell into the 1st XV. For the next two seasons he was to have a huge influence on my Rugby and on my growing up.

We went through that first season undefeated. We were virtually unstoppable. We were a very physical team, and sombody made the observation that an average of three players left the field against us. This was not caused by dirty play, but by the sheer power and determination that we exerted. We were all tough country kids and played the game with tremendous vigour. I played well enough to make the ACT schools representative team for the Australian schools championship in Melbourne. We beat NSW that year, but lost the final to Queensland. In that match I only came on as a replacement near the finish because of an injury, so I had no chance of making the Australian schoolboys team which toured New Zealand.

That season it was planned that we would play against Chevalier College in a curtain-raiser to the England v Country representative game in Goulburn and, as it happened, the Country side trained at our school. It was my first experience of senior representative football and, quite frankly, I was stunned by it. Country's hooker was the Test representative Peter Horton, and I couldn't believe how he screamed and raved at the rest of his forwards as he tried to get their scrum working properly. I thought he had a few marbles loose. If that was big-time football then they could keep it. But it paid dividends because on match day we annihilated Chevalier College and Country had a tremendous 14-13 win over England.

The next season I was vice-captain of the 1st XV—and also vice-captain of the college—and we were again formidable, losing only two matches. Even at that early stage it seemed the captaincy of Rugby teams was avoiding me, as Claude Assen, who had been captain the previous season, repeated the school year.

I had become as keen as mustard on my football. During the school holidays I'd even go looking for extra matches to improve myself. Sometimes I'd go across to see Andy at the Australian National University and urge him to get me a run in one of their lower grade teams. I even had a run one day with a mob known as the ANU Foresters. There were blokes in the team playing in army boots and running shoes and you name it. They were the most bizarre mob you can imagine, but great fun to play with.

That season I again made the ACT schools team which had two outstanding coaches, Max Green and Al Thomas. In the Australian schools championship in Canberra we again beat NSW to make the final, which was no mean feat seeing they had schoolboy internationals Steve Williams and George Gavalas. From there we went on to meet Queensland again in the final. They also had a couple of useful hands in

Chris Roche and a fellow named Wally Lewis. The Queenslanders were too good for us on the day but that match was the first time that I'd ever experienced full-blooded rucking. The boots were really flying, and if you were in the way of them then just too bad. Throughout that game I also had a fierce personal war with Roche, the first, it turned out, of many we were to have on football fields in the years ahead.

St Patrick's College, Goulburn, First XV, 1976. I'm the long-haired lout, third from left, back row.

After the championship, they picked the Australian schoolboys team and I was included, along with two other mates from St Patrick's—prop Nick Manikis and breakaway Claude Assen. I could be wrong, but I don't know if any other country school has had that many representatives in the same national schoolboys team. Although we didn't tour anywhere, a game was arranged for us against Sydney Colts. I played most of that game but towards the end Wally Lewis, who was the five-eighth, told me to fake an injury and take a dive. Very reluctantly, I did. But then, blow me down, who should come on but Roche, his Queensland teammate and my keenest rival. The smoke was really coming out of my ears over that incident.

Scholastically, I managed to do well. I certainly wasn't any Dumbo at school and my HSC results were good enough to get me into any of the university courses I was thinking of doing. But I decided not to go to university immediately. I wanted to spend some time thinking about what I wanted to do, so I had a year working for a road contractor around

FOR LOVE NOT MONEY

Goulburn, swinging a pick and shovel. I also worked for some concreters and builders named Peter (Tracker) McAlister and Pat Moore. Tracker and Pat were unbelievably hard workers—and also unbelievably big drinkers—and to this day Tracker claims that the ten- to twelve-hour days I put in labouring alongside them was largely responsible for any increase in my strength. He also did an enormous amount in opening my eyes to life—his nickname for me in those days was always Boy.

In that winter of 1977 I played Rugby for the Goulburn Club. That was a great experience, not only because it was my first time in senior football but also because it was where I had my first introduction to the social aspects of Rugby, for which it's so famous. From being a clean-nosed, non-drinking schoolboy, I quickly learned all the Rugby graces of boat racing (where two teams race each other in beer-drinking contests), skolling, and singing about ladies of dubious moral standards.

That season we won the grand final in the Southern Tablelands competition, defeating Bowral. I also made the Southern Tablelands team for Country Week, and it was a big experience for a kid like me even to go to Sydney, let alone play in such a competition. I was offered a lift up to Sydney in a car driven by a couple of hard old country Rugby guys named Snowy Maloney, who was from out Taralga way, and Frank Piggott, a stock and station agent from Goulburn. When we were leaving Goulburn they said that they were going to stop for a beer or two at every pub in every town that began with the letter B. That was all right by me. They wouldn't be drinking too much. There was only Berrima and Bowral that I knew of. We got only about 30 kilometres to Marulan and they pulled up at a pub. 'What are you stopping here for?' I asked. 'It's called Barulan,' they told me, and went in for a few beers. Then came Berrima (a few more beers) and after that Mittagong. They stopped again. 'This is Bittagong,' I was told. And on they went, making this ultra-marathon pub crawl 200 kilometres up the Hume Highway to Sydney. I'm just pleased the police didn't have any reason to stop us that day.

In that Southern Tablelands team was a likeable and experienced old campaigner named Steve Streeter, who had been a Wallaby winger some years before and had plenty to teach youngsters like me. I learned a lot from Steve. It's amazing how destiny works, because for a few years Steve worked under me in the Sydney stockbroking firm of McNall & Hordern Limited.

Shortly after Country Week (in which we didn't do any good) our Southern Tablelands coach Des Ross entered us in the Sydney seven-a-side competition at T G Millner Field. I'd never heard of sevens football, nor had most of the other boys. But Des told us: 'You've got no choice. You're all playing.' So off we went again to Sydney, as innocent as you like about the particular skills needed for this compressed form of the XV-a-side game.

Lo and behold, we won our first match, then the second, then the third and suddenly we were in the semi-finals against Eastern Suburbs. They were well ahead, but we desperately fought our way back and scored again in the last minute of play to get within a try of them. But by the time they kicked off again to restart play, there was less than 30 seconds remaining. Well the ball came directly to me and I ran the full length of the field to score. We kicked the goal to win the match, and this bunch of country nobodies was suddenly thrust into the final against none other than Randwick, with all their international players.

Realistically, we didn't have a hope in hell of beating them, but the whole crowd was behind us. Amazingly we were winning the final until the very last minutes of the game when their Wallaby five-eighth Ken Wright cut through our defence with four or five of those marvellous sidesteps of his and they won the final. Little did I know that six years down the track I'd be playing for that same outfit, but at least I know the feeling that so many opposing footballers have experienced over the years of desperately wanting to beat Randwick and not quite being able to.

But at the same time I really didn't have any awareness or even ambitions about top level Rugby, and was, if anything, more interested in Rugby League because of the way we were bombarded with it on television and in the newspapers. I had more interest in how Craig Young and his St George Rugby League team were doing every week than what was happening in Rugby.

That, however, was soon to change.

In 1978 I decided it was time to give the labouring away and get down to the serious business of carving out some kind of career. I wanted to do a degree in agricultural science and had the choice of going either to the University of New England at Armidale in the northern country region of the state or to the University of NSW in Sydney. Two legends from the University of NSW Rugby Club, Geoff James and Lindsay Cotterill, had already been down to Goulburn to see if they could woo this former schoolboy international with stories of what a top club they had and the great social life that revolved around it. If these two were examples of the Sydney social scene then there definitely were some good times ahead. And they did a good job, because I decided to go to the Uni of NSW.

So off I went to the big smoke, full of ambition and desire for success. I enrolled in a course at the university called 'wool and pastoral science', and took up residence on campus at Phillip Baxter College.

University of NSW was a first division club in those days and, after a few matches in reserve-grade, I won my way into first-grade. I'll not forget my opening first-grade match in a hurry. It was memorable, not for the result or anything I did personally, but for the fact that I ran out for it looking like I'd been waylaid on my way home from hospital. I was carrying about thirteen stitches around my left ear. I'd copped a boot in a 'friendly' university match the previous Sunday and so I had to go out all bandaged up against Hornsby at Waitara Oval.

Hornsby's first-grade team in those days was full of Fijians who looked a cross between some of Colonel Rabuka's infantry troops and those massive policemen you see in the streets of Suva with feet the size of plates. Among them was the huge prop-forward Jo Sovau, who had been sent off in the third and final Test of Fiji's 1976 tour of Australia, causing the rest of his teammates to walk off the Sydney Cricket Ground and refuse to continue for ten minutes.

In that initial first-grade game of mine, I must have looked a good target with all my bandaging, because Sovau threw a punch at me. I'm pleased I ducked—I felt a wind-gush of hurricane proportions whistling overhead. My poor old noggin, bandages and all, would have finished in the grandstand had he connected.

During that season, I became a lot more aware of international Rugby and a lot keener than I had been to make it into the representative teams. I began to admire, even idolise, some of the current Test players. One Saturday night, after one of the Test matches against Wales, some Test players turned up at Randwick Rugby Club, where I was among the crowd having a few drinks with some of my mates. I spotted Paul McLean and Stan Pilecki at the bar and went up and asked McLean if he'd mind having a drink with us. He politely refused. Although I was disappointed then, I was later to understand just how much Test players get badgered like that and how they like to be left alone. The irony was that this shy country kid was going to be playing against those two internationals the very next season.

In my second season with the university in 1979 we had a schoolteacher named Graham McLennan for a coach. He had coached lower grades with Randwick, but left them to join us so that he could get a first-grade team. He had an unshakeable belief in the running game, perhaps even more so than any of the coaches he'd left behind at Randwick. But to be able to run the ball, he reasoned, you had to have extreme fitness. So we began that 1979 season with some of the hardest fitness training I've done in the whole of my career. He found a conditioner from Maroubra, Chris Armstrong, who was nothing less than a psychopath, and he absolutely drove us into the ground night after night.

I'd played pretty well in one of our trial matches at Prince Henry Hospital, against Randwick of all teams, and as I walked off the field a fellow came up to me and introduced himself as Maurice Goldberg. He congratulated me on how I'd played, said he was a representative selector and that he thought I had potential. He took my name and contact address and telephone number and said I might be hearing from him later in the season. At the time I didn't think much more about it.

Graham McLennan's presence, if not the fitness training, had drawn some good players to the club, but we were very unlucky in a lot of our matches that season. We were beaten on the bell in our very first match by Parramatta and just lost the second one against Manly. Then our luck changed and we beat Randwick. That Randwick match was something else. I got into a fight with Ian Kennedy, now among the senior detectives in the NSW Homicide Squad. John Maxwell and I also kept belting one another most of the afternoon. I didn't quite know what this rough stuff was all about, but it was all part of a great learning experience.

Before long, Maurice Goldberg's influence had its effect. I was picked to play in the Sydney and NSW under-23 teams and also for Australian Universities. By then I was really enjoying my Rugby. I played in these teams in curtain-raisers before major representative fixtures, and that gave me a tremendous buzz. One of these games for the NSW under-23 team was against Queensland under-23s at Ballymore before a Test match. I scored a try under the posts from about 50 metres out by outrunning their fullback Roger Gould. I'll remember that until the day I die.

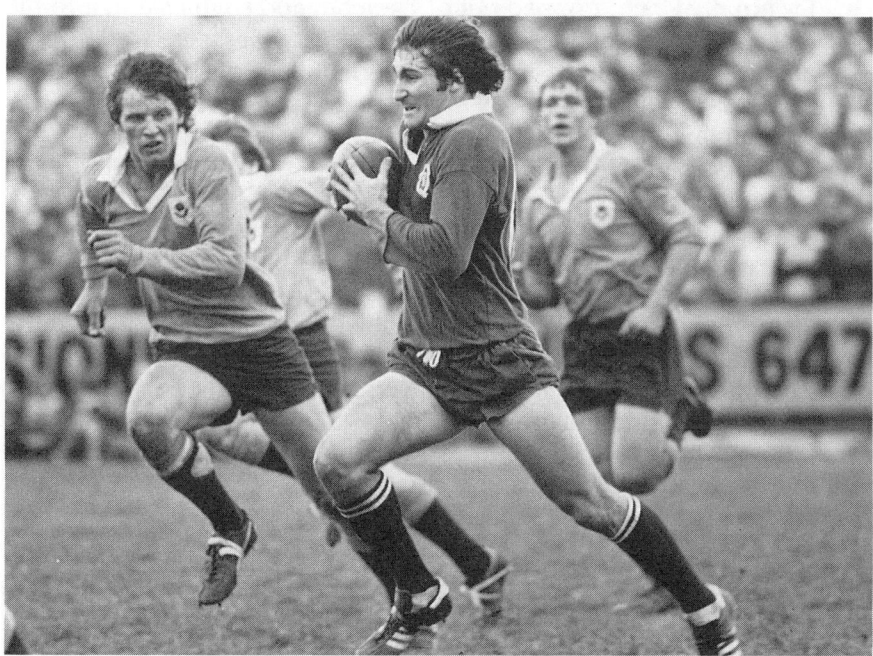

A youthful Poidevin cover defending against Peter Grigg, NSW v Queensland, 1979

SYDNEY, CRITTLE AND THE DREAM COMES TRUE

I was called to the phone in my college one night in August 1979. It was Maurice Goldberg. This time he wanted to know if I would be available to play for NSW against Queensland in the return interstate game, because Greg Craig was injured and looked like having to withdraw. Very politely, he asked would I be available for training.

I was stunned at the invitation and the question of being available didn't need to be answered. I'd have done anything to get the opportunity of playing against Queensland.

At first it was hard for me to digest Goldberg's offer, because I was still very much a starry-eyed fan of all the current Test players, and thought back to less than twelve months before when I'd asked McLean and Pilecki to join me and some of my mates for a drink for the simple pleasure of wanting to share their company. Now I was possibly going to be playing against them. Goldberg's presence at that trial several months beforehand—and I guess his judgment—was finally starting to pay dividends for me.

Eventually Craig dropped out of the team and so in I went, into the back-row alongside Don Price and Andy Stewart. I was a great admirer of Stewart. I'd watched him closely during Australia's tryless 12-6 win over the All Blacks to regain the Bledisloe Cup in the one-off Test the previous month and couldn't imagine there ever having been a more courageous player. He took an unmerciful battering that day, but just kept coming back for more.

My feelings about playing in my first interstate game were mixed. Of course I was over the moon with delight, but also very aware of Queensland having given us an absolute hiding by 48-10 in the first interstate game at Ballymore back in May. That left me feeling a little insecure, to say the least, about our chances this time around.

And of course the other NSW players would hardly be lifted by my presence. Here was an unknown being tossed in alongside them in what ranks traditionally with the fiercest domestic confrontations in world Rugby. NSW against Queensland compares with Auckland v Canterbury or Northern Transvaal v Western Province. In games like these you take no prisoners.

Queensland came south with a team bristling with talent. Every one of their players was an international, and I daresay they would have posed a threat to any team, international, provincial or otherwise, on the face of the earth.

For the record the Queensland lineup was: Roger Gould, Peter Grigg, Andrew Slack, Geoff Shaw, Brendan Moon, Paul McLean, Rod Hauser, Mark Loane (c), Greg Cornelsen, Tony Shaw, Peter McLean, Duncan Hall, Chris Handy, Peter Horton, Stan Pilecki.

Not a bad outfit in anyone's language, and their back-row of Shaw, Cornelsen and Loane, especially Loane, were real heroes of mine.

A decade later, that game at T G Millner Field still sticks in my mind as being unbelievably hard—definitely one of the hardest games of Rugby I've ever played.

The two teams climbed into each other like I've rarely seen teams do. The sheer pace of the game, the toughness, even the brutality was something you could never imagine. At one point I looked up from the bottom of a ruck and Duncan Hall appeared over me and then dropped both knees into my back with all the force he could muster. I thought to myself 'Well, I guess this is what playing in the top stuff's all about.'

Despite a very gallant performance by us, they were much too good and too physical. They won by 24-3, scoring four tries to nil. After the final whistle, as we were walking off, I felt like I'd just spent 80 minutes in a mediaeval torture chamber, either being stretched on the rack or dangling from the wall in chains. Hardly a bone in my entire body wasn't aching and I was bleeding from a dozen scrapes and cuts. Then I caught sight of my socks. The tops of them were intact and the binding I used to keep them up was in place, but the rest of them, from the tops of my calves virtually to my ankles, had been ripped to pieces. I'd been to war.

In the dressing-room, when we began stripping to have our showers, someone called our attention to the bare back of Warwick Watkins, our hooker from Armidale. It wasn't a pretty sight. So severely had the Queenslanders raked him with their boot studs that he looked like he'd been repeatedly clawed by a lion.

After it was all over and the aches and abrasions started to subside, I gave my representative baptism of fire a lot of thought. Call me mad if you like, but I really enjoyed it. Despite the physical hurt, the fierce competitiveness had appealed to me, as it had right from those earliest days playing League back in Goulburn. Having that adrenalin pumping as much as it was and pitting my strength against another's had the same effect as a junkie hitting himself with a fix. I was hooked.

There was a selection trial the following week between an Australian XV and The Rest to help choose the Wallaby team to go to Argentina. Although a few of my mates at college had been geeing me up about being ready to make the fairytale change from a nobody to a somebody, I didn't do any more than warm the reserves' bench.

After the trial I hitched a lift in the bus carrying the Queensland players from Concord Oval to the airport for their flight home to Brisbane. They agreed to drop me near the university, which was on the way. Immediately after the very fierce game the previous week, I hadn't exactly wanted to share any beers with them, but on that bus ride they treated me like there had never been a tough interstate game and made me extremely welcome. They appealed to me as a fairly decent bunch, and I felt that somehow I'd develop a close affinity with many of them in the future.

At the start of the 1980 season I went on my first overseas Rugby tour with the University of NSW to the west coast of North America. The tour took in games against the University of British Columbia in Vancouver, then down to the United States to play against the universities of Stanford, UCLA, Long Beach State and Berkeley.

It was terrific fun playing against these great universities, even though their Rugby wasn't in the same class as their academic status. Still, it was a great experience for a bunch of young university students like us. We had a wild old time and tremendous fun, and even tried to set a beer-drinking record during the flight across the Pacific. But while we played hard off the field, we also did the same on the field. The whole atmosphere really whetted my appetite for touring with Rugby teams. What made that particular tour doubly enjoyable for me was that my brother Andy was also in the team.

Soon after we came back, the Sydney representative squad was announced, and I was in it. Our coach was Peter Crittle, who had been a clever, resourceful forward during the John Thornett era and had played in 15 Test matches in the sixties.

Crittle's among the great characters of Rugby. He has a brilliant and perceptive mind, which he deploys so effectively these days at the NSW Bar, and by all accounts was a hilarious character to have in any team. I gather that he used to keep his teammates constantly laughing with his witticisms and his antics. He also liked the unusual. During his career, which included four Wallaby tours, and his subsequent wanderings to the far-flung corners of the earth, he behaved like a bowerbird, collecting the largest and weirdest objects to take home for souvenirs. Nowadays, he's surrounded in his chambers by hand-crafted masks from South-east Asia, a mountain tiger's head, a python skin and an elephant's foot, which is used as an ash tray.

This man was to be my first Sydney coach.

Early on I knew him less for his humour and loquacity and his odd ways—it was the intensity of his training that struck me. Hell, he drove us into the ground. He was an extremely hard coach, who believed in a high degree of fitness in his teams.

You either loved or hated Crittle, but as the season wore on most of us in the Sydney team grew to love and respect him.

Soon I was chosen for a short tour of New Zealand in the Sydney team, with just three games against Waikato, Thames Valley and, the toughest game of all, Auckland. While preparing for the tour, we witnessed an extraordinary occurrence one night during training at Woollahra Oval. We were scrummaging against the Eastern Suburbs' pack. In the very first scrum one of our props, Declan Curran, suddenly came reeling out of the scrum with his forehead split open as if he'd been belted with a hammer. Nobody knew what had happened and we all rushed to help. But he brushed us aside saying it was nothing to worry about and that he'd merely bumped his head against the rival front-row while packing down. So the scrum went down again and immediately a player went reeling out of the Easts' second-row, oozing blood from his head. Just what was going on here?

When we saw who this fellow was, the whole crazy situation began to add up. The Easts' forward was none other than Frank Curran, Declan's older brother.

In an unusual display of brotherly love, he'd punched Declan in the first scrum and then Declan had kicked him in the next! The younger players in both sides couldn't believe this extraordinary scene, with the two brothers fuming and snarling and spilling buckets of the family blood between them.

Both demanded that the scrummaging should continue. God knows what they had planned for each other next, but Crittle stepped in and called a stop to the night's scrummaging. Then he pulled Frank aside and asked him what the dickens had brought that on. Frank told him with considerable wisdom: 'Oh, Declan's new to the Sydney side and has to be toughened up if he's going to New Zealand. So I thought I'd give him a belting.'

That Sydney team had wonderful team spirit and was to bring many young players to the forefront of Australian Rugby ... players like Glen and Mark Ella, Dave Cowlishaw, Phillip and Mitchell Cox, Michael Hawker, Mick Martin, Don Price, Steve Williams, Mick Mathers, Declan Curran (who didn't find the opposition nearly as brutal as his big brother), Bruce Malouf, John Coolican—and me. A few of them had been to Argentina with the Wallabies the year before, but it was on this New Zealand tour that we really all progressed in leaps and bounds.

We won the first game against Waikato very soundly at Hamilton, and afterwards the team had an enormous drinking session to celebrate the victory. That's when I first saw the Manly forward Steve Williams in action. His nickname is Swill, presumably derived from his name as well as his ability to swill beer, for he could skol jugs of the amber fluid like nobody I've ever seen before. But Swill wasn't the only one to put away vast quantities of beer that night. We all did. Lots of it. We all let our hair down because Crittle had promised us only a light training run the next morning as a reward for winning.

That taught me never to accept Crittle's word in such matters, for the next morning our team of very sick individuals had a road run around the streets of Hamilton, then went to the ground and had an hour's training of fiendish intensity. Players kept dropping out, collapsing on the ground and being violently ill. Finally, there were only about ten or eleven of us left when Crittle ordered us literally to run into a fence, and only then called it quits.

Then up to Thames, where we were to play Thames Valley, a not-very-exciting or successful provincial team known as the Swamp Foxes. We stayed there at the Brian Boru Hotel, which was to gain so much notoriety during the Wallabies' tour in 1986, when the team walked out because of the standard of accommodation. More of that later, but the Sydney players weren't as choosy and put up with the tiny rooms which had no bathrooms or toilets and beds so small that some of the players had to sleep on the floor on mattresses.

We struck a bit of local gamesmanship at Thames. Before the game, local Rugby officials arranged a bus trip for us to see the Coromandel Range and then go to a club for lunch. As the journey turned from minutes to an hour and then two hours, we wondered what was going on. We seemed to be driving from one end of New Zealand to the other. There was obviously an ulterior motive here and, the further we went, the more Crittle, who was sitting at the back of the bus, kept bellowing, 'Food ... get us food'.

Eventually we arrived at a delightful little Rugby club on the water's edge, and when lunch was over the local officials wanted to take us further on to see some lovely Kauri trees, hundreds of years old. Thinking that we should be grateful for this, we headed up into the range again, then got off the bus and began a long hike through the forest until we came upon the Kauri trees. Both of them. Imagine taking us all that way to look at two trees! If the local officials were trying to tire and annoy us they had definitely succeeded.

The players couldn't believe it. Crittle shook his head in bewilderment, made the shortest speech he ever has to the officials in thanking them for taking us there, and then ordered us all back to the bus. We'd been there about 30 seconds.

On the way down the bush track, a few of the boys decided to play a trick on Crittle. He'd been regaling us throughout the tour with tales about the safaris he had been on in South Africa in 1963. And just how fearless he'd been in the presence of all the wild animals he'd seen there. Well Lance Walker and one or two other players found a snake-shaped stick, hid in the undergrowth and then tossed it out in front of Crittle as he walked by. Quite forgetting that New Zealand doesn't have any snakes, our fearless leader leapt backwards like a startled rabbit and the players fell about in fits of laughter.

Despite the needless bus journey and mountain hike, we easily beat Thames Valley and then headed for Auckland and the biggest game of the tour against one of the great provincial Rugby teams of the world.

I mentioned in the opening chapter that the dressing-rooms at Eden Park separate you from sounds outside only by some louvre windows and that the Rugby fans know this and abuse visiting teams before matches. Well they bit off more than they could chew with Crittle. When the smart-arsed Kiwi comments started drifting through to us, Crittle went off his brain and turned on them through the louvre windows with invective like I've never heard before. I'd hate to be in the witness box under cross-examination whenever he lets rip, having heard him in full cry that day.

He shut them up instantly, but the incident provided us with just the motivation we needed before such an important game. All steamed up, we went out and defeated Auckland by 17-9 in what was a very important victory.

Altogether, it was a great result for the team to beat Waikato, Thames Valley and Auckland on the tour, and when we arrived home Crittle went about telling anybody in the media who cared to listen that players like Williams, Mitchell Cox, Martin and Poidevin should be chosen to play for Australia before the season was out. Charlie (while he preferred his middle name, Peter, everyone else called him by his first name) didn't mind stirring up a bit of publicity, but I didn't think I was nearly ready for that sort of honour. As far as I was concerned, it was a matter of first things first, and Sydney had a game coming up against Queensland.

Because of the results in New Zealand, we had tremendous spirit in our team and we were dead keen to even the score after what had happened in the interstate series the year before.

Crittle had a great little motivational device that he always used on us. When the representative season first started, he produced a small blackboard with the names on it of all the teams Sydney would be playing that season. Before we went out for each match he'd challenge us to see if we could wipe that particular team off the list. And in the dressing-room after each victory he'd ceremoniously cross out the name of another victim, to the players' immense delight and satisfaction. As infantile as it might have seemed, this ritual grew into a very useful source of motivation for us.

At that stage, given the three preparatory matches that we had against Victoria, the ACT and the President's XV, and then the three-match New Zealand tour, we had wiped out six opponents. Crittle went through his little exercise once more in the cavernous dressing-room beneath the grandstand at the Sports Ground. Sure enough, it worked perfectly once more, because in another very tough game we beat Queensland 18-10. Seven out of seven.

Next came NSW Country, who had made their annual, and mostly inaccurate, boasts that this was the best team they'd gathered for ages and that they were ready to show Sydney exactly where the source of Rugby power lay in New South Wales.

It rained heavily before the game, but we wiped them out in the heavy going by 66-3. There had been much criticism around at the time that our winger Mick Martin didn't have enough pace to play for Australia. As Mick galloped over in the corner for his fourth try that afternoon, I could hear Crittle bellowing from the grandstand like a fog-horn: 'Mick Martin's not fast enough ... Mick Martin is not fast enough to play on the wing for Australia.' The whole crowd got his point.

In the very last minute of that game, a big-framed Country forward named Ross Reynolds fell on me when I was on the bottom of a ruck and I heard a crack. I'd popped an AC joint in my shoulder, which put me in doubt for the coming interstate game against Queensland. As much as I wanted to play in that, I was eventually forced out, and NSW beat Queensland in a typically ferocious encounter by 36-20.

The following day the Wallaby team was announced to go to Fiji and, as thrilled as I was at finally being chosen to play for Australia, I was almost as pleased that we had twelve of our Sydney boys in the touring team. As well as me, there were Mitchell Cox, Michael Hawker, Mark Ella, Phillip Cox, Peter Carson, Donald Price, Mick Mathers, Steve Williams, Bruce Malouf, Keith Besomo and, finally, Mick Martin.

Australian Rugby owes a lot to Crittle for the role he played in developing those players. If you look down those names, you'll appreciate just how much influence they were to have on the future of the game.

One other character closely associated with that Sydney team and almost every representative player in NSW was Rick Moore. Rick was 'dad' to all the players and the most fun-loving gent I've ever met. He was also our baggage man with the biggest set of ears seen this side of the equator. Hence his title, 'OBE' (Old Big Ears). If there was ever a soul to any Rugby team I've been in, it was Rick Cyril Moore, OBE.

I was pretty lucky to make the Fijian tour. My shoulder was still very sore during the training runs before departure, although I managed to hide it from the team management. But Peter Carson knew the score. Aboard the aircraft the little halfback came up and said: 'Frenchman, I can't believe how you got on this plane, because you've been carrying that injury at training. It's definitely not right, is it?' It sure wasn't.

In Fiji, it couldn't have been any hotter if you were being burned at the stake. During training for our first game against Lautoka, the ground had been baked so hard that Peter Grigg even snapped a couple of sprigs off one of his boots! So the tour was obviously going to be a great test of physical endurance.

I had my shoulder well-strapped for the opening game before we went out in extremely debilitating and claustrophobic conditions and beat Western Unions by 25-11. We won the next game more easily against Eastern Unions at the National Stadium in Suva, and so began the countdown to the one and only Test on the same ground four days later.

We went down to Pacific Harbour, the lovely resort just along the Coral Coast from Suva, to train and have a game of golf, and it was there that the Test team was announced. Number six was Simon Poidevin. I've made many, many Test teams since, in varying and sometimes surprising circumstances, but nothing will ever replace the elation at hearing my name read out that first time.

There was an awful lot of talent in that touring team and, consequently, some controversy with the Test lineup. Hawker was five-eighth, which meant Mark Ella missed out. Mark was God over there. Everyone knew who he was and the ethnic Fijians were very disappointed that he wouldn't be playing. Mitchell Cox also missed out. Wouldn't it be lovely nowadays if we had those same selection problems and could leave out such gifted backs as Ella and Cox because of the abundance of talent. Our backline was Phillip Cox, Hawker, Moon, Slack, O'Connor, Martin (remember Crittle's shouting at the match against NSW Country!) and McLean at fullback.

In the first 30 seconds of the Test, I got in the way of a pass from the scrumbase by Peter Carson and wrecked a promising move. I thought, 'What a hell of a way to start a Test career'. I had some work to do to make up for that. We won the Test 22-9 in a dour sort of game, and afterwards we had some hilarious celebrations, with Tony Shaw and Chris Handy putting on an imitation bout of rock'n'roll wrestling that had us all rolling around the room in fits of laughter.

Then we returned home for what was the far more important assignment of facing the New Zealand All Blacks in a three-Test series for the Bledisloe Cup, which Australia held.

Never have I faced such an avalanche of brutal, high-powered Rugby, for it eventuated that I played against the All Blacks on *six* separate occasions—for Australian Universities, Sydney, NSW and in each of the three Test matches. They must have been sick and tired of the red-headed breakaway by the time it was all over. I'd certainly had my fill of them, and to this day I still carry scars on my back from the extremely fierce rucking

I struck in my marathon playing stint against them.

Sydney had the honour (is that the word?) of the first tour game against them. Crittle had the team really fired up for this game. He went to extremes to get us charged up for it, even to the extent of coming to training in an All Black jersey and inviting the forwards to ruck him off the ball just as hard as they liked to simulate a realistic match situation. We obliged. Our hatred for the All Blacks grew every minute the game drew closer.

At one of these sessions Crittle appealed to us to repeat the rucking routine in his most endearing terms. 'Come on you mongrel dogs, come over the top and ruck me off the ball.' We did, but he wasn't nearly satisfied. 'You're a bunch of big sheilas. What do you think this is all about. I'm lying here with an All Black jersey on me and nobody has really laid a boot on me.'

Next time any anger over his painful training sessions throughout the season and our dislike for the All Blacks really came pouring out, and Crittle was raked and booted like no man ever deserved to be. Most of the pack would have been ordered off had it happened in a match. One particular player, Bruce Malouf, thought that all his Christmases had come at once, because there was always lots of ill-feeling between him and Crittle.

'That's better, you bunch of mongrel dogs,' he eventually told us, getting gingerly to his feet and very much the worse for wear. Then he went down on the ground and called for us to do it again! After the training session, the cuts and scratches criss-crossed Crittle's back like the LA freeway system. When he got home that night his wife couldn't believe that anybody would go through that in trying to prepare his team. And he wasn't even being paid! To me it merely emphasised the strength of the man's character, that he would go through such punishment for the sake of his players.

We didn't let him down. We drew 13-all with the All Blacks. We came back to the dressing-room feeling a little disappointed about not having won, after scoring two tries to one. Out came the blackboard again but Crittle was reluctant to put a cross through the name NEW ZEALAND as we'd not beaten them. But Don Price walked over, grabbed the chalk from Crittle and took over. 'We mightn't have beaten them, but we bloody well didn't lose,' he said, and with that he put a big cross right through the name while the rest of us cheered.

The All Blacks went on their merry way after that, rolling over every other team they encountered, including NSW. Just minutes before the State team went out to play them, the skies bucketed down on the Sports Ground as if ordered by the All Blacks. It didn't do much for our spirits, as we knew how much they love the heavier conditions and, sure enough, they won 12-4.

Somehow our hooker Bruce Malouf had his jaw broken in a scrum early in this game. He was taken off to St Vincent's Hospital to have his jaw wired, but Bruce is one of those people who believe very much in the finer things in life. He wanted nothing of the public hospital system, so he checked out and walked up the road to St Vincent's Private Hospital where he booked himself a private room, which was more his style. You couldn't say Bruce wasn't a mover and a shaker.

The first Test at the SCG really felt like my Test debut. Sure, I'd played against Fiji but that wasn't the same. Here was arguably the best Rugby team in the world, and we were definitely in with a fighting chance of beating them before our home crowd.

I'd learnt a lot in the short time the All Blacks had been in the country—that their rolling maul was very effective, for one thing, and that it was permanently open season on any man lying on the ground. Believe me, I learnt very quickly to fight fire with fire. I followed the dictum that if it was black, tread on it.

Although the All Blacks dominated possession during that opening Test, we still scored two tries to nil through our backline and got home by 13-9.

The scene later in our dressing-room was marvellous: sitting on the benches in those timbered and historic surroundings, with people everywhere, our coach Bob Templeton's oval face lit up like the man in the moon, champagne corks popping and tinnies being torn open, and Greg Cornelsen singing *I Did It My Way*. Then there was the delight of walking out into the Members' Bar, which separates the rival dressing-rooms, and having hundreds of people cheering and whistling. It was all fantastic.

Unfortunately, the ecstasy wasn't to last very long.

A week later we went in against them again in the second Test at Ballymore in Brisbane. We started well that day and got to 9-0. We'd even had the opportunity to score a few more tries. About that time I got caught on the bottom of a ruck on the side of the All Blacks. I couldn't move for love nor money. Then suddenly I heard someone call out 'Get him, Axle'. Their prop Gary Knight's nickname was Axle, and the next second I had a size twelve boot ripping across my head. Although I finished the game, I came off spattered in blood from a nasty wound and looking very much the worse for wear. There was some humour in the fact that one of Goulburn's loudest Rugby personalities, Terry Tilden, who used to call me Bloodnut, had been yelling this nickname from the crowd throughout the game loud enough for me to hear. The All Blacks apparently decided to make the nickname fit.

They took care of Steve Williams that day too. He had his jaw broken by a punch from Mark Shaw and was replaced by Mick Mathers. Steve had been really asserting his size and authority but, with one quick punch, they managed to nullify him.

I was sorry to see Steve go (not half as sorry as he was, I'm sure). I always enjoyed playing in the same team as the big second-rower. In fact, I even made a point of always running out onto the field immediately behind him. It seemed to help my confidence to run out there knowing this man-mountain, who was also such a fierce competitor, was on your side.

While losing Steve was a very telling blow, in the end we were beaten by one of the best orchestrated tries you could ever hope to see on a Rugby field. The ball passed through eleven pairs of All Black hands as they swept from one end of the field to the other before their hooker, Hika Reid, who had started the move when he burst clear of a maul near his own line, eventually crossed our line. It meant that they took the Test 12-9, and what made it even more unpalatable for me was hearing all those boozed Kiwi imports on Fourex Hill, who had obviously adopted this country in name only, going absolutely delirious over the result.

Yet in the dressing-room later, there was still a strong feeling among our players that we were better than this mob, and we resolved to prove it in the third and deciding Test.

In the meantime, I packed my bags and headed from the sumptuous surroundings of the Parkroyal Hotel to far less salubrious accommodation at some pub in Kangaroo Point, where our Australian Universities team was preparing to play the All Blacks in a mid-week game. What a comedown that was! The rooms were small and shoddy and the starving students almost had to fight the management to get more and better food than what was normally served the guests. What's more, we got flogged by 30 points.

Then down to Sydney for the last Test, for which the selectors had made some drastic changes.

Phillip Cox was dropped at halfback for Peter Carson and Peter Grigg came onto the wing for Mick Martin, who was injured. The forward changes were much more sweeping. They brought in Declan Curran to the front-row. His style of play would be largely unsuited to Test match Rugby these days, because he was purely and simply a scrummager. The engineroom of the scrum seemed the main concern in his life and, believe me, this big, beefy solicitor was good at it. Tony D'Arcy, another real powerhouse, was brought in on the other side of the front-row to add even more muscle and authority to the scrum. Our skipper Tony Shaw was also shifted into the second-row and Duncan Hall moved into a

The early clashes sometimes made me wonder if it was all worthwhile.

reshuffled back-row. The only enforced change was Peter McLean in the second-row for Williams. Hooker Bill Ross and I were the only forwards who had been left in our positions.

The team changes didn't seem to make the slightest difference to our resolve. On the morning of the Test, the confidence of that team as we breakfasted together was unbelievable. We were acutely aware that the fate of the Bledisloe Cup hinged on this game, and that Australia hadn't beaten the All Blacks in a series on home soil since 1934. We had the chance to make history, and were determined to.

The New Zealanders had some problems in their camp before the Test with food poisoning. The obvious rumours circulated about it being done deliberately by some pro-Aussie sympathisers, but that was bunkum. Closer to the truth was the story that some of their supporters had brought across a few crates of the famous Bluff oysters, and that the All Blacks had hoed into those a night or two before the Test.

Whatever their physical state, the All Blacks could never have won. We were so revved up that nothing was going to stop us that afternoon.

In the very opening minute of the Test, the ball went along the Australian backline. New cap Peter Grigg chipped ahead to the right-hand corner of the field and the ball bounced into his arms as he raced after it for an unconverted try. The crowd went bananas. Our spirits went through the roof, and after that we sustained one attack after another.

They simply couldn't contain us and towards the end of the Test the whole crowd was singing Waltzing Matilda. After another of our tries, as we were walking back to halfway, Tony Shaw called to us: 'Listen to that! Just listen to that crowd! We're not going to let them down. We're really going to nail these All Blacks to the wall.'

And we did, comprehensively. By 26-10. And there was no greater buzz than doing a lap of honour at the great Sydney Cricket Ground with the Bledisloe Cup in our hands.

So the Bledisloe Cup was ours—our first victory over New Zealand in a home series in nearly half a century. And afterwards, the old wooden rafters in the SCG dressing-room almost lifted off with the celebrations.

In my first season of international Rugby, it was a dream start to my career. After succumbing for generations to All Black-forward power, it looked like we had at last found a dominant pack of our own to complement the marvellous backs that Australia always seems to produce year in and year out.

CUT DOWN TO SIZE

*H*aving been undefeated the previous year, Sydney were very anxious to build on their record in 1981; coach Peter Crittle even declared publicly that he wanted to again win every game.

He brought us together for training in February and pushed the 'mongrel dogs' just as hard as he ever had. While the backs and the back-rowers were able to hack the tremendously hard work, the front and second-rowers found it almost too much. At one fitness workout he put us through a torturous series of time trials and, to finish off, we each had to run a mile in under six minutes. If you couldn't, then you were penalised an extra two laps of the oval. Our lumbering props Declan Curran and John Coolican had no hope of doing that at the end of a long series of sprints and the rest of us sat back and laughed our heads off while watching the 'water buffaloes', as Crittle called them, doing the extra laps. We might have laughed at them then, but we all knew we could never get by without those two tanks.

Before the season really got under way, I went off to Japan with the Australian Universities team for a short tour, which was to finish with a mini-Test against All Japan. The tour was seen as a way of fence-mending after the Australian Colts tour there a few years before, when there was a lot of on-field fighting, which greatly disturbed the Japanese. They like their Rugby played without any rough stuff, and so it was impressed on us by our coach Brian (Boxhead) O'Shea and skipper Roger Davis to keep it clean at all costs, which we obliged in doing.

The Japanese are really unsurpassed as hosts and it remains one of the most enjoyable and funniest tours I've ever been on. We won the four games against their university teams, but then lost to All Japan, which was to all intents and purposes their Test lineup, by a single point. It was amazing seeing the tremendous elation of the Japanese players for about 30 seconds after the fulltime siren before their inherent discipline suddenly returned. They stopped cavorting around with excitement, bowed their heads, shook our hands and solemnly walked off the field. At the official dinner that night the sister-in-law of the Emperor, Princess Chichibill, was present in her capacity as patron of the Japanese Rugby Union.

Back home again I was picked to play for Sydney in early April against a World XV, which was all part of the razzle-dazzle which the

Australian Universities v All Japan, Tokyo, 1981. Aust. Uni. players l to r: Roger Davis, Dick Davis, Mal Washbourne and me

executive director of the Sydney Rugby Union, Ken Elphick, had dreamed up to make the game more commercial. Nonetheless, it was one of the best invitational lineups you could imagine, with players like Bruce Robertson, Hika Reid and Andy Haden from New Zealand, Graham Price from Wales, the monstrous Alejandro Iachetti from Argentina, who was 203 centimetres in his stockinged feet, and his genius of a countryman Hugo Porta, as well as a sprinkling of Queenslanders, including Mark Loane as captain.

A new face in our Sydney team was the Fijian Villie Vai, who was going to mark the World XV's Japanese winger Masaru Fujiwara. Before the game, so as to get Villie all steamed up, Crittle called the team into a huddle one night at training, pointed to Villie and solemnly told him: 'This is a very, very important game for you, Villie, because you're playing against a team which has a Japanese playing opposite you. And Villie, do you know what the Japanese did during the War? They bombed Fiji!' The rest of us began scratching our heads and trying to recall whether Japan really had bombed Fiji. Well, Villie wasn't too hot on his wartime history and didn't even give it so much as a second thought. His eyes were already rolling with anger. We went back to tackling practice and Villie started hitting the tackling bags so desperately hard that he was almost knocking the stuffing out of them. And by the time he got out onto the Sydney Cricket Ground for the match he went after Fujiwara with so much vehemence that you'd have thought he'd finally found the pilot who led the bombing raid. He almost took Fujiwara's head off every time he tackled him. You could never take it away from Crittle. He was as cunning as a sewer rat when it came to things like that.

Much of the pre-match publicity centred on the individual duel between Porta and Mark Ella, who were undoubtedly among the best five-eighths in the world. Both were genuine artists, but there was no question which of them was the better that day. Porta finished clearly ahead and, as well as playing all over Mark, he kept me and the other breakaway Greg Craig constantly bamboozled with his sidestepping. We couldn't get anywhere near him to slow him down and consequently he had a field day.

Given the opposition, Sydney did tremendously well to draw that game 16-all. Loane said afterwards that, given the way the Sydney forwards had played, Australian Rugby was really blooming and looking healthier than it had for years.

Mark Ella's skills were limitless as illustrated by this innovative pass

Sydney then undertook a procession of representative games over the next few weeks, which included playing Queensland at Ballymore. We hadn't been beaten in the fourteen matches we'd played over two seasons before that. But all our confidence and feelings of invincibility came crashing down with an awfully loud bang that day, for the Maroons whipped us 30-4 and four tries to one. Afterwards there were plenty of questions asked about our performance, but what stuck in my mind was my first clash since schooldays with the little Queensland terrier Chris

Roche. He was to become my toughest opponent at home as well as the greatest threat to my Test position.

Then in quick succession, Sydney lost again to Canterbury from New Zealand, then bounced back by beating Auckland under lights at Redfern Oval. Regulars at the home of the South Sydney Rugby League team would have rubbed their eyes in disbelief and sworn off the booze for life if they'd seen the ground lights on that night and wandered in. Rugby had never been played at Redfern before. But having this game under lights at the home of the Rabbitohs in the very heartland of Rugby League was another of Elphick's weird and wonderful ideas aimed at making Rugby more commercial.

In the next outing we beat NSW Country, again at Redfern Oval, before the NSW team was picked for a series of games. Our State coach was Jeff Sayle, one of Rugby's greatest characters, here or anywhere else in the world. He's misunderstood by many because of his laughter and light-hearted approach to many things, but his knowledge of the game and his loyalty is limitless. I'll come back to him in more detail later in the book, but at the time I became not only one of his players, but also his chauffeur. I'd drive him to training, then on the way home I'd be instructed to stop at one of his mate's pubs for a schooner, then detour to Harry's Cafe de Wheels at Woolloomooloo for a cup of blood (tomato soup) and a South Sydney (pie, peas and tomato sauce) alongside all the sailors and assorted Sydney riff-raff, then stop for just one more schooner at the Randwick Rugby Club, and then finally be made to go into his home for a few glasses of wine and to watch his dog Sonny play the xylophone!

NSW's first game was against Manawatu, another of those tough provincial teams from over the water with five All Blacks in it. Yet we thrashed them unmercifully by 58-3 and ten tries to blot. Then we cleaned up Waikato and Counties, before playing Queensland under lights at the Sydney Cricket Ground at the end of May. As was the case with Sydney, the Maroons spoiled everything, stopping our advance by 26-15, which was a very big disappointment.

A week later we had the chance for revenge when we went back to Brisbane for the return game. With Queensland having beaten both Sydney and NSW, their supporters were baying for blood more loudly than ever. But they didn't get it. Our forwards gave it everything that day, we completely dominated the lineouts and beat them 7-6. In the dressing-room later, all Sayley could do was walk around and around just laughing his kookaburra laugh in relief and happiness.

That was an important victory for the NSW players in terms of Test selection, because the French touring team was arriving in mid-June and everyone was scrambling to grab a spot in the Test team. None more so than me.

Given my ancestry, I had a natural affinity for anything French, and was particularly keen to play against their skipper, Jean-Pierre Rives, about whom I'd heard so much and watched so intently on television. Rives stood out on a Rugby pitch like a shining beacon, not just because of his mane of Persil-white hair but because of his tearaway style. There wasn't much doubt about Rives being the world's finest breakaway at that time, and trying to match him presented me with a fierce challenge.

He'd brought a pretty fair team with him. France were the Five Nations champions, having beaten England, Wales, Scotland and Ireland in that order just a few months before. Besides Rives, they had several other players with exceptional reputations, such as their massive prop-forward Robert Paparemborde and a new young fullback or winger everyone in Europe was talking about named Serge Blanco. In his first year of coaching them was the former French halfback and captain Jacques Fouroux, who was a dead ringer for Napoleon. Fouroux was to shape the destiny of French Rugby for well over a decade, and become one of the game's best-ever teachers. Incidentally, had he ever turned to crime he'd have done very nicely at that too because his favourite party trick, which he does with amazing dexterity, is picking pockets and lifting watches!

Why the French accepted the itinerary that they did I'll never know. It was a suicide mission, as they were drawn to play Queensland first up on June 14. But after the many arduous tours the French had put on for Australia over the years I guess this was a case of getting even. But to make them play Queensland . . . that really was over the odds. Yet despite this they won the game 18-15, which ranks as one of the most courageous victories by an international side that I've ever seen. The fierceness of that encounter had to be seen to be believed and included some savage rucking of their halfback Pierre Berbizier, who had his ear so badly ripped that he had to return to France. That incident did not make me proud to be an Australian Rugby player. Many might have forgotten that injury, but the French certainly didn't. It came back to haunt us on the Wallaby tour of France in 1983, because in the opening game at Strasbourg the first scrum partly collapsed and we immediately heard the call from the French side: 'Queensland! . . . Queensland!' The French second-rowers then set about trying to kick in the heads of every Australian forward lying on the ground.

But back to 1981. France's game against Sydney was under lights at the Sydney Cricket Ground. There was a tremendous build-up for this, given that Sydney hadn't been beaten by any international side since 1974, but on the night the skies opened and the rain came down in buckets. It became heavier and heavier as the game wore on. But after the teams had slogged it out for the whole game in the torrential rain, the result finally rested on a single penalty kick by our fullback, Geoff Richards, in the dying seconds. France were ahead by a point when Queensland referee Col Waldron awarded the decisive penalty. Richards, the unflappable Pom, took all the time in the world and his kick from a long way out hit the crossbar and skipped over for us to win 16-14. The French were totally distressed by that ending, so much so that Rives led the lot of them straight off the field and into the dressing-room without so much as one of them shaking hands with any of us. The next day, after the media had highlighted their extreme rudeness, there were excuses from the management about the players not wanting to linger in the rain, but at the time there was no doubt that Rives and his men were just steaming mad at losing.

Skin and hair were set to fly when NSW played them, because of the way they'd lost to Sydney and the 'no handshakes' episode. And it did. There was no quarter asked or given by either side, and the fellow who took more punishment than anyone was their second-rower Daniel Revallier. He'd obviously been told by the coach Fouroux to go down on the ball in the rucks and thus stop NSW from getting it at all costs. And if he was kicked a thousand and one times while he was doing it, then to remember it was for the glory of France.

Revallier—who was called Samson by his teammates because he could lift a car on his own—proved a wonderfully loyal, if foolish, Frenchman, because he did exactly as ordered. But though we climbed all over him while he kept constantly lying on the ball, he never once blinked an eyelid. I can't really believe the punishment Revallier absorbed that day.

France won that game 21-12, but in the process lost their skipper Rives, who injured a shoulder when sandwiched in a tackle by Parramatta teammates Mick Martin and Don Price. He was so troubled by that injury that he was virtually out of action for the rest of the tour. One of my rival back-rowers that afternoon was Pierre Lacans, with whom I was to enjoy the odd glass of wine or two during the tour and become very good mates. But when we arrived in France with the Wallabies two years later, we learned that in the meantime he had been tragically killed in a car accident.

There was so much talent around at the time that competition for spots in our first Test line-up was red hot. Loane was back from a footballing-working adventure in South Africa, during which he captained Natal and also the South African Barbarians against the touring British Lions. He became a Junior Springbok and looked certain to win the rare honour of playing for South Africa when he returned home to play against France, realising he would have to play in that series to be chosen for the Wallaby tour of the British Isles later in the year. He took the lock-forward's spot, Tony Shaw was made captain on one side of the

Concentration plus against the French in 1981

scrum and I won the other breakaway spot ahead of my old adversary Chris Roche.

Geoff Richards was fullback instead of Roger Gould, John Hipwell was halfback again after three years' retirement and, in a selection which gladdened every Queenslander's heart, Paul (Spoofer) McLean nudged Mark Ella out of the five-eighth role. But given the way Queensland had dominated our lead-up games, nobody could deny Spoofer his place. I felt the unluckiest guy to miss out was Mick Mathers, who was the most honest footballer you'd ever come across.

That first French Test at Ballymore held special significance for me because I was playing alongside Loaney for the first time. In my eyes he was something of a god, and I guess my feeling was the same as a young actor getting a bit part in a movie with Dustin Hoffmann. Loaney was a huge inspiration, and I tailed him around the field hoping to feed off him whenever he made one of those titanic bursts where he'd split the defence wide open with his unbelievable strength and speed.

Sticking to him in that Test paid off handsomely, because Loaney splintered the Frenchmen in one charge, gave to me and I went for the line for all I was worth. I saw Blanco coming at me out of the corner of my eye, but was just fast enough to make the corner for my first Test try. I walked back with the whole of the grandstand yelling and cheering. God and Loaney had been good to me.

Although we won the Test by 17-15, we should have won by a country mile. France weren't nearly as potent with Rives missing because of his injured shoulder, and we diced with defeat because our kickers couldn't land enough goals. McLean landed only one from seven shots before Richards took over and got one from three.

Then down to Sydney for the second Test and the only change to the lineup involved Spoofer McLean going to fullback, with Mark Ella coming in at five-eighth.

The team was quartered in the Hyatt Kingsgate Hotel at Kings Cross and, apparently due to an oversight by the Australian Rugby Football Union, we were allowed to eat from the a la carte menu. Now if Loane was the best lock-forward in the world in those days he also had strong claims to being the world's biggest eater. It was like watching a front-end loader at work seeing him shovel away the tucker. He just seemed a bottomless pit, and I watched in awe at one meal as he polished off three half-lobster mornays ... for his entree. I and some others managed two each. Our food bill must have been massive, and someone within the ARFU must have had his behind kicked for allowing us to eat the fancy a la carte dishes rather than sticking to the set menus which are the norm for football teams.

Much interest in the second Test revolved around Rives and whether or not he'd play. His shoulder was still troubling him a lot, but he was such an inspiring leader that the French were desperate to get him onto the field in the hope of lifting them to victory and squaring the series. In the end, they left it to Rives himself and he said he'd play, although when he ran out onto the SCG he was so heavily strapped that he looked for all the world like the Hunchback of Notre Dame. And he was obviously in great pain every time he got bumped on the shoulder. We capitalised on his injury, calling a lot of throws to me at the back of the lineout where, with Rives opposite me so handicapped, I was able to tap down to our forwards coming around. Yet late in the Test I vividly recall a tremendous covering tackle when he came from nowhere to take out one of our backs. It must have hurt like hell doing that, and I was in awe of Rives and his courage. Mark Loane was later quoted as describing it as 'courage to the point of insanity'.

Even with such inspiration from their injured skipper, the French didn't have much chance that day. There were more than 41 000 spectators on our side, our backline of Hipwell, Ella, Hawker, O'Connor, Moon, Martin and McLean fired, the penalty count was 17-4 our way, and McLean finally found his kicking boots. This time he potted six out of eight for 16 points in our 24-14 win.

In the early hours of the next morning I found myself with their halfback Jean Pierre Elissalde at the Hyatt Kingsgate pouring out the last drops of a bottle of cognac which we had polished off between us. He'd had more practice with cognac than me and, while they'd lost the

New Zealand, 1988, Concord:
Wayne Shelford, All Black inspiration
(**Action Graphics**)

World Cup: Japanese captain Toshiyuki
Hayashi (**Action Graphics**)

France, 1986: Nick Farr-Jones looks on
hopefully (**Nick Jacomas**)

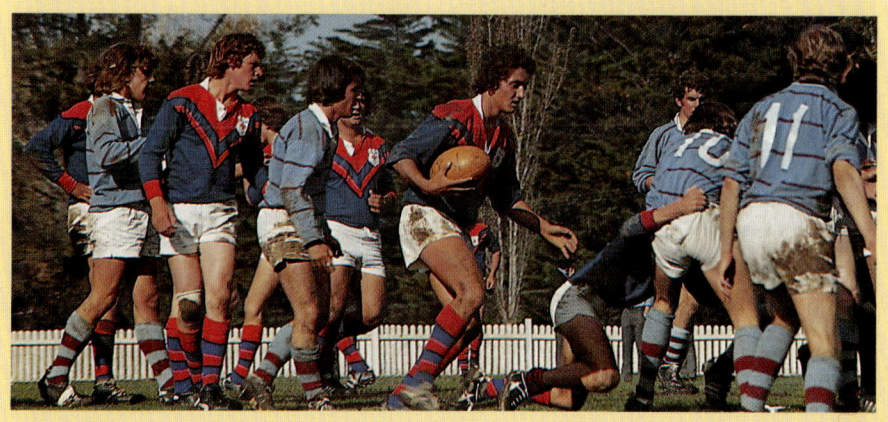

Schooldays: St Patrick's Goulburn against arch-enemy Chevalier College—we won,
of course!

France, 1983: the boys having a bleat—Andy McIntyre, Steve Williams, Roger Gould, Steve Cutler and a hungover Poidevin

The Vatican Museum, 1983: Bob Dwyer and Ollie Hall, as Steve Cutler takes another bath

series, he won the drinking bout hands down. My head confirmed this the next day.

In mid-August the ARFU had the Wallaby trials to choose the team to go to Britain, but I was a non-starter. I'd broken my thumb in a club game. University of NSW were then in second division and, because I was a Test player, I found I was always a marked man. A Test player obviously posed a greater threat than anyone else, and if the circumstances arose where he could be quietened then so be it. Well this particular afternoon playing against Drummoyne I tackled their Tongan five-eighth a little late and was set upon by about six of his teammates—all of them Tongans. I made the mistake of hitting one of these blokes on the head and consequently broke my thumb.

So I missed the trials, but was still selected for the British Isles tour in what was hailed as the most talented Australian touring side ever chosen. We had skills to burn in almost every department. The media also made much of the three Ellas being in the team, and Hipwell was selected at 33 years of age for what was his third tour of Britain, having been there in 1966–67 and 1975–76.

So good were the personnel that our captain, Tony Shaw, made the fairly provocative statement before we went that the Seventh Wallabies were capable of winning all four Tests, if not all 24 matches, which immediately put added and unnecessary pressure on us. We had more than enough as it was. Having beaten New Zealand in four of our last five Test encounters, and more recently the French by two Tests to nil, and coming after the success of the marvellous undefeated Australian schoolboys team of 1977–78, which included the Ellas, an inordinate amount was already expected of us. Australian Rugby was undergoing a renaissance and everybody naturally wanted that to continue by having the Wallabies wipe everything before them in Britain. So I doubt if any other Australian side has left these shores carrying such fervent expectations.

I was very sad to see Don Price miss the touring team. He had a hard time living in Ray's shadow. I don't know how many times I'd heard him tell people: 'Don't call me Ray Price's brother. I'm Don Price.' He always fought extremely hard for his own identity, and it was just a pity he was around at the time of so many good back-row forwards, because he was a terrific player. I'd have also liked to see Keith Besomo make the tour. He was a fantastic second-rower, who could really jump and was very aggressive. It was amazing how Keith had overcome his complete deafness to get where he had in international Rugby and, as time would tell, we could really have done with his lineout skills in the UK. But sadly they couldn't fit everybody into this very talented team.

We arrived in London to much the same expectations as we'd heard back home. Typical of the headlines was the one which screamed RUGBY MESSIAHS EXPECTED TO PRODUCE MIRACLES. So much was still being written and said about us in those early days that the pressure was starting to reach bursting point. Nevertheless we were confident of living up to all those lofty predictions.

In the opening game against Midlands Division, with the English captain Peter Wheeler leading them and on a miserable day, we were all at sea. We were under pressure at both the scrum and lineout, which were going to be telling points throughout the tour, and at the end of the day had been beaten 16-10. Suddenly our hopes all came down to earth with a crash and we realised just how much work had to be done, especially with the weather experts forecasting that Britain was heading for its worst winter in a century.

We won only one of our first four matches and then just scraped home 10-9 against Wales B. Obviously things were getting pretty grim by this stage as we weren't exactly setting the world afire. There was a lot of criticism of our performances in the media and this really started to get to the players. We desperately needed a strong victory to lift our spirits.

The sixth game was against Pontypool, the Welsh club whose forward pack at the time made it probably the best non-international team in Britain. By then everyone in the Wallabies wanted to spank this outfit to show that we shouldn't be written off this early.

We went into the game all revved up and took them apart in great style by 37-6. It was an enormous lift for our deflated confidence. Hipwell had a great game, as did McLean at five-eighth.

It looked like the tour was back on the rails and we had two more wins before heading for Belfast, where we were all anxious to have a first-hand look at life in the strife-torn city. The Wallabies stayed at a hotel just outside the city and two armed detectives were assigned to us during our stay. It was a fascinating and sometimes chilling experience seeing all the armed foot patrols and armoured vehicles on the streets, while the people went about their daily chores as if nothing at all unusual was happening around them. One night when some of us were walking back from a pub down the road from the hotel a guy jumped out of the darkness brandishing what looked like a sub-machine gun. We all scattered in fear, then realised it was our court jester of a captain waving a lethal-looking stick.

We defeated Ulster 12-6 then flew out of Belfast the next morning on a chartered aircraft, which we were told was the only flight taking off that day. A high-ranking official had been gunned down and the airport had been closed while searches were made. We were all a bit tense in this atmosphere, and just after we took off Peter (Spider) McLean looked out the window and then turned to the extremely-nervous flier Bob

Templeton and remarked that 'the view's much better now the wing has fallen off.' Our coach went into hysterics. Seriously though, being in Belfast in that atmosphere finally brought home to us the seriousness of the 'troubles' there.

The British Isles tour, 1981, weather and conditions sub-arctic. l to r: Michael Hawker, Paul McLean, Phillip Cox with ball, Mark Loane, Mitchell Cox, myself, Mick Mathers and Chris Roche

About that time I was beginning to feel a lot of pressure with regards my Test position. I knew that I really needed a very big performance in our next game against Munster if I was to stay put for the Test against Ireland. So in that particular game I just kept tackling everything that moved and, although we lost, one of the boys told me later: 'Gee mate, you really looked inspired out there today.' It paid off, because I made the Test line-up. This meant, however, that Tony Shaw was moved from his normal position in the back-row to second-row, which was significant in that it robbed us of some height and weight. The most disappointed player to miss out was our prop Declan Curran, who so much wanted to play because of his Irish ancestry and because his brother Frank (the one who had decked him) was coming over especially to watch this one Test match.

When we arrived in Dublin for the Test we found we were staying right in the centre of the city at the old Shelbourne Hotel. Nothing wrong with that, except the Irish team was staying there too! Normally that's just not done for obvious reasons. So in the days leading up to the Test the two teams had to play cat-and-mouse at meal times or while passing through the foyer in order not to bump into one another. We even found ourselves sharing adjoining team meeting rooms on the Friday afternoon before the Test. At that stage we were watching a comedy video, rolling around with laughter, while the Irish next door were talking about tactics for the next day. We knew this, because you only had to put your ear to the keyhole to pick up a fair amount of what was being said. The Irish, on the other hand, must have thought the Australians were taking a light-hearted approach to the game with all the screams of laughter coming from our side.

Our dirt-trackers (the non-Test players) had a whale of a time being in Dublin that week and seemed to spend every night out on the tiles drinking Guinness at either social functions or the pubs with the extra-friendly Irish, then stumbling home in the early hours and waking up the rest of us.

Australia won the Test 16-12 at Lansdowne Road. Although we suffered in the scrums, where we conceded three strikes against the head, as well as the lineouts, the forwards showed great spirit and we tackled our hearts out, particularly towards the finish. Our back-row played exceptionally well, and Hipwell had an absolutely tremendous game behind the scrum.

On the Sunday, the Wallabies spent the day at the Wanderers club and, in all the elation over our victory, I ended up with the greatest hangover I've ever had in my life.

We continued the tour with a last-minute win over Leicester, the English county champions, and then had good wins against Swansea and Pontypridd, giving us the encouraging record of nine wins in our last ten matches. The thing which stands out in my mind from that game at Pontypridd was the fervour of those Welsh fans way up there in the valleys. I've never seen so many autograph hunters waiting for us after our official dinner that night. They must have been 50 deep and had been lined up for hours waiting for us to emerge. It proved to us just how fanatical the Welshmen are about their Rugby.

We went into preparation for the Test against Wales at the Arms Park with our Grand Slam hopes alive and with great expectations. But from the outset there was constant pressure on our scrum, which gradually took its toll as the game went on. We led 13-6 after three minutes of the second half but, although we won a fair share of loose ball, we squandered many chances and couldn't put the result out of reach. Midway through the second half we also lost Hipwell with a rib injury. Slowly the tide turned and the Welsh overhauled us. McLean also had a rare bad day when he managed only two goals from six attempts. So while we scored two tries to one, Wales won by 18-13. This loss was one of the greatest disappointments I've experienced in Rugby. To smell victory in the 'cauldron' and then see it slip away was heartbreaking.

Our next game was against Lancashire at the beautiful Vale of Lune ground. There were doubts about the game being played, because it was snowing and bitterly cold. But the organisers spread hay on the ground to stop it freezing over and we were able to play in fridge-like conditions. We had a good victory there, then easily defeated Glasgow in Edinburgh on a day when the now-appalling weather saw the temperature plunge to minus five degrees. The game had been shifted from one side of Scotland to the other because everything in Glasgow was under snow and only Murrayfield's underground electric blanket could thaw out a surface for us to play on.

Then we headed even further north to Aberdeen. By then it seemed to be snowing constantly. We had to train indoors and Michael O'Connor hurt himself in a gymnasium, which ruled him out of the game against North and Midlands and also the Scottish Test. To lose a player of O'Connor's ability at that stage of the tour was a heavy blow.

Again straw was laid on the ground at Aberdeen to enable us to play, but we won quite easily and I produced another very good game to ensure that I was still in the Test line-up. The most noticeable change for the Scottish encounter was bringing Ella into five-eighth and shifting McLean to inside-centre, because Hawker and O'Connor were both unavailable through injury.

We scored three tries to one against Scotland, but again lost. We couldn't believe it, although we'd been forewarned about what might happen. Everybody had been telling us not to allow Scotland's fullback, Andy Irvine, too many kicks at goal, but he sank us well and truly. He scored 17 points in their 24-15 success. The complete frustration at scoring more tries than the Scots yet seeing the Test slip away caused Tony Shaw to belt their second-rower Bill Cuthbertson late in the game right in front of the referee, and he was extremely lucky not to be ordered off. And Spoofer McLean had another shocker with his kicking—just one goal from seven attempts. Even though I scored from a charged-down kick, there wasn't much joy from any of us in the dressing-room afterwards. The atmosphere was one of absolute depression.

What was becoming very, very apparent was that in the internationals we didn't have the power up front. The forwards were under great pressure from the opposing packs, who could keep us pinned and then capitalise on the penalties when they occurred. And McLean's kicking had deteriorated so much that he simply couldn't respond when it was our turn for kicks at goal.

We won the next two games, during which we had a break for Christmas. While many of the team had their wives and girlfriends over there and went off with them, unattached souls like myself, Steve

Williams and Mick Martin stayed in the hotel by ourselves and had the time of our lives. My sister Jane was working at a nearby pub and I'd drag all the available players down there at every opportunity. But Jane must have gone close to losing her job at times because, apart from all the noise, Wallabies would occasionally fall over in dead-ant falls (lying on the ground with your arms and legs in the air, kicking like a dying ant) and frighten the regulars half to death. We had a wonderful white Christmas, and those of us still in the hotel would go out for an early morning run in the snow where the dead-ant falls again caused so much delight for anybody watching, especially tourists with cameras.

The Test against England was our final chance to at least even up the results of the internationals. The days leading up to it were very tense, and there was great interest in whether the tour selectors would make any changes to the line-up in a last-ditch attempt to salvage this Test. On the day the Test team was to be announced, the manager Sir Nicholas Shehadie, coach Bob Templeton and captain Tony Shaw walked together into our team meeting-room at St Ermin's Hotel. You couldn't read anything on their faces. I even detected a smile on Shawy's face. But when the team was read out he was not in it and Loane was our captain. The specialist second-rower Steve Williams had been brought in to bolster the scrum. McLean was fullback instead of Roger Gould, with Ella still five-eighth. And Hipwell was back from injury after missing the Scottish Test.

Again, we could well have pulled off this Twickenham Test, even though our scrum was still under pressure, and Bill Beaumont and Maurice Colclough won an ever-increasing amount of lineout ball. At the final whistle, we'd scored two tries to one and yet were again beaten, this time by 15-11. In what was now becoming a regular accusation, McLean received most of the blame for failing to convert either try and for getting only one penalty from three attempts.

The statistics relating to McLean's kicking throughout the tour are certainly very damaging. We scored eight tries to three during the course of the four internationals, and he kicked a total of only seven goals in twenty-three attempts. Yet in no way could you lay the blame solely on Spoofer for the failure of the Wallabies. The fact was simply that we didn't have the ascendancy in the set pieces to take the pressure off him, although the backrow of Loaney, Corny and I received tremendous accolades for the way we played.

We also struck the vilest British weather imaginable, and were often forced to play ankle-deep in mud and snow when essentially we were a highly mobile team best suited to firm grounds.

There were other problems, smaller maybe but problems nonetheless. We were hampered by a succession of injuries, with Hipwell, our most experienced player, being able to complete only two of the internationals. The tour selectors also had something to answer for in giving certain players too few games. For instance, selecting Mick Mathers for only six games out of the 23 we played was quite ridiculous given his ability. Also the training was often monotonous, which doesn't help any team's enthusiasm and attitude. Tempo must take some blame for that, although the weather made many of the training sessions abnormal, like the time we trained on packed ice before the Scottish Test, and it was so cold that the team had to be physically pushed out of the dressing-room and onto the paddock by Tempo.

But these were matters we could only mull over in retrospect after the England defeat. The tour was virtually over.

When we headed off to play West Wales for our penultimate match, an extraordinary story written by Sydney journalist David Lord hit the press back home, claiming that the team had failed because it had split down the middle into NSW and Queensland factions. That was absolute nonsense. There was certainly discontent, simply because we'd lost three of the four internationals, but there was complete camaraderie between all the players. You couldn't differentiate New South Welshmen from Queenslanders by the way they socialised, trained or travelled together.

The last port of call for us was Porthcawl for the game against the Barbarians. We were hoping to recover some dignity by really breaking loose in this traditional tour finale. But the locals were forecasting atrocious weather, and the night before the game the whole countryside disappeared under nearly two and a half metres of snow. It was a bizarre situation. The game had to be cancelled, and we had nothing to do but eat and drink for four or five days until we were scheduled to leave for home. We got so bored that one day some of us even tried to dig the team bus out of the snowdrift for something to do. At one stage Corny wanted to lead those who wished to chance it on a hike across the snowdrifts to a roadway leading to London. Nick Shehadie quickly canned that idea. But other challenges and amusements were found, the most vivid being Mick Martin and I running for over one and a half kilometres through the snowdrifts in togas to get to a fancy-dress night in a local nightclub. Eventually they had to fly the Wallabies back to London in helicopters so that we could catch our flight home to Australia.

Cancellation of the Barbarians game was a sad way for the tour to end, but it was symptomatic of that tour. It's all captured vividly in the magnificent video of the tour called 'The Running Game'. We never really got going. Although Tony Shaw's men finished with sixteen wins and one draw from 23 matches, we've got to live with the fact that history still judges us to be failures.

ADVENTURES IN THE LAND OF THE LONG WHITE CLOUD

After our return from the British Isles tour, I didn't quite know how to feel. The 1981–82 Wallabies had gone away billed as potentially the greatest Australian team of all time and had come back with very little to show from the four internationals. One win and three losses. I felt deflated ... disappointed ... call it what you like. But given the mood I was in, it was a good time to change Rugby clubs. I'd been thinking about it for a while. University of NSW had spent the previous two seasons in second division and I very much wanted to play my future club football each week at an ultra-competitive level, so that there wasn't that huge jump I used to experience going from club to representative ranks. So I left Wales after four very happy years and switched to Randwick where, with Greg McElhone turning to League and Gary Pearse going to Port Hacking, I walked into the first-grade line-up. I know many people would have liked me to have gone somewhere other than Randwick. Traditionally they always have heaps of representative players and one more wasn't going to make that much difference to them, whereas I could have been invaluable to one of the weaker first division clubs. But I've only ever wanted to play with the best and against the best, and that's why I threw in my lot with the famous Galloping Greens, a decision I've never regretted one iota.

I wasn't with them long when Randwick had the Australian club championship match against Brothers at Ballymore and I found myself opposing my Test skipper Tony Shaw. It was the first time Shawy had played in front of the Queensland crowd after the Wallaby tour and he seemed determined to exorcise all that pent-up disappointment on the redhead playing opposite him. He gave me a tough old time that afternoon. Although we beat Brothers, I can remember walking off and thinking it was nice to have Shawy on your side occasionally and not have to play against him week in and week out.

The Sydney team had a new coach in Peter (Fab) Fenton, with Crittle moving on to coach NSW. After warm-up matches against Victoria and ACT, Sydney headed off to meet Fiji in Suva. Playing there in the National Stadium is always a tough assignment, but we beat Fiji that afternoon 21-18, after Mark Ella scored a terrific try and then popped over the conversion to pull us out of the fire. While the trip was successful in the playing sense, we had problems off the field because our team manager, Norman Watson, was new to the job and trying to find his way. His heart was in it, but he made a few silly blunders—one of the forwards got so riled that he had to be dissuaded from belting him on the nose.

A week later Sydney faced Queensland at Concord Oval. We had so much spirit that afternoon that we absolutely blasted them off the paddock by 25-9, despite their having a complete line-up of internationals, including Pilecki, Hall, Loane, Shaw, Lynagh, O'Connor, Moon, Slack and McLean. We played fantastically well and there would be few, if any, teams in the world which could have thrashed Queensland as comprehensively as we did that day.

Our next game was against NSW Country and, with Michael Hawker injured, I was named Sydney captain for the first time. My rival skipper was their outside-centre Paul Southwell, who came from Goulburn and had played alongside me for ACT schoolboys. We'd also played against each other in the local competition down there and then together in the Southern Tablelands side. It turned into the easiest of victories for us, as we ran away with it by 43-3.

NSW then undertook a three-match tour of New Zealand, with Crittle as coach and a new face entirely as team manager. His name was Alan Belford Jones. A former schoolteacher, he had moved on from there to become executive director of the NSW Employers' Federation. I didn't know anything more about him. He certainly didn't look the Rugby type. I tried to picture him being on the bottom of a ruck or whistling through an opening and setting-up his winger, but couldn't. He looked too soft and too slow altogether.

The first time I ever spoke with him was after the Sydney-Country game when he pulled me aside, suggested that I virtually ran the NSW team, and wanted to know what we would need for the New Zealand tour in the way of physiotherapy, equipment, clothing etc. Mind you he didn't manage to get everything I asked for, but at least I was very impressed with his interest in the team's welfare.

When we got across there, the ritual in the dressing-room before each game was that Jones would give a short inspirational speech to the team before Crittle would come forward, say a few encouraging, or sometimes critical, words about each player, and then also try to inspire us collectively. Both were such fantastic orators that having them motivate us before each game was like being hit with a double dose of Norman Vincent Peale. While we had a very talented side regardless, with Mark Ella the captain and weaving magic with his brothers Glen and Gary, the stimulation from Jones and Crittle was nevertheless able to lift us each time onto that higher plane.

We convincingly beat the tough mob from Waikato 43-21 in our opening game, despite Steve Cutler being king-hit, and so that evening we indulged ourselves much more than normal. Waikato was always a prized scalp. Crittle led the revelry, and everyone was forced to skol a jug of beer. Even Jonesy put one down easily, which made us all think that maybe he wasn't just an academic toff who idolised Pavarotti and was heavily into the Liberal Party and reading Kazantzakis.

But nobody in the team that evening, or any evening, came remotely near Steve Williams when it came to syphoning jugs of beer down his throat. He put away three or four before we all retired for dinner. The locals in the hotel who had watched this couldn't believe anybody could drink so much beer so quickly. They reckoned there was only one fellow in town who might match Swill. Someone asked them to produce him and, before you knew it, one of them disappeared and arrived back a few minutes later with the local beer-skolling champ. From his weather-beaten looks and large belly, he obviously spent his working life outdoors and the rest of his time drinking beer. With the rest of us urging him on, Swill excused himself from the dinner table and accepted the challenge. Soon the bets were flying thick and fast. The NSW players had so much faith in Swill that we all got a piece of the action. The fact that he was handicapped by having already had three or four jugs didn't worry us at all. Well they lined up at the bar for the showdown, Swill and the local, the starter gave the signal, up came the jugs of beer to their mouths and down it went. Swill's empty jug hit the bar again a matter of seconds later, fractionally ahead of the local's. We collected all our winnings, the local staggered off somewhere and Swill went quietly back to his unfinished meal.

We should have learnt our lesson from the previous Sydney tour, because the next morning Crittle again summoned the troops for a training run approaching the horrific proportions of 1980. He ran us into the ground. The team then headed for New Plymouth, where the Taranaki team always provides tough opposition on a soft pitch. With this in mind, Crittle trained us extremely hard beforehand. We were doing one exercise where the forwards run bent over with our hands scraping on the ground to impress upon us the importance of staying low when driving into rucks. Crittle finally referred to the exercise as 'Triffids'. We must have covered the length of the fog-bound field a dozen times over. It was killing us. But, 'once more', Crittle demanded. When we got to the end, the backs, who as usual hadn't been doing much at all, were huddled in a tight circle singing 'my baby takes the morning train . . .' and tossing the ball to each other to that rhythm. We couldn't believe it. We stopped, quizzed Crittle about what was going on, and he called us a bunch of 'mongrel dogs' and punished our insubordination by making us do our back-breaking exercise a few more times. As usual, the flashy and pampered three-quarters had got their way. If I ever come back in a second life ...

We defeated Taranaki 14-9, and the next morning went by bus down to Palmerston North. During this trip Jonesy got to his feet in the aisle, took the driver's microphone, and provided the team with a phantom race call of one of the Melbourne Cups. We hadn't known, but he has the most phenomenal knowledge and recall of Melbourne Cups, and can give an amazingly accurate race call of virtually any Cup you care to nominate. The new manager really was starting to impress us.

At Palmerston North it had been raining cats and dogs. What with that and the fact that Manawatu had a heap of All Blacks, it didn't look too promising for us. But in a very physical game, during which a fair amount of blood was spilt on both sides, we won 40-13. Afterwards at the local hospital there was a queue of players from both sides receiving stitches. That night some of the Manawatu players came along to our toga party, but two of them who disliked each other intensely finished up having an almighty blue. One of them had to be taken back to the hospital for further repair work to his head. They're a strange breed these New Zealanders.

With the tour over, we headed home all very impressed with the combination of Crittle and Jones as coach and manager. Both were highly intelligent individuals with professional backgrounds, they had many beliefs and values in common, and got on very well together. They were very successful on that tour, and I've often wondered what they might have been like running an Australian team together.

The NSW Rugby Union had another of those invitational matches arranged for us. It was against a World XV but, because some of the European players withdrew, the pack finished up with a predominance of All Blacks, including Graham Mourie, Andy Haden, Billy Bush and Hika Reid, which we could have done without. Their presence in the forwards really stiffened the opposition, and although we won 31-13 it was at great cost. Glen Ella, Michael Hawker, Sandy Muston, Gary Pearse, John Coolican and I were all hurt during the game, which tended to break up the momentum of our New Zealand tour. The injury which put me off the field that afternoon—or rather what caused it—created a tremendous stir.

Among the 25 000 spectators was my mother. She had decided that this would be a nice social game to watch me play. Not too serious and therefore not too rough. So she and dad drove up especially from Goulburn. About twenty minutes into the game I found myself pinned on the bottom of a ruck with my head suddenly being kicked and scraped repeatedly. Try as I might, I couldn't protect or defend myself. I could only brace myself, and next thing I felt and smelt blood spilling down my face. The wide-angled lens of the media photographers caught several boots making contact with my head, and publication of these photographs the next day caused a huge furore. I went off in a terrible mess. After being stitched in the dressing-room without anaesthetic by our medical officer there was still so much blood dripping onto my shirt that the late Dr Syd Sugerman took me to his Bondi surgery for some additional mending. When this was all finished I proceeded to the reception where Haden

NSW v The World. Yes that is my head.

denied to my face that he had done any of the serious damage. All evidence then seemed to point to Bush, who was the other prime suspect. But years later, Mourie told me that he had been shocked at the incident and, being captain, had spoken to Haden about it at the time. Haden's response? He accused his captain of getting soft. Apart from making my head look like a patchwork quilt for a long while, it stopped Mum from coming to many future matches involving New Zealanders.

Over the next few days there were calls for an inquiry into the incident, and Alan Jones really took up the fight on my behalf. But in the end no action was taken. Often I think what might have happened had this occurred in contemporary Rugby League, with their examination of videos and fairly efficient judiciary committee, and have come to the conclusion that the culprit(s) concerned would have spent a very long time out of the game.

All the injuries from that World XV game badly disrupted the NSW team for the two games against Queensland. Because it was the Queensland Rugby Union's centenary year, it had been arranged that both interstate games be played in Queensland, the first up north at Townsville and the second at Ballymore.

I was determined to play in Townsville, even though I still felt like I'd been kicked in the head by a mule. Or an All Black. We had some others feeling sick and sorry for themselves and had to make a few team changes, with my flatmate at the time, Tony McGeoch, being plucked from nowhere at the last hour to replace Glen Ella. It so happened that Tony played an absolute blinder at fullback and certainly equalled Roger Gould on the day.

Queensland barely outlasted us by 23-16. We played extremely well in very hot and trying conditions, and really felt afterwards that our patched-up team had been robbed by referee Dick Byres, who disallowed several tries that we thought were legitimate. I still laugh about Dr Mark Loane coming into our dressing room after the game to kindly remove the stitches in my head, something he'd tried to do a number of times on the field that day.

We suffered a few more injuries in that game, so we went south to Brisbane, for what was being billed as the real highlight of Queensland's centenary celebrations, looking fairly knocked about. Among the Townsville casualties was Mark Ella, so yours truly was made captain of NSW for the first time. It obviously wasn't their fault, but the backs we had that day bore no resemblance at all to the set we had fielded against the World XV a fortnight before. There was just no way we could hide their extreme inexperience, and they constantly fouled up the mountain of ball we won in the forwards. It meant that the match followed the script with Queensland rejoicing in their centenary year by climbing all over us 41-7.

With Scotland about to arrive, the competition was really hotting up for Test spots, none being more contested than the breakaway positions, where there wasn't much between Tony Shaw, Peter Lucas, Gary Pearse, Chris Roche and me. Lock-forward Loane seemed the only fly-by-nighter guaranteed his place in the backrow.

The Scots began well with a 44-16 win against Queensland Country at Mt Isa, but lost the next two matches when Queensland beat them 18-7 and then Sydney 22-13. Their tour was at a critical stage then, and I'm sure their captain Andy Irvine and coach Jim Telfer were compelled to do some impassioned talking and make some strong threats to get things in order. The remedy worked, for they took care of Victoria easily enough and then made an unexpected return to form with a comprehensive 31-7 defeat of NSW. Headlines before this match included POIDEVIN NEEDS A BLINDER. The inference was pretty clear and, while I thought I had played well in the interstate series and also in this loss to the Scots, I missed out on the Test team, with Shaw and new cap Roche the breakaways. That hurt a hell of a lot, especially after having played in all four internationals on the British Isles tour.

Sydney v Scotland at the SCG, 1982. Sydney forwards intent on taking care of our halfback, Peter Carson

But if the omissions of me and Paul McLean from the Australian line-up were surprising, they were nothing compared with the choice of Glen Ella at fullback ahead of Roger Gould. That really was a bombshell. Queenslanders were ready to get a lynch mob together and go hunting for the new national coach Bob Dwyer. It was clearly his logic. The three Ellas played with our Randwick club where Dwyer was the coach. He was blinded by their ability, as considerable as it was, and wanted the Test XV to revolve around two of them. He'd obviously been able to convince the other national selectors, John Bain and Bob Templeton, to give him his way. It was a bad mistake. Queensland Rugby Union's executive director Terry Doyle demanded to know: 'How can the world's best fullback not make the Australian team?' And I agreed with him. As a clubmate, I greatly respected Glen as a courageous and extremely skilful player. But when it came to choosing the fullback for a Test match, there really was no choice to my way of thinking. I say emphatically here and now that Gould is the best fullback I've ever played with or against, and I'd never leave him out of any side for which he was available. As a fullback, he was without peer. What made Glen's selection even more ill-conceived was that the Test was to be played in Brisbane, Gould's home ground. So when poor Glen ran out, the capacity crowd booed and jeered him as if he was from another planet, which wouldn't have done much for his spirit.

What the omission of McLean and Gould did, apart from causing almost a Rugby civil war, was to leave Australia without a recognised goalkicker against the Scots. Michael Hawker, playing out of position on the wing, did the goalkicking after mid-week lessons from soccer coach Jim Hermiston, and landed only one goal from five attempts. With a try apiece, Australia should have won through goalkicking, but Scotland crept in by 12-7.

For the second Test in Sydney, the selectors dropped Mark Ella, Glen Ella and Andrew Slack, reinstated Gould and McLean, returned Hawker to the centre and Peter Grigg went to the wing. Bob Dwyer hadn't got his way this time and the Queenslanders' wrath marginally subsided. The changes worked and Australia registered a record 33-9 victory, the highest score ever against a member country of the International Rugby Board and the biggest margin ever against Scotland. McLean's 21 points—eight goals from nine attempts—was five points higher than his previous Test scoring record, which he shared with Greg Cornelsen. As if to emphasise the error of leaving McLean and Gould out of the first Test team, Gould became the first fullback to score two tries in a Test for Australia.

As for me, the Australian Rugby Football Union couldn't even see its way clear to allow me any complimentary tickets to the Sydney Test, despite providing every tin-pot official with ample tickets. Alan Jones provided tickets for me and Tony McGeoch and we watched the Test with him. Having played ten consecutive Test matches before that, I squirmed uncomfortably in my seat throughout the whole 80 minutes and then got myself nicely smashed afterwards in one of the Paddington pubs.

Despite my feelings, the world didn't in fact come to an end, and towards the end of the season I was named in Mark Ella's reshaped Wallabies for the tour of New Zealand. I say reshaped, because nine of the most experienced players declared their unavailability. There had been a growing feeling among Queensland's senior players that they were being used unmercifully by the Rugby authorities, who were content each season to arrange fixture after fixture and one tour after another involving the representative players without giving any thought at all to compensating them for the time lost from work and their families. Their grievance had a lot of support from the public at large. Loane, for example, was a doctor doing post-graduate work in ophthalmic surgery and it really was laughable to expect him to forgo the huge salary he could command for the pittance paid amateur Rugby players. Yet Loane, who became the spokesman for the disgruntled group, never wanted to be reimbursed for salary, but merely to receive a nominal amount to defray mortgage costs and car expenses. At any rate, nine of their most senior players pulled out of the New Zealand tour in protest—Loane, Shaw, Peter McLean, Tony D'Arcy, Bill Ross, Stan Pilecki, Brendan Moon, Michael O'Connor and Paul McLean.

In some ways, it was a blessing in disguise. I understand that during the Scotland series there was almost a revolt when McLean and Gould weren't there for the first Test. Loane and Shaw had begun to exert a strong influence on the team, aimed somewhat against Dwyer for his part in those sackings. So it was probably a good thing that they didn't go to New Zealand under him as coach.

It meant that the Wallabies were largely a new team with a dozen fresh international players among the 30. Mark Ella deserved to be the touring captain, and Alan Jones gave him some pointers on after-dinner speaking to help him with this part of a touring captain's responsibilities.

We were also lucky to have Dr Charles (Chilla) Wilson as manager. Chilla was the most disorganised bloke you could ever meet, which was surprising for an obstetrician-gynaecologist with a large Brisbane practice. How he ever kept track of his patients I'll never know. But he was such a delightful and popular character that everybody easily overlooked any of his organisational failings.

Just as in Britain, the Australian team was viewed as the potential saviours of Rugby in New Zealand; the players to bring the crowds back to the game as a united force after the agitation and hatred created the previous year by South Africa's tour which had so polarised the country's

Sydney Representative Team, 1980
Back Row: L Walker, D Curran, R Moore (Baggageman), D Cowlishaw, P Cox, B Malouf. Middle Row: M Martin, B Lyons, B McLean, D Price, S Williams, S Poidevin, I Robertson, J Coolican. First Row: M Cox, M Ella, M Goldberg (Manager), M Mathers (Captain), P Crittle (Coach), M Hawker, G Ella. Absent: P Carson (**Action Graphics**)

Australian Rugby team to New Zealand, 1986
Back Row: J L McInerney, D J Frawley, R J McCall, S A G Cutler, W A Campbell, S N Tuynman, R J Reynolds.
Second Row: T A Lawton, M N Hartill, M T Cook, M A Murray, J M Gardner, W J Calcraft, A Leeds, P C Grigg, J S Miller.
First Row: G S Craig (Hon. Physiotherapist), B A Smith, E E Rodriguez, N C Farr-Jones, G H Burrow, M P Burke, S L K James, D I Campese, M P Lynagh, J E Moulton (Hon. Doctor). Seated: B W Papworth, M I McBain, R A C Evans (Assistant Coach), A G Slack AM (Captain), K P Grayling MBE (Manager), S P Poidevin (Vice-Captain), A B Jones (Assistant Manager/Coach), G J Ella, I M Williams (**Melba, Sydney**)

The Premier, Nick Greiner, with the 1989 Grand Final winners—Randwick

On top of Mt Olympic—Perisher Valley—Ski Patrol and the legendary Lindsay Cotterill. Snow skiing could be the only sporting substitute for Rugby

The Poidevin Clan—SPP, Jane, dad, mum, Andrew, Anna, Lucy and Joanne

opinions on whether the Springboks should have gone there or not.

We were blessed with good weather early in the tour, which is unusual for New Zealand in the depths of winter. Largely as a result of playing on firm grounds and the team starting to click much quicker than expected, we won the first five games.

Before our tour opener against Taranaki, a disturbing incident occurred in our hotel. Two of the forwards, Ross Reynolds and Shane Nightingale, were sharing a room when Nightingale was awoken in the middle of the night by someone running a hand up his leg under the bed clothes. Now Nightingale's a huge red-haired bloke and not the prettiest looking individual in the world. Why anyone would want to make amorous advances to him I've no idea. His first thought was that it was Reynolds playing a joke on him, but Reynolds was fast asleep in the other bed. Then Nightingale spotted a shadowy figure fleeing from the room. The Queenslander took off after him, out of the room and down the corridor, making a terrific noise as he went looking for the mysterious sex deviate. He never found him. I'd hate to have been the culprit if he had. But imagine if you were that way inclined finding you'd accidentally picked on an international Rugby forward! Hopefully, it cured the deviate of his nocturnal sexual escapades for life.

There was another amusing incident at Timaru before the match against South Canterbury. Touring teams are allocated a certain number of tickets before each match for family and friends. Invariably there's a lot left over and teams sell them and put the money into a tour fund that they use to buy birthday presents, gifts for the management etc. This day it was Mick Martin's turn to sell the tickets outside the ground before the match. He came back with a mass of money. It seems Mick had not only sold all the spare tickets, but also all the tickets to the seats that the Australian officials, non-playing team members and reserves for the match were sitting in. So very soon this group was surrounded by a mob of furious locals wanting the seats they'd paid for. They had no chance of shifting them, and after screaming blue murder to no avail these luckless Kiwis went away, cheated and very angry, and our tour coffers received a handsome boost.

Having five wins from five matches by our young and inexperienced side put us in very good spirits for the opening Test. We were just praying the skies would remain as clear as they had been. While our forwards hadn't been playing all that impressively, Dwyer reckoned that if we could get only 40 per cent of possession then our backs could bring off victory on the dry pitch. Even that was asking a lot from us against this topnotch New Zealand pack, which contained Mourie, Mexted, Shaw, Haden, Higginson, Knight, Dalton and Ashworth. They'd been together for years, but four of the six new caps in our team were forwards.

On Test morning in Christchurch the weather was fine, which pleased us no end. But by the time we ran out onto Lancaster Park a near gale-force wind was blowing. You could barely force your way out of the tunnel. Mark Ella lost the toss and Australia were forced to run into this wind in the first half. With the All Black forwards having this wind behind them early, they soon put points between us. In the end, they were much more commanding than the final 23-16 scoreline indicated. Out on the field it felt like a real flogging, and personally I'd been well outplayed by their skipper Graham Mourie, a player of great intelligence and an inspiring leader.

The real highlight between then and the next Test was the team's cricket match at Buller across on the desolate west coast between the odds and evens (determined by our touring numbers). The odds lost after scoring 140 runs. I didn't help our cause by getting only six runs and one wicket.

We won at Buller and also our next two games against Otago and the strong Waikato line-up, which really put a spring back into our step for the second Test. We lost John Griffiths for the rest of the tour in the Waikato game with a torn Achilles tendon. Griffo had been a surprise selection: a man with a very large and bulky frame and 34 years of age. Hardly an ideal choice as a new Rugby international, and he was really unsuitable for such a demanding tour. This caused some ill-feeling in the side and brought added pressure on the other props, which was unfortunate, as Griffo's a terrific style of fellow and very smart. The illustrious Stanislaus Joseph Pilecki was sent for as his replacement.

The team flew into Wellington for the second Test very much on a wing and a prayer. The aircraft lurched from side to side coming into the capital's airport and was forced to make a landing as harrowing as any I've experienced.

That second Test produced one of the most courageous victories by any of the Australian sides with which I've been associated. I didn't go out to warm-up that day, preferring the silence and isolation of the dressing-room, where I concentrated so deeply and intently on the Test that I was wound up like a coiled spring when we eventually ran out onto Athletic Park.

Another gale was blowing, but this time Mark Ella won the toss and now it was our turn to have first use of the wind. And from the word go, every player in that Australian line-up was like a tackling machine, knocking over everything black in front of them. In the first 30 seconds of the game Mark Shaw came at us; Rochey hit him low, I crunched him high, and we smashed him to the ground. Even now I can recall the questioning look on his face as if he didn't believe it. But the whole team had a huge roll on from the outset. We knew we had to build up a big lead while we had the wind and, sure enough, our points started to come. Then a nasty incident occurred when Mark Shaw buried his knees unnecessarily into Duncan Hall's back as he lay on the ground and he had to go off with what was a fairly serious injury. I've always respected Shaw for the toughness of his play, but occasionally he went overboard and did totally inexcusable things like this.

Hall's replacement was the one and only Steve Cutler. Just before halftime David Campese completed a magnificent try which Gould converted to give us a 19-3 halftime lead. Then we hung on against a massive All Black finishing effort. The harder they came at us, the more determinedly we cut them down in their tracks. We were desperate and we fought desperately. In the last 30 seconds of the game, I dived onto a loose ball and the All Blacks swarmed over me and Peter Lucas and started rucking us like fury. They were dancing up and down my back. But we knew that if the ball went back our way we'd win the Test, and when Luco and I saw it heading back our side we actually started laughing with joy. We all began embracing and congratulating each other in highly emotional scenes. Against all odds, we'd beaten the All Blacks and suddenly had a chance to retain the Bledisloe Cup. D J Cameron, the great New Zealand Rugby writer, summed it up when he wrote: 'But only the Wallabies had that deathless desire for victory, for making the kick or tackle tell, for making the headlong plunge for the loose ball, for playing in a team in which all members were utterly consumed by that burning ambition for victory.'

But from that point things started to turn bad for the Wallabies. For a start, the weather became foul, with rain and cold. Then we were taken apart by the Bay of Plenty by 40-16 and in the next game against Counties by 15-9. Team morale plummeted about as quickly as the barometer had.

Our penultimate game before the third and deciding Test was against North Auckland. We played very poorly and still won 16-12. There was altogether too much talking by our players during the game and they didn't have their minds on the job. So much so that Bob Dwyer went off

NSW v Manawatu, 1982. Gary Ella looks on in amusement as his centre opponent gets a lift

his head in the dressing-room afterwards. I had a fair bit to say too. It was hardly the ideal preparation for the Test match that was going to decide the fate of the whole tour.

In Auckland it was pouring rain for the Test at Eden Park, the sort of weather the All Blacks relish. However, the skies cleared on arrival at the ground and in brilliant sunshine the Test started for us in bewildering fashion when Gould steamed into the backline after the first scrum and took a long pass to go in untouched. He converted his own try for Australia to lead 6-0. We couldn't have had a more perfect start. But then rival fullback Hewson joined their backline to score a similar try, which he converted. Had he been stopped, our chance of winning would have been much, much better. At halftime we were leading 15-12 and it could have been 21-12 if a try equal in skill and drama to the Campese try at Wellington hadn't been disallowed for a forward pass. As the second half progressed the All Black forwards began increasing their amount of lineout possession and were crashing up the centre making valuable ground with Mourie directing the onslaught. While they continued holding territorial command, Hewson kept lobbing over the goals and the All Blacks ran out deserving winners by 33-18.

With the tour finished, we headed home reasonably satisfied and certainly very proud of our second Test victory. But in the end we just didn't have the necessary firepower to hold back the All Black forwards. Nevertheless, even crusty New Zealand media types like T P McLean gave us some wonderful wraps and complimented us, especially our backs, for playing such an attractive style of Rugby and bringing people back to the game. After all, we'd scored 316 points, including 47 tries, which was a fair effort overall. Eight of them had gone to the goose-stepping newcomer Campese, about whom we were to hear so much in the next few years. Dwyer had done fantastically well as coach during the tour, and also Mark Ella as captain, even though Mark was more of a leader by example than a thinking, scheming tactician like Mourie had been for New Zealand.

Typical of the comments at the time were those by Jim Woodward of the Sydney *Daily Telegraph*: 'That Dwyer could in his first season of representative Rugby, go to New Zealand minus ten of the country's best players and then force the All Blacks to wait until seven minutes before the end of the third Test to realise they had finally clinched the series with a 33-18 win, is a huge tribute to the Australian coach.'

I arrived home in time for another Queensland Rugby Union centenary game between the Barbarians and Queensland in front of the Duke of Edinburgh, and then played for Randwick when we beat Warringah 21-12 in the grand final to win the Sydney premiership. I notched two tries that day, but far nicer than any personal achievement was sharing a grand final triumph with my new club, the Galloping Greens.

PUMAS, FROGS AND PAIN

A few eyebrows were raised at the start of the 1983 season when Mark Ella, Steve Tuynman, Bruce Malouf and I began pre-season training in January with Eastern Suburbs Rugby League Club and the media got wind of it. We made it pretty clear that we weren't about to become Leagies and were only getting in some early fitness work before our own pre-season training began. Tommy O'Neill, who had been Randwick's trainer, had gone across in the off-season to Easts Rugby League Club and arranged for us to join their training. We asked the national coach Bob Dwyer if it was all right and he encouraged us to go. We thoroughly enjoyed the training. It was tough work, harder than what we were used to, but we more than held our own. In fact, the Leagies couldn't believe that someone of Steve Tuynman's enormous size could move so fast in the 400-metre time trials they had. They reckoned that he'd have made a sensational lock-forward in League.

The four of us were merely wanting to get a jump on the rest of our international players in view of the very heavy representative season coming up. The American Eagles were coming, then Argentina, a one-off Test against the All Blacks, and finally the Wallabies tour of Italy and France. Despite the arduous tour of New Zealand the previous season, I was feeling surprisingly fresh, hence my keenness to get in that extra pre-season work.

An interesting appointment for that season was Alan Jones as coach of Manly. He'd finally shed his team manager's image and was anxious to coach a senior Sydney club team, though he had coached The King's School 1st XV, Kings Old Boys in the sub-district competition, and his college team at Oxford University. Typically, he had a lot to say about what the Blues would do and about his approach to coaching.

The first weeks of the season were soon rumbling with tales of David Lord's proposal to introduce professional Rugby. The likely ramifications of this echoed round the world and grabbed countless column inches in newspapers from Auckland to Durban, Sydney to Dublin. If Lordy's grandiose scheme eventuated, it would globally turn the game upside down and inside out. He was talking of 200 players from all the major countries wanting to join his professional Rugby circus and playing for massive amounts of money compared with the peanuts they were paid as amateurs to cover incidental expenses. Had Lordy been better organised his whole extraordinary creation might have come off.

A number of meetings were held between players and Lordy, at which he outlined his plans for the series of professional tournaments. I remember meeting with him at the Brooklyn Hotel, where Grosvenor Place now stands, and going through his whole game plan. The only catch was that he wouldn't say who was the principal behind the plans. That made us all sceptical. It's like a political party saying vote for us, without disclosing any of its policies. We had another meeting at Bruce Malouf's Golden Grove Hotel at Maroubra Junction. Much the same. Lots of talk, but not many facts.

Further down the line I had a telephone call from the president of the Australian Rugby Football Union, Sir Nicholas Shehadie, charging me with being the proposed baggageman for the Rugby circus. That really was absurd. I'd certainly had talks with Lordy, but with the view to being a player and not somebody's bag-carrier.

I wasn't really concerned with the money Lordy was offering. I just wanted to be part of whatever was going on. I didn't want to miss out on anything where the best Rugby players in the world might be coming together in an amazing tournament. That's how the idea was sold to us and I was very keen to be part of it. And I think a lot of players felt the same way I did.

Just why did the whole thing fail? I don't really think that Lordy ever had someone like Kerry Packer to back his venture financially. I feel he was trying to market the philosophy of this world Rugby circus before selling the whole concept to some rich individual or company and, fortunately as it turned out, he didn't ever manage to do it.

The Sydney representative team had its usual run of early season matches, including another against a World XV like we'd had the season before. This time, the World XV gave us a 33-16 hiding, which was the first time in eight seasons that Sydney had been beaten by an overseas team. The All Blacks in that team couldn't quite understand the motivation behind Ken Elphick, the Sydney Rugby Union executive director, who masterminded these type of games. We'd fought ourselves to a standstill against the All Blacks over there the previous season, and then he turned around and pitched Andy Dalton, Gary Knight, Mark Shaw, Gary Whetton, Graham Mourie, Andy Haden, Mark Donaldson and Steve Pokere in against us again.

But Elphick would go to any lengths to stage these matches. I was never sure whether it was for the game's sake or simply to satisfy his ultra-ego. But he'd go to any expense to get the best international players here. Most of them brought their wives or girlfriends with them, they stayed in the very best accommodation and none of them ever seemed short of spending money. I couldn't believe the extravagance, especially as I had an enormous row with Elphick about trying to get casual shirts for the

Sydney players to wear in Fiji the following week instead of their having to wear shirts and ties in the heat and humidity. He wouldn't come to the party, yet he'd spent money willy-nilly the week before.

As it happened, Fiji defeated Sydney rather easily, but then we turned around and beat Queensland 27-22 (to end the Ballymore hoodoo for us), and also North Auckland and NSW Country.

Then NSW lost to Queensland at Ballymore in June in a very vicious game in which I had my head opened up once more. A significant newcomer in that game was Brett Papworth at inside-centre. Only Ken Wright among the world's contemporary Rugby players has had a sidestep like this fellow. He went over for a try that day at Ballymore in which he left half the Queensland team flat-footed and bamboozled as he zigged one way and then zagged the other. But Pappy's defence wasn't the best in those days and he was dropped for the return game the next weekend at the Sydney Cricket Ground.

Putting on an interstate Rugby game at the SCG was an enormous gamble by Elphick! As you might have expected, the crowd was only 7599. The public support just wasn't forthcoming and the poor souls who did turn up looked lost in that great barrel of a ground, but at least they had the pleasure of seeing NSW win a grafting game by 7-6.

The American Eagles arrived that same month. I support the Australian Rugby Football Union in feeling that it has to play its part in encouraging Rugby in nations where the game isn't strong, but the way international tours are funded means that such tours are financial suicide. In Rugby, the host side pays everything for a touring team and keeps all the profits. While that means the Wallabies are big money-spinners wherever they go because of their success and the popular way they play the game, it doesn't work when we bring minor Rugby nations here, where we don't get vast crowds even for the All Blacks or any of the Home countries. Of course, the ARFU could concentrate on bringing out only major nations and let New Zealand and the United Kingdom, where they get good crowds irrespective of the standard of the opposition, encourage tours by the lesser Rugby nations. But the Australian administrators seem to have a better perspective of the future of world Rugby than some of their more powerful counterparts. There's no doubt, however, that, to compensate for the financial losses caused by the tours of lesser Rugby nations, the ARFU has to push much stronger than it has in the past for receiving an even share of the gatemoney that the Wallabies generate when they're abroad.

I thought for a while that I might have been on the wrong track, when the Yanks won their opening three games and were then only narrowly beaten by Sydney and Queensland. Before the Sydney game against them, our coach Peter Fenton arranged to take us all to a special movie preview.

He's an exceptional sound mixer, who has worked on many of the finest of the Australian movies, so he was able to arrange for us to go to a small city theatrette to get a sneak look at the movie 'Phar Lap'. There were a few country boys in the team, including Ollie Hall, Phil Clements and me, and we were particularly touched by this wonderful film about our greatest racehorse. It was real tear-jerking stuff at the end when Phar Lap died in America. Just before the night game at the SCG, Fab gave us the usual motivational talk and then ended by saying: 'Listen you blokes. If there's only one reason why you're got to beat these Yanks tonight it's the fact that they poisoned Phar Lap!' Well, we started rolling around the dressing-room with laughter. In fact, it was so funny and took our minds so much off the game that it had a diabolical effect on how we played. We only won 13-9.

By the time of the one and only Test match, the Americans had built a very respectable record and everyone was beginning to ask whether it was going to be much harder than at first imagined. As it turned out, Australia simply walloped them at the SCG, winning 49-3 with David Campese scoring four of the nine tries. The game marked David Hillhouse's return to the Test pack after five years' absence pursuing his career as an airline pilot, and I couldn't believe that any player could leap as high unaided in lineouts as he did. The next day, the poor Yanks went home shattered men after being blown out of the water worse than they had been at Pearl Harbor. I wonder how they ever recovered from that and what it did for the game's development over there.

Overlapping the end of the Eagles tour was the Golden Oldies Festival, claimed to be the largest sporting event ever held in Australia and based at our Randwick Rugby Club in Sydney. One hundred and eighteen teams attended, representing 4070 players aged from 35 to 83. They came in all shapes and sizes, but the most common characteristics were round bellies and bald heads. They played and socialised throughout the week, then had their closing ceremony and dinner at Randwick Racecourse. A modest affair. The attendance that night was 5700, making it the largest dinner ever held in this country. The Golden Oldies put $7 million into the NSW tourist industry, but more than that it was fantastic to see so many veterans still wanting to play Rugby, and it was a wonderful advertisement for the game.

I was amused before Argentina arrived to see them being written off by so many critics, when only the previous year they had beaten the Springboks 21-12 in the second Test when they toured South Africa masquerading as the American Jaguars. They might have been underestimated by some, but I certainly wasn't about to take them lightly. I knew they'd be heaps better than the Americans.

To emphasise just how good they'd be, the Pumas gave NSW a hiding by 19-7 in their opening game. Their captain, Hugo Porta, scored all but four of their points that day. One of their props, Serafin Dengra, also turned in a remarkable performance. This flamboyant character—who's a Conan the Barbarian lookalike—would more than hold up his side of the scrum and the next minute be screaming around the field like a centre three-quarter. We couldn't figure out how he had so much energy and speed left after all the scrummaging. While their tight-head prop was a much quieter achiever he was the one who really caught our attention and gave us such a headache. Enrique Rodriguez was his name. They called him Topo, or the Mole. He reminded me of a Spanish buccaneer with his jet-black hair and goatee beard and dark features, and believe me, with his immense strength and scrummaging technique, he was just as damaging.

The Pumas also beat Queensland, so the first Test shaped up as quite a battle. Bob Dwyer said beforehand that he thought Australia's backs of Vaughan, Ella, Hawker, Slack, Moon, Campese and Gould would be altogether too fast for them. Rival captain Porta simply replied with the warning: 'We shall see who gets to the ball first.'

In retrospect, I imagine Porta was quietly chuckling to himself. They had their strategy in place. It was all worked out. They knew they had the power to kill us in the forwards and that, after they had dominated us in the scrums, our forwards would simply not have the energy left to scrounge for the ball elsewhere.

It's part of Rugby folklore what Argentina did to us in the forwards that July 31 at Ballymore. They bled us to death in the scrum with more power and technique than any of our forwards had ever experienced before. Not the All Blacks, the French or any of the Home nations had ever shown anything like this. It was frightening at times. You'd hear them call in the scrums for a 'bajada', then suddenly you'd feel this immense thrust coming through the scrum and we'd all start skidding uncontrollably backwards like we were being pushed by some mechanical monster. The long, deep tear marks in the Ballymore turf as we fought desperately to keep our grip were there for days later, as a never-to-be-forgotten reminder of Argentina's herculean scrum. Never in my 50-odd Tests have I experienced an opposing scrum as destructive as that. And the cornerstone of it all was that blasted Topo.

Given this platform, Argentina beat us comprehensively by 18-3. It was a sad Test match in other ways, because our lock David Codey walked off injured and this simple act of walking off saw him banished to the wilderness for sometime. He'd hurt his back, but the unwritten laws of Rugby stress that a bloke playing his first Test simply doesn't walk off. He gets carried off. So it was no accident that he wasn't picked for the second Test or for the Wallaby tour of Italy and France later that season.

After the Test, our front-row was knackered. Declan Curran and Stan Pilecki reckoned they'd never felt pressure like it before. Something had to be done to counter the Pumas' scrummaging, so for the second Test the selectors brought in John Meadows, who had then recovered from the malignant cancer which he'd had removed from his groin, and was recognised as the finest scrummager we had. Meadows had done a great job in New Zealand the year before and, for a bloke of his size, he had unbelievable strength and technique.

We sought all the scrummaging help we could before the second Test, with Tony Miller among those who pitched in with some advice. We also did much more scrummaging than ever before. All the work we did and the fact that this Test was at the SCG, where Australian teams invariably play better, made us feel confident we could reverse the result, and sure enough we did. We won 29-13. Early in the Test the Pumas had us camped near our line when a scrum was put down. It was their feed. They were looking for a pushover try. We heard the call 'bajada', and then the power started coming through. We dug in even further, clenched our teeth and pushed back with every ounce of strength we had. The blood vessels in my neck felt like they were going to burst. My back was breaking. We were teetering. I felt that we couldn't hold an instant longer. Then suddenly they relaxed a moment before we heard 'bajada' again, and for a second time they came at us. Again, we held. Then 'bajada' a third time. Please, no more. But when they backed off this time, they were finally finished. The reaction of the crowd was extraordinary after watching this enormous war of attrition and they went berserk. We knew then that we had the Pumas and the Australian backs finally began to cut loose. A remarkable aspect of this Test was the penalty try awarded to Australia by that showman among showmen, Clive Norling. Twenty-two metres out from Argentina's line, Mark Ella was passing the ball to me when it was knocked down by their breakaway Tomas Petersen. The next instant the Welsh referee was running from the spot across to the goalposts. I looked at Mark. He looked at me. Neither of us knew what was happening, but Norling had ruled that by intentionally knocking the ball forward Petersen had prevented me from scoring a try. Suddenly we all realised what had happened. A penalty try! Awarded 22 metres out! Unbelievable! The Pumas went crazy. There has been much written and much analysis done about that try in such unusual circumstances. The ruling may have been technically correct, but it was a real showman's effort by Norling and we didn't really deserve it.

A fortnight later, Australia faced the All Blacks in another of those one-off Test matches. Despite having shown our resilience by retrieving that second Test from Argentina, it was expecting a lot for us to wipe out an All Blacks side with Knight, Dalton, Ashworth, Haden, Higgensen,

Hobbs, Shaw and Mexted in the pack, and with Loveridge behind them. While they were virtually impregnable there, the three-quarters looked the only place where we might be able to exploit them in any way. But our own backs were weakened by the withdrawal of Roger Gould, which meant Campese remaining at fullback where he had played in the second Test against the Pumas. While Campo was always full of running and injected tremendous sparkle into teams, the only fullback I ever wanted behind me against the All Blacks was Gould. Having him behind you gave the team a huge psychological advantage.

Without Gould, the Australian backs failed to perform at all, despite the forwards playing heroically against this world-class pack. It was a fierce old slog up front. I was really stirred up for this, after the team copped plenty of lip from lots of Kiwi supporters crossing the SCG No 2 while we warmed up there. I went out ready to go berserk and got into a few stouches early in the game. I remember swinging one punch at Haden and finding I didn't have the reach to connect with his chin, then racing off to the other side of the SCG to the next breakdown and hoping to hell he wasn't on my tail. But despite the fierce commitment of our forwards, we came nowhere near matching them in the backs. Our fellows couldn't fire, and Campo couldn't kick any goals. So while we scored two tries to one, Alan Hewson put over five goals from six attempts for them for an 18-8 victory. The most pleasing thing for me was scoring a try right in front of the Members' Stand. Campo broke through a set move from the backs and I followed, trailing him like a drover's dog. He tossed the ball back to me, I saw the line open and went with everything I had. I saw the black figure of Bernie Fraser coming at me, and though he got to me a metre out he couldn't stop me and over I went. There are no more satisfying moments in Rugby than scoring at the SCG in front of all those people, knowing your family and all your mates are out there among them.

The following month I had another important Rugby appointment: the Sydney premiership grand final. We'd won five premierships on the trot at Randwick and went in as favourites for our sixth against Manly. But there was one factor in this grand final which we'd not encountered before. Manly had been taken into the grand final by Alan Jones in his first season of club coaching. He'd never coached much higher than schoolboy level before, and had performed an extraordinary task in getting Manly into the grand final. He'd given them a new vitality and direction and had been a fresh personality in a club which traditionally always looked the goods but had never delivered. Even in the week leading up to the grand final Jones showed that he was going to make it tough for us at Randwick. He went into print calling the attention of referee Dick Byres to what he insisted was Randwick's apparent ability to ride roughshod over referees. Byres wouldn't have been human had he not taken heed of that and determined that he wouldn't allow us a centimetre of latitude in any area. It was smart thinking. While Jones did a mighty effective job beforehand in every way to ensure Manly won, the players followed up his words with action and they beat us 12-10, with Mark Ella missing a drop goal in the final minutes which would have changed everything. Jones had struck again. He was having an ever-increasing influence on my Rugby career.

The tour of Italy and France was just around the corner, and typically the national selectors couldn't help but throw in a few curly choices. One day selectors will stop gambling with players and merely choose the logical candidates. With this team, for example, Peter Grigg, Peter Lucas and Declan Curran were all surprise omissions. Luco was dead unlucky, as he'd had a tremendous season in the Sydney representative team. The player picked instead of him was Queensland's Jeff Miller. While I've got enormous admiration for him now and count him among my best mates in Rugby, at the time Miller's selection didn't add up, particularly as Chris Roche and I were similar types of breakaways. On that score, one didn't have to be a genius to figure out that we were going to have problems at the back of the lineout where none of us were jumpers. Only one player in the team, David Hillhouse, had toured Italy and France in 1976. He kept saying that he couldn't understand why he was going back a second time, a point which was largely lost on the rest of us at the time.

The tour began with a brief stopover in Rome, so hot and steamy but extraordinarily captivating, where all the boys rushed around from one tourist spot to another—the Trevi Fountain, The Colisseum, the Vatican (particularly necessary for good Catholic lads like John Coolican and me), Via Veneto, Spanish Steps, and so on.

Then we went north-east by bus to L'Aquila for our first game against Italy B, and won that fairly unimpressively by 26-0. Playing for L'Aquila at the time was the South African international Rob Louw, whose lifestyle opened our eyes for the first time to just how well visiting players fare in Italy. He had a magnificent apartment, an easy-going lifestyle, and drove a BMW with ROB LOUW painted on the side. It was no coincidence that since then there has been a steady stream of Australians going over to play in Italy.

The team travelled much further north after that to Rivogo, where we stayed in an amazing hotel in which the occupants were mostly German tourists who flock there to relax in the hot baths. Our stay was enlivened by the number of fat old Italian maids who somehow always walked in to clean your room when you were about to step in or out of the shower. We were very much more embarrassed than they appeared to be.

The Test was played at Padova, not far from Venice, and we had a good win by 29-7. While we treated the match fairly seriously, it was real life-and-death stuff for the Italians, and they were devastated afterwards by the loss. It had been a rare chance for them to do well against a recognised Rugby power and they'd blown it. We were lucky to finish with fifteen players, as our fullback Glen Ella hit one of the Italian players with the worst head-high tackle I've ever seen, precipitating an all-in brawl. Still, it didn't stop us all sampling a fair bit of Chianti with the Italian team that night.

The next day the Wallabies went across to Venice and spent the day floating around the waterways of this wonderfully romantic city in gondolas and sipping coffee in Saint Mark's Square. It served as a timely reminder that Rugby has a lot to offer compared with Rugby League and Australian Rules, which never touch those parts of the world. Nigel Holt became so carried away with the romance of Venice that he got lost. Roger Gould had to stay behind at the hotel to wait for him to turn up, then make a mad dash by car to the airport to join us on the flight to Paris.

Our first few days in Paris made us begin to wonder if all the horrific stories of French Rugby were true, because we stayed at a splendid hotel on the outskirts of the capital and the Rugby officials couldn't do enough for us. It's here that we first met our beloved liaison officer for the tour, whom we affectionately nicknamed Monsieur Blockhead.

The opening game was against a French selection at Strasbourg, up near the German border, and was promoted very heavily to try to boost Rugby in what was primarily a soccer region. It was a night match, and that morning we went through the Adidas factory and had lunch in the executives' dining room in the most opulent surroundings many of us had ever experienced. And the gear offered to us was fantastic, far better than any Australia-made gear we'd seen.

During the day we'd also had our interpreter tell us what was in the local newspapers, and the French Rugby president Albert Ferrasse was quoted as saying that France wanted to avenge those defeats of 1981. He also emphasised the point that the first game for any touring team was of very special interest, and it didn't escape our attention that Queensland had given them curry in their first game in Australia two years before.

When the first scrum packed down that night, I heard an extraordinary call from the French side: 'Queensland ... Queensland.' I was puzzled, until the front-rows on both sides suddenly collapsed. Then the French second-rowers started kicking the heads of our front-rowers with everything they had and immediately there was an all-in brawl. Of the team which had toured Australia, prop Jean Paul Wolff, second-rower Alain Lorieux, lock Laurent Rodriguez and the winger Laurent Pardo were also in this French selection. So suddenly things started to add up.

Then came the first lineout. While the ball was still in the air Rodriguez turned around and knocked Steve Tuynman as cold as a mackerel. So it was on again. When the referee eventually got the fighting under control, Tuynman was still out to it. We brought him around and he chose to continue.

But the viciousness continued unabated. It was unbelievable. Just before halftime another brawl developed between me and Lorieux, which led to one of the biggest and nastiest brawls ever seen on a Rugby field. Almost the whole 30 players joined the fray. We were punching and the French were punching as well as kicking, something they're very fond of. This squirming mass of violence moved from the 22-metre line right up to the halfway line before it quietened down. At the end of this great brawl I was called out by the referee, cautioned and penalised for starting it all.

You got the feeling at halftime that the French felt they weren't going to win the fight, and both sides started to play Rugby in the second half. We won 18-16 in what still rates as the most vicious game I've ever been part of. Sometime later I met one of the Frenchmen from the 1981 tour with whom I'd become friendly, the halfback Jean Pierre Elissalde, and I mentioned the viciousness of the Strasbourg game. His first response was a long 'Oohhhh . . .'. Then he explained that the players chosen for that game contained all the known thugs of French Rugby, so the intention was very clear indeed: to get revenge for what Queensland had done.

To help douse the memory of this night of disgrace, a few of us drank till five o'clock in the morning, but paid for it with enormous hangovers. So I wasn't at all amused during the next day's bus trip when we got out for a comfort stop and someone in the team rolled a huge bunger between my legs. Not only did it give me an almighty fright, but it started my headache all over again. After that, throwing bungers became a popular recreation with the lads.

The Wallabies drew the next game against French Police at Le Creusot, then won well against another French selection at Grenoble. So everything was moving nicely. We hadn't been beaten in five games on tour, the hotels were much better than we'd been led to believe they would be, and we were enjoying the countryside.

Then we arrived at our next hotel outside of Perpignon after an eight-hour bus drive. It was a two-star hotel, with only one bathroom on each floor and beds not nearly long or wide enough for giants like Steve Cutler or Steve Williams. So we moved out and directed our bus into Perpignon, where we decided on a hotel from the outside that looked somewhat more liveable. But the hotel management wasn't too keen for us to stay there, because a Rugby League team had stayed there the year before and had almost wrecked the joint. They had performed little niceties like throwing television sets out of windows. The management thought the two codes were similar and took some convincing that we'd behave ourselves better than the Mungos.

We lost that game mainly through some bad refereeing. Then came another long bus journey to Agen, where we got landed in another low-class two-star hotel way out of town. We couldn't figure out why they wanted to keep putting us out in the sticks. The players in this French selection (the fourth of these teams, in which their national selectors simply parade all their likely Test talent) were the toughest-looking mob you've ever seen. All their noses were bent and twisted. And while they gave the Wallabies a 36-6 hiding, looks deceive because it was a clean game. Nevertheless, two of these tough characters picked Michael Lynagh up during the game and drove him into the turf so hard that he broke his collarbone and was finished for the tour. It was a big blow to the team, as he was playing extremely well and consistently kicking goals.

The first Test at Clermont Ferrand produced a tremendously gutsy performance by Australia. We were literally so short on lineout jumpers that it was decided I should jump at number two in the lineouts against Lorieux. Well at the first lineout he had one look across at me and simply laughed. I had no hope of matching him, so I just tried knocking him sideways out of every lineout.

The team put up a determined effort in a Test which never rose to any heights. It was tight, unattractive and closely fought, and at the finish we managed a very satisfying 15-all draw. This Test was significant in that it was young Tuynman's first Test. Certainly his ability to get up and continue playing after being decked at Strasbourg in our first game had won him a lot of fans, and The Bird has, of course, gone on to make many, many Test appearances.

There was one isolated incidence of foul play during the Test and it was a real shocker. Late in the game a scrum went down and one of the French forwards kicked our hooker Mark McBain in the head in one of the most vicious acts I've ever seen. It was a full-blooded blow and as soon as it happened you could tell Mark was in serious trouble. In the dressing-room later, some of us honestly thought he was going to die. He had any number of doctors working on him, and there was a good deal of distress about his condition. His skull was fractured and he had cerebral fluid dripping into the back of his throat. There was no way Mark could play again on tour and it took him several years to recover from that diabolical act.

The backrow of Chris Roche, Tuynman and I got tremendous wraps after the Test for outgunning the French trio, which included Jean-Pierre Rives. What I couldn't understand was the change in Rives' personality from 1981. He was head-butting, he was throwing punches and generally

The ugly bunch: the French front-row in the first Test in France, 1983

Australia v French Selection, Grenoble France, 1983. I look for support with halfback Dominic Vaughan at my shoulder.

I feel the intensity of the defence in the first Test in France, 1983.

A Rugby fan who holds a special place in the players' hearts— Matt Latham.

carrying on like a madman all day long. It wasn't the Rives legend I'd known, and I wondered if it wasn't because he was playing in front of his countrymen this time.

We beat the French Army in the game separating the Tests, then headed for Paris and the second Test. Again, we were put up in a hotel way out on the outskirts of the capital, which disappointed all of us. We had to catch the metro if we wanted to do any sightseeing. We were so far out that we even had to get a police escort all the way into Paris to the Parc des Princes on the afternoon of the international. The two motor-bike police assigned to our bus put up a spirited performance clearing the freeway on the way to the game, on the way back to the hotel for happy hour, and yet again for the trip to the official function in Paris. They blew whistles with style and kicked car doors with gay abandon.

That Test was an excellent defensive effort by the Australian team. The French won so much possession it wasn't funny, and they came at us in wave after wave. But we cut them down time and again. How we held them out as much as we did I'll never know. It was another vicious game. I was kicked in the head early on and walked around in a daze for a while. Tuynman also had his nose broken. And late in the game he was slippered in the ear, but stayed on. It didn't look as bad as it was, but in effect his ear was torn from top to bottom. Courageously, this 20-year-old kid kept playing and finished with a broken nose and his ear hanging half off, which probably ended any hopes he might have had of a Hollywood career. Later in the dressing-room the two doctors attending him finished stitching his ear and found a bit of cartilage still hanging out. They tried pushing it back unsuccessfully, then simply snipped it off with a pair of scissors as poor Bird screamed his head off. Back home, he needed plastic surgery. Among the other casualties in the Test was the French prop Michel Cremaschi, who had been deemed responsible for McBain's shocking injury in the first Test. Coincidentally, Cremaschi went off after 38 minutes of this Test to have his head stitched . . .

We had the chance to win this game. We were down only 9-6 when our hooker Tom Lawton was penalised in a scrum five metres from the French line for an early strike and the Frogs were out of trouble. Mark Ella also had a drop kick charged down by Rives late in the game. Finally the French pulled off a blindside move, scored a remarkable try, and won 15-6.

At this stage, the players all wanted to go home, but we had one game left against the French Barbarians at Toulon, which we won 23-21 in the most exciting game of the tour. I haven't trusted an Irishman since Fergus Slattery, who was playing for the Barbarians, strolled into our dressing-room before the game and quietly told us that the French were approaching the game in a very light-hearted manner. Nothing could have been further from the truth. We were also hammered unmercifully by the referee, and our captain Mark Ella spent the whole time arguing and pleading with him. The ref even started marching him back ten metres at a time for back-chatting. Mark appealed to Rives, his rival captain, to speak to the referee in order to gain some consistency, but it had no effect. There was plenty of viciousness in this game too. They came at us at 100 kilometres an hour, not with the same callous brutality we'd struck elsewhere, but with plenty of stick all the same. But we hung in there, scored some fantastic tries, defended like we were trying to save our lives and so finished the tour on a tremendous note.

The flight home in late November was the last low-cost flight out of Europe for the year, so there were more families and kids on our plane than you could imagine. It was a horrendous trip. All we wanted to do was get home, but we couldn't stretch out or even sleep.

Picture the sight of Steve Cutler, Steve Williams, Ollie Hall and me trying to get comfortable in a row of economy-class seats at the back of a Boeing 747. Sleep wasn't easy to come by I can assure you, so we had lots of time to recall David Hillhouse's scepticism at backing up for a second tour of France. The thought of being reunited with wives and girlfriends at the end of the flight was the only way that the players could maintain any degree of sanity.

Meanwhile, back in Australia, forces were at work to remove Bob Dwyer as national coach. Those criticising him in Australia were unaware of the extreme difficulty of the French tour, both on and off the field, and the relative inexperience of the team.

Not many tries had been scored but it is impossible to score tries without the ball. We consistently played against packs with significant height and weight advantages. Without quality ball we did a lot of defending, and this aspect of our game was for the most part faultless.

Dwyer, given these severe limitations, should have been applauded for going within a whisker of coaching an Australian team to a series win in France. Instead the knives were flashing in alarming numbers.

THE BEGINNING OF THE JONES ERA

I'd regarded Alan Jones as a first-class manager when he was looking after the NSW team. I'd never seen a more competent person in that position. But, other than one training night when Peter Crittle was away and he stepped into the breach as coach, I'd never so much as thought of him as having any coaching ability. He stuck exclusively to being team manager and left our training completely to Crittle. But in 1983, when he took over the coaching of Manly, he emerged as being extremely competent in that role also. To take them to the Sydney premiership in his first season of senior coaching was an extraordinary feat, particularly in a club which traditionally had been resistant to outsiders.

His success with Manly came as a real surprise to me, although on reflection it shouldn't have been considering his background. In business, he had been Prime Minister Malcolm Fraser's speechwriter, so not only did he have considerable skills in communication but if he could get on with our acerbic national leader then he could get on with anybody. On the sports field, he had been a tennis player of state-level ability, a very useful athletics coach, and he had also had his share of success with the school, college and sub-district Rugby teams he had coached. So while he hadn't done much serious coaching before 1983, he quite obviously understood people, the conditioning and training of athletics and how to extract the most from them both physically and psychologically. And, most important of all, there seemed to be very few things in life at which Jonesy had failed. In a nutshell, he was a winner.

Once he was in charge at Manly his unbelievable ambition in the area of coaching really emerged. Having lifted Manly to the club's first premiership in 33 years, there really seemed no bounds to what this extraordinary man might be able to achieve in terms of coaching any Rugby team.

By the time 1984 dawned there was some strong feeling among influential members of the Rugby fraternity that Bob Dwyer wasn't really the answer as Australia's coach. He certainly hadn't set the world on fire, despite having worked under difficulties when so many players withdrew before the New Zealand tour in 1982, and there were doubts whether he was really the man needed that season to help the Wallabies overcome the All Blacks and then succeed on the major tour of the British Isles.

In the wings, a closeted group of power brokers led by the NSWRU chairman Ross Turnbull urged Jones to stand against Dwyer for the national job and promised that they'd get him the full support of the NSW Rugby Union, which was easily the most dominant Rugby state. To this day, Jones claims—and I've every reason to believe him— that it was more the urging and insistence of these people than any burning ambition at the time on his own behalf, that made him agree to stand against Dwyer. Knowing the way Turnbull works, I could see that as a real possibility, although once committed Jones would go ahead hammer and tongs.

So Jones threw his hat into the ring and, when it was apparent that he had an excellent chance of winning given the NSWRU's support, a tremendous hue and cry developed. As I saw it, the whole crux of the argument was not so much either man's ability or lack of it, but that Dwyer deserved another chance and that Jones should have served some time as a senior representative coach before being considered for the national job.

I stuck up for Dwyer, even though Jones had become a very good friend of mine during his period as NSW manager. Even while he was coaching Manly the previous season we saw a bit of each other socially. But I and the other players who had been on the New Zealand and French tours with Dwyer had developed a close association with him. He had been a strong supporter of the players, an excellent coach, and was a thoroughly likeable character—so that was where my loyalties lay when it came to the national coaching job, and I came to Dwyer's defence whenever it was suggested that he might be ditched.

On the afternoon preceding the Australian Rugby Football Union's vital council meeting on February 24, I was even rung by one of the ARFU council members, Daryl Haberecht, and asked my opinion of Jones as a coach. I didn't back away from anything I'd said or thought. I told him that I hadn't played under Jones as coach, but thought he was a fantastic team manager. I hadn't seen any better. But I simply couldn't recommend him to be our national coach.

I'd be lying if I didn't say that I was still smarting from the arrogant way in which Manly had beaten us for the premiership the previous season, and how Jones had very skillfully manipulated the media and hence the referee before that grand final. Even allowing for my annoyance over that, the clear light of retrospect would not change my view: I said then and I say now that Dwyer did not deserve to lose his job. He had been a courageous coach, certainly deserving of another season.

Obviously, my opinion counted for nought, because the whole matter when the ARFU met the following afternoon was determined as swiftly and efficiently as a turkey's future on the chopping block at Christmas time. Dwyer's head rolled. Jones had the bloc vote of the five New South Wales delegates, and Dwyer the five from the smaller states.

Given that Dwyer had evoked unremitting anger from Queenslanders when he omitted Paul McLean and Roger Gould from the first Test team he coached against Scotland, it wasn't hard to figure where the Queensland preferences would go when Bob Templeton dropped out of the ballot. Alan Jones was given the job, amid thunderous editorials and public rebukes of the ARFU from Sydney Rugby sources for having ditched the extremely popular Dwyer.

No sooner was Jones in office than I had a call from him, summoning me to visit him for a tete-a-tete at his combined terrace and office in the inner city suburb of Chippendale. For the first fifteen minutes he ripped into me, accusing me of speaking out against him as regards his running for the coaching position. I listened as the words shot out like a burst water-main, then had my say. I told him Dwyer had gained my loyalty through New Zealand and France and I wasn't about to discard that, even though Alan had become a friend. The good thing about this whole conversation was that once he got his gripe off his chest and I'd been open about my position, he simply said, 'Right, that's out of the way, let's get down to talking about where we're going to this season.' While the friction between us might outwardly have ended there and then, I suspected that he might hold against me what had occurred. That suspicion increased when the season began and Bill Calcraft, the breakaway Jones had coached at Manly, seemed to be in the new coach's inner circle. That really made me filthy and I began to sense a threatening situation.

During our heart-to-heart talk that day, Jones laid down the guidelines for what he wanted in Australian Rugby. He stressed that 'there have to be players in this country of 6ft 8in who can win us the lineout ball we haven't been winning in the past and at the same time get around the field, and powerful front-rowers who can both scrummage and play a team game.' He made no secret of the fact that he would leave no stone unturned finding a tight five that could hold its own against any pack in the world in the set pieces and then deliver enough ball to our three-quarters to allow them to run wild. The tight five was the crucial component to the Jones plan, because without that we couldn't dominate a game to the extent that was needed to win Test matches. In the previous decade, we'd received many accolades for the way we had played in Tests that we hadn't won. It was starting to get people down, none more so than Jones. His big aim was to secure our scrum, get together a lineout that could win us ball all day, and so finally make the most of the skilled backs we'd developed through the seventies and eighties. We'd always had the backs, seldom the forwards, and he was about to change that come hell and high water. Even if he had to borrow a couple of giraffes and gorillas from Taronga Park Zoo, he was going to find himself the tallest, heaviest and strongest set of forwards that Australian Rugby had ever had.

In the meantime, I left him to his nationwide search and his quite obvious lofty ambitions and headed off to Europe the following month with the Sydney representative team.

Hindsight's always the most marvellous teacher and I often wish now that I could make that tour all over again, because I'd have approached the whole thing entirely differently.

I was captain of the 23-man team for the six-match tour of Italy, France, England, Wales and Ireland and, if I were able to relive that time over again, then I feel I might have become captain of Australia a lot sooner and remained in the role a lot longer. It was a terrific opportunity for me to show just what I had to offer as the captain of representative teams, but I blew it.

How? Andy Conway was a terrific manager because of his efficiency and high standards, but he was a born worrier. Our coach Peter (Fab) Fenton was another fantastic bloke and very knowledgeable on Rugby, but hardly the most organised or toughest coach you'd ever meet. It meant that I felt in the unfortunate position of having to both set and impose the discipline on the players on what was going to be a fairly demanding tour. And that task became very onerous to me. We also had several new young players in the team, and they needed help to fit into the way of a touring team. I had the added problem of having broken a finger before leaving and spent the whole of the tour in a fair bit of pain, which wasn't helped by the extremely cold weather we encountered. Personal problems at home also added to this dangerous cocktail.

All these factors added up to my not being able to give the captaincy role the complete attention it required. I wasn't nearly as good as I should have been and I daresay that some of the players returned from the tour with fairly mixed feelings about my leadership qualities. And I've no doubt that the Manly players in the team who had Jones's ear would have told him so too.

This was only the second time the Sydney team had undertaken a major tour since 1977 and, to keep costs down, the Sydney Rugby Union worked out the cheapest ways of getting us everywhere. While it didn't mean having to hitch-hike or sleep on park benches, we didn't exactly travel like Arab sheiks. It took us 36 hours to get to Zurich travelling on Air Garuda, followed by a twelve-hour bus trip the day after we arrived. Still, we had some funny characters in the team like Brett Papworth, Lance Walker, Phil Clements, Peter FitzSimons, Peter Lucas and our coach Fab, who kept us laughing all the way and took our minds off the less than sumptuous travelling conditions.

We easily won our first game against the Zebre Invitation XV at Livorno in Italy, then defeated Toulon 25-18 at Toulon, which was a pretty fair result, then narrowly lost our third game to Brive Athletic Club, the club which FitzSimons was later to play for during several of our off-seasons. Then across to Britain, where we romped home against a Brixham XV at Brixham and lost to Swansea in Swansea by eight points. Our final game was against Ulster in Belfast and by then we were carrying a string of injuries a mile long. Before the game we had a training run in the coldest conditions I've ever experienced, but there was so much laughter and mischief during the run that it helped lift our spirits enormously. Coach Fenton even found himself stripped of all clothing at the end of the run.

Ulster are always a tough outfit who have knocked off many international touring teams, but we were leading them 16-0 at halftime before letting open the floodgates, and they won by 19-16. It was a very disappointing end to the tour, for the team generally and for me in particular. Still, if you're ever going to get beaten at Rugby, there's no nicer place in the world to have it happen than in Ireland. The Irish are terrific people, and they soon make you forget whatever showed on the scoreboard. While in the Northern Ireland capital, Lance Walker, Gary Ella, Phil Clements and I found our way to the Royal Hotel smack in the middle of Belfast. Calling it a pub is a poor description. It was more of a bunker, as it had been bombed and rebuilt about five times. Barbed wire and chicken wire were strung everywhere inside and outside this dingy little place to help hold it together in anticipation of the next explosion, and here, in what was very much a symbol of the sectarian mess they've got themselves into over there, were four crazy Aussies standing at the bar heartily singing Waltzing Matilda.

By the time we arrived home, the controversy over Jones's appointment was dying down, but certainly not some malicious attacks on his character. And isolated sections of the media still persisted in attacking his appointment. This was the dirtiest game they could play, aimed at destroying the guy's credibility even before he got started. It is of immense credit to the man that he was able to cope with all this and proceed so well with the job he had been given.

By then Jones was well into the business of rounding up the players he thought could help carry the day for Australia. He indicated that he was after the Queensland tight-head prop Andy McIntyre, who had played his first Test against New Zealand in 1982 but had been dropped in 1983, and had even spent a fair amount of time warming the Queensland reserves' bench. They also had a 203 centimetre second-rower up there named Bill Campbell. He wasn't in their State selectors' favour either, but he fitted Jones's criterion for huge, mobile forwards exactly. And Jones was prepared to stick with Steve Cutler, a man of the same enormous height, who had been in and out of representative teams for several seasons and who many thought looked and behaved about fearsomely as a flamingo. Jones also had his sights firmly set on a young kid who had been plucked from Sydney University, then in second division, and sent with our Sydney team on its European tour for experience. His name was Nick Farr-Jones. Having played alongside him on that tour I couldn't help but be impressed with his tremendous talent. But I thought he was a terribly undisciplined player; that he didn't want to do what the rest of the team was doing. It frustrated me at the time, and at the end of that tour I had a very long talk to Nick and told him that if he wanted to have a part in any future international teams then he couldn't just go off and do whatever he wanted to do. Nick now says he's very glad I spoke to him the way I did and that, when he became the Wallaby skipper, he had to say exactly the same thing to other players. Back in 1984, what Jones saw was this very big halfback who was as strong as an ox, just the sort of halfback he could use behind his monster pack like a fourth back-rower. The name was pencilled in. Another one he wanted was Enrique (Topo) Rodriguez, the magnificent prop from Argentina who had destroyed us in the front-row the previous season and had since migrated here with his family. No sooner was Rodriguez in the country, than people were declaring that he was going to be the saviour of the front-row. But Jones wouldn't act until Rodriguez's residency status had been clarified. Only when it was determined that Rodriguez and his family had obtained permanent resident visas did Jones declare that Topo would henceforth be considered eligible for senior representative selection.

In his own determined way, Jones was gradually marshalling his forces for this season of tremendous challenge. He had incumbent Test players like me to work with, but with the addition of these five, plucked from the scrap-heap, second division and another land, he believed that he would eventually be able to take on the might of world Rugby. Besides everything else Jones did for Rugby, it should always be remembered that he was primarily responsible for nurturing and developing McIntyre, Campbell, Cutler, Farr-Jones and to a lesser extent Rodriguez (who had been a Test regular with Argentina) into the truly great international players that they were to become. That alone is worth a line on his epitaph.

In April, Jones introduced a national training squad of 50 to 60 players for the season. It was that size, he argued, because the fringe players would feel they all had something to strive for, and that, in turn, would help lift the standard of the NSW and Queensland teams. At the same time he started to coordinate those he considered to be the superior Rugby coaches in Australia—Dick Marks (the fulltime national coaching coordinator), Alex Evans (national under-21 coach), David Clark (Queensland coaching director) and Arthur McGill (NSW coaching director). He talked to them, let them in on the plan, then told them to go out and help him make it happen. To this day, Marks remains one of the strongest supporters of Alan Jones, which is a very telling comment given his own ability.

Jones also spent countless hours on the telephone to individual players, advising them on areas of their game that needed improving, implementing training programs for others, and even conducting special workouts on the running track for those based in Sydney to help with their speed. The man never seemed to sleep, and had the most energy of anyone I'd ever met. He also worked behind-the-scenes in many, many ways to ensure that the home lives of his players were happy and their careers secure. He chased jobs for some; found new ones for others. As a new immigrant, Topo came in for special attention. At every turn, Jones offered him help. When Topo bought his first home at Cromer on Sydney's northern beaches the hand that did the successful bidding at the auction didn't belong to Topo, but to the Australian Rugby coach. Whether Jones gave him any financial help in the purchase of the home is between the two of them, but he did everything possible to make Topo, his wife and two small children feel wanted in their new land.

He singled out the more senior players like Mark Ella, Steve Williams, Michael Hawker and me for long talks and went to Queensland for further discussion with Andrew Slack, Michael Lynagh and Tom Lawton. He plundered our ideas and then passed on to us his own thoughts and strategies on how the Jones vision was going to work. I'd never had any coach appear so thorough or so committed.

At this stage I also began to develop a better understanding of the other side of Alan Jones. I'd go to the Newtown warehouse he'd recently bought and converted into a home/office and find myself spending more and more time looking at the expensive paintings on the wall and browsing along the bookshelves crammed with books of poetry, politics, business, history, sport and the arts. It all made me think a little more about life as a whole. There'd be opera blaring from the hi-fi system, or you might even interrupt Jones singing along at the top of his voice to an aria from 'Madame Butterfly'. (It often used to make me wonder what the factory workers in the street several floors below used to think was going on.) He was obviously a very cultured man. At Oxford University he had become a friend of Benazir Bhutto, later to become Pakistan's Prime Minister, and also of the best-selling author Jeffrey Archer. At every turn, there was some new surprise to this man, and as time wore on I found him to be an extremely likeable and fascinating person.

Everything about Jones seemed so consummately learned and professional, and he always seemed so totally convincing. Listen to him and you'd think: 'Hey, everything this guy says is great common sense; it's very logical. The big plan is in action here. This bloke really thinks about what he's saying and knows what he's doing.'

Layers of confidence soon started to develop around Jones and his grand vision. He obviously knew precisely what he was doing in terms of our national Rugby team, and he was going about it in a more professional manner than any sporting coach in this country had ever done before. Indeed, I would think that only Iron Curtain efficiency could have matched what Alan Jones did in preparing for the entry of the Australian team into the international Rugby arena in 1984.

However, we didn't exactly begin by jumping in at the deep end. We had a gentle beginning, with the Wallabies scheduled to visit Fiji for a three-match tour in May–June to prepare us for the All Blacks visit and the British Isles tour later in the year.

THE CALM BEFORE THE STORM—
FIJI AND NEW ZEALAND

The 1984 season for me was interrupted when it had hardly begun, because of the broken finger I'd painfully nursed through the Sydney team's European tour in March. It was in such a sorry state that I had to have surgery, and had my first game back on May 19 for Randwick against Sydney University at University Oval.

As I was about to run onto the ground for that game, I looked around at the small crowd lounging around in the sunshine at the very picturesque setting and could scarcely believe who I spotted. It was Dr Bruce Conolly, the hand surgeon who had performed the operation. Talk about Big Brother watching! Obviously he was there to see how his work stood up to the rough treatment it was about to receive. I guess a Rugby game was as good a post-operative examination as he could ever hope for. During the game I couldn't help having the occasional glance his way and, whenever I did, he was staring straight back at me through a set of binoculars. His concern was all about dedication to one's profession and pride in one's work. And at the end of the 80 minutes he could only have been happy, because I'd come through the game without any worries and the finger felt fine. What's more I'd bagged two tries in the process.

The Wallabies were about to be chosen for Fiji but I felt my selection was questionable. I wasn't sure how Alan Jones would react to my having been off the paddock for a few weeks, and I still wondered if he was secretly harbouring a grudge for my having backed Bob Dwyer for the national coaching job in February.

That was all fanciful thinking on my part, however, because when the team was announced for the three-match tour I was in it. So were Andy McIntyre and nine new Wallabies, including, rather significantly, Bill Campbell, Nick Farr-Jones and Topo Rodriguez. Jones was gathering his chosen troops around him. It was interesting how quickly Jones had changed his attitude on Rodriguez once the Argentinian had gained his permanent residential visa and he ushered him into that Australian touring team almost before Topo had unpacked his bags. Another chosen for that tour, but who withdrew through injury, was Queensland fullback Greg Martin. It just goes to prove that in Rugby it's a case of 'out of sight, out of mind' because it took Marto until the 1989 season against the British Lions to be selected again for Australia.

One particularly contentious selection issue was Mark Ella being sacked as captain by Jones and his co-selectors and the role being handed over to Andrew Slack from Queensland. This was very surprising to me as Jones had always been a strong supporter of Ella. It would be interesting to discover from where the real push came to relieve Ella of the job and that is a question that only Alan Jones, Bob Templeton or John Bain could answer. But suddenly the writers' quills were being dipped in poison once more, for Mark was an extremely popular personality in Sydney Rugby as well as being a unique talent. At the start of the season he had been dropped by the Sydney selectors when he decided to discover the sights of Beijing on a short holiday rather than attend squad training, and later he lost the NSW captaincy to Michael Hawker. Despite all that, it was still unpalatable to many to see the incumbent Test skipper being hoisted so hastily by the new national coach.

When the Wallabies came together before the tour at the Camperdown Travelodge it definitely wasn't a case of old buddies being reunited and all of us looking forward to this Rugby adventure in the Pacific. I, for one, was seething. I felt very strongly that Jones was grooming Bill Calcraft, whom he'd coached at Manly, to replace me on the side of the Test scrum and, in fact, I became very aggressive towards Bill at training one afternoon and did everything to him physically in the rucks and mauls short of hooking him one. Bill was the innocent party. He was oblivious to what had stirred me up so much and must have wondered what this red-haired lunatic was on about. If I was a friend, then he must have wondered what the enemy would be like. His presence wasn't the only thing that had made me angry. The other was the fact that Jones had named Chris Roche as vice-captain of the Wallabies, when I'd held that position at times on the New Zealand and French tours the previous two seasons. So it just seemed to me as if I was on the outer in this Jones regime whichever way I looked and that I was going to find it very hard to make it back into the Test lineup.

Fiji is always an incredibly tough place to tour, given the flint-like playing surfaces, the stinking humidity and what feels like complete isolation. There are very few whites over there who follow the game, yet the natives are absolutely besotted by it, so when you run out onto any ground all you can see is this press of jovial-looking, coal-black faces.

Our first game was against the Western XV at Churchill Park in Lautoka. A tiny ground. People jammed in the miniature grandstand, on top of buildings, hanging from trees. Black faces everywhere. Every empty space was taken. And the heat was claustrophobic. It was a very important game for me, because I so wanted to get my name back up there in lights for the Test team. Also, it signalled two most significant Australian debuts: those of Jones as coach and Rodriguez as prop-forward. And for the first time ever we saw the pairing of Ella at five-eighth and Michael Lynagh at inside-centre. Everything went fairly well for us, we shook off all the cobwebs and overcame the heat to win 19-3.

The following day the Wallabies had a day off across on Beachcomber Island, the exquisitely beautiful and intimate honeymooners' island eighteen kilometres off the coast from Lautoka. It was really a fun day, with all the players letting their hair down. But can you imagine Alan Jones in that setting? Here's a character who always has to be doing something, sleeps about two or three hours a night and classifies leisure as seeing how many pages of Darwin's 'The Origin of Species' or some deep political treatise he can get through in a day. Lying on the beach on a sun-baked Pacific island in Speedos and suntan cream sipping cocktails is definitely not Jonesy's way of relaxing. His reaction was typical. I can hear him now complaining that 'I'm not spending five hours in this place, but one hour five times over ...' One local journalist observed that the executive director of the NSW Employers' Federation finally understood, at least for five hours, what it was like being unemployed. His attitude towards anything relaxing was prejudiced even further by his worry about the team not training with a Test match just down the road and about one or more of his prized players either drowning themselves or getting a nasty dose of sunburn as they frivously enjoyed themselves.

We finally left Beachcomber Island, much to our coach's delight, and headed off for the eastern end of Fiji where we were to play the Eastern Selection at the National Stadium in Suva. We moved into the Isa-Lei Hotel, but were only there overnight before Jones decided that it wasn't nearly good enough for his team and ordered that we move out. It wasn't the last time he was to take charge and order a hotel evacuation. The Fiji Rugby Union was thrown into an immediate spin and quickly had to find us alternative accommodation at the Suva Travelodge, which thankfully met the Jones criteria. While the Wallabies were in the midst of their hotel shuffle, the local newspapers were full of the story about the Eastern Selection having trained on the previous Sunday. Being the devout Methodists they are, doing anything on the Sabbath was normally unthinkable behaviour so it really exemplified the extraordinary hold Rugby has on their lives over there.

I was among those rested for this game, with Chris Roche captaining the Wallabies. It had been raining cats and dogs beforehand and the game turned into a mudbath as well as a bloodbath. Ross Hanley was clobbered and someone tried to decapitate Bill Calcraft. But the real fun and games occurred when in an all-in brawl erupted. We'd all been warned not to get isolated if something like this happened, to stay with your backs to each other so that no-one could hit you from behind. Well Nigel (The Shredder) Holt either hadn't listened to the warning or forgot about it in the heat of battle, and the Queenslander was out in the open spilling a few drops of Fijian blood by flaying into everything that was mean-looking and black when suddenly one of his rival second-rowers came from behind and connected with one of the best king-hits you've ever seen. Down he went, mixing a bit of his Aussie blood with what was already on the ground, and the next day he looked like he'd been hit by a double-decker bus. But the performance of The Shredder elsewhere in that heated 15-4 win saw him earn his first cap for the Test match at the same ground four days later.

The day the Test team was announced, Jones began summoning various players to his room. And it seemed that the players NOT in the team were being summoned. Peter FitzSimons ran into my room and wanted to know if I'd been called, because he had. I told him I hadn't. 'That could mean only one of two things,' he declared, 'that you're in and I'm out or I'm in and you're out.' Five minutes later there was another knock on the door, and there was the big jovial oddball looking very dejected. Fitzy had been told he wasn't in the Test team and thereby missed his first chance of playing in a Test match. My inclusion suddenly eased all the tension and anxiety that I'd been feeling in the lead-up.

Australia won the Test in pretty foul playing conditions by 16-3. Heavy rain had made it hard going under foot, but we played very controlled Rugby against the Fijians, who really find the tight XV-a-side game too much for them. They much prefer loose, broken play when their natural exuberance takes over and then they can play brilliantly. Afterwards, the Fijian media singled out the fullback and one of the wingers and blatantly accused them of having lost the Test— a type of reporting you don't normally see elsewhere in the world. But it wasn't the fault of any of the Fijian players. In fact, our forward effort that afternoon in difficult conditions was outstanding, and Mark Ella also had a terrific game. He kicked a field goal that many of the Fijian players disputed, but the referee Graham Harrison thought it was okay and that's all that mattered. Mark also set up a brilliant try, involving Lynagh and Moon and eventually scored by Campese, who was playing fullback. An interesting sidelight to that Test is recalling the fellow playing five-eighth for Fiji. He was a 23-year-old technician from the Nakelo Club in Rewa named Acura Niuqila, who four years later was to wind up on the end of the Australian backline.

During that short tour, Jones had clearly shaped his forces. The front-row of Rodriguez, Lawton, McIntyre. A giant of a second-rower in Campbell (later to be replaced by Cutler, who had been unavailable for Fiji). Ella at five-eighth with Lynagh alongside him. Slack outside-centre. Moon on the wing. It was all coming together. The new coach had also shown that he wasn't in the least frightened to make the hard decisions. That he was prepared to involve himself in the management of the team was shown by his act of shifting hotels. On the field, he trusted his judgment and authority by going for Ella at five-eighth when Lynagh had been the dominant player there in domestic matches, and also by substituting Rodriguez for Coolican, who had served Australia well.

Rodriguez was becoming part of the outfit in another way. Everybody was helping him with his English but he was being told more slang than correct grammar. Topo finished with a better grasp of Australian slang than anyone I've ever met. And he didn't seem to mind at all being nicknamed the Dapto Dog by his teammates.

When the tour ended, a few of us, including Matt Burke, Mark Ella and Peter Lucas, broke from the rest of the team and spent a night and a day at the sumptuous Regent Hotel. We'd all experienced Mark's remarkable popularity in Fiji at first-hand when the small kids would run after him at training or even chase the team bus shouting 'markella ... markella ...', but we went into Nadi to do some shopping and everywhere we went it was like the Pied Piper all over again. Adults as well as kids followed him everywhere. If ever they want someone other than Rabuka to organise a coup d'etat in Fiji then he's the man, because the Fijians absolutely adore him and treat him as though he's a ratu (chieftain).

Back in Australia, several of us declined to go on the NSW team's three-match New Zealand tour. Among those who went was Rodriguez, who hadn't seen much of his family since his arrival but was obviously very keen to cement his position in the representative teams.

The All Blacks were shortly to arrive. I was chosen for NSW against Queensland, but because the new State coach Barry Taylor stayed loyal to many of those who went with him to New Zealand the team was not as strong as it could have been and Queensland beat us at Ballymore by 13-3. Steve Cutler played a blinder for NSW that day. He had not been in Fiji, where Holt and Campbell played so well in the second-row, and obviously had all stops out that day to do well. But the game generally wasn't of a particularly high standard and Queensland coach Bob Templeton summed it up nicely with one of his quotable quotes by declaring: 'It wouldn't have made Andy Dalton's All Blacks quiver with fear.'

NSW played the All Blacks in their second tour game. Barry (Tizza) Taylor arranged for the NSW team to stay at the five-star Manly Pacific International Hotel on the beachfront at Manly, which was a great move on his part. We all thoroughly enjoyed the atmosphere, rather than being closeted in the city, and it's a pity more teams don't stay at such locations. Taylor also had some martial arts instructors come along to our training and they talked to us and got us to scream out the way they do as a means of ... come to think of it, I'm not exactly sure what it was supposed to do. Most of us found it pretty amusing. On the way to the game, Taylor came up with another innovation. He ordered the bus to stop about ten minutes from Concord Oval and told us he was going to play a tape which he wanted us to listen to carefully. It was the theme from Chariots of Fire, which he turned up so loudly that the All Blacks probably heard it as well, wherever they were.

Despite Taylor's careful planning, the All Blacks ran all over us by 37-10, the most significant point about the game being the injury to their glamour winger John Kirwan. Matt Burke drove him so hard into the pitch that he seriously damaged his shoulder, a telling blow for the All Blacks considering that Kirwan was their major strike force in the backline and probably the best winger in world Rugby. Afterwards, the feeling among our players was that in the Test series we could undoubtedly make a mess of their backs, who lacked some flair, if only we could get enough possession from their forwards. But that wasn't going to be at all easy.

Australia's Test XV, which was the first one where Jones had everyone at his disposal to select from, was: Gould, Moon, Slack (c), Hawker, Campese, Ella, Cox, Reynolds, Roche, Poidevin, Williams, Cutler, McIntyre, Lawton, Rodriguez. The only surprise was Lynagh's absence, given the good season he'd been having at home, his form in Fiji, and the fact that it left us light in the goalkicking department.

Where our playing strength was fairly evenly divided, the All Blacks were top heavy in the forwards through tough men like Ashworth, Knight, Shaw and Mexted. They also had an excellent coach in Bryce Rope. Plenty of spice was added to the series by the New Zealand team manager Dick Littlejohn, whom the Australians loved to hate. He was very arrogant and certainly knew how to rub people up the wrong way. We heard, read about and saw lots of him during the tour and at almost every turn he gave us another reason for wanting to beat the All Blacks.

In the period leading up to the Test, those of us in the Australian team began receiving the first of the flood of memos Alan Jones used to send to his players. They went into a lot of our statistics, provided considerable detail about the tactics we'd employ, and discussed at length the strengths and, more importantly, the weaknesses of the opposition. They were the kind of things you'd read in a quiet moment and, while you could hardly be expected to absorb everything he wrote, an awful lot of it would stick and make you think about what was ahead.

In a memo written by him on 11 July 1984—ten days before the first Test—and running to five pages, Jones began with a quote: 'Life's battle doesn't always go to the biggest or strongest or fastest man. But sooner or later the fellow who wins is the fellow who thinks he can win.'

Then he told us to remember:
- Australia has only won 69 Tests out of 204 that it has played, a 34 per cent winning percentage, but
- the last ten years has shown this country, above all others, reaching for the top of the Rugby tree.
- We've played 49 Tests and won 25, which indicates that the defeats of the past are becoming more and more infrequent.
- New Zealand has won 70 per cent of all the Tests it has played against Australia,
- but in the last ten years they've won just over 50 per cent.

The lesson is, we are improving, we have improved and we are going to sustain that improvement. We are never underestimating them nor are we underestimating ourselves.

We must be:
- committed
- disciplined
- fast
- physical
- unapologetic.

What we do in the next few weeks will live with us for life. But we won't get where we want to go by talking about it. We are going to have to make things happen. Remember several things:
- Predictability in what we do reduces pressure on the opposition.
- Skills done aggressively equal success.
- Skills done aggressively breed confidence.
- Confidence breeds composure and composure gives us time.
- All of these make you look like the winning outfit.

Then he went into detail, insisting that 'we must find touch, kickoffs and 25 drop-outs can't be out on the full, 25s must cross the line, tackled players must release and not fiddle with the ball, binding at the scrum is important, the tackle line has to be straight all day, our defence on the blindside has to be water-tight through the breakaways, No 8 and blindside winger etc.'

The most telling observation in the whole memo, and one that I marked with three crosses and read and re-read said:

'This game is about denying these people (the All Blacks) time and space and adding to that denial total physicality. Our men will do that. We must make our minds up now. We will yield to no-one. We are not interested in the papers, the crowd, the officials or the opposition. We must now be unyielding in what we seek but we have to have skills and discipline to match our ambition.'

His analysis of the All Blacks' weaknesses was very telling and would have been of immense interest to all in the Rubgy world who thought they were almost unbeatable.

Jones argued that:
- When they are not in the box seat they lose cohesion and purpose.
- They hate the ball being behind them.
- How mobile are the tight five? We must put them to that test.
- I've said predictability reduces pressure. We have the backline that can create the element of surprise—they don't.
- The French showed them vulnerable on the loose head.
- They have a preference for the blindside which must enable us to bottle that up.
- Eventually we will put the fullback under pressure, not early but, when it happens, comprehensively.
- He will be arguing with the No 8 as to who takes the high ball and that will assist us.

The forwards received another memo five days later; two pages detailing the finer points of what to do at the lineout when it was their ball, our ball, and then all the variations we would use.

This was in addition to all the hours and hours of work that we put in on the training paddock, where Jones drove us relentlessly.

As the Test came closer, Jones started to use the media more and more to help his campaign. This was something that became a very significant part of his coaching over the following few years. He'd raise matters in the press which would focus on areas where he thought we were in danger, with the idea of neutralising them. The classic example here was the situation with Steve Cutler, whom he was sure would be an All Black target. He went into print saying: 'The All Blacks won't put up with Cutler's presence for more than two minutes before attempting to take him out. If the referee doesn't take care of him, we will.' Of course, he was assuming the English referee Roger Quittenton would read the papers.

All that said and done, it then remained to be seen whether on July 21 at the Sydney Cricket Ground we could put it all together.

Well we did. We won 16-9, scoring two tries to nil before 40 797 spectators. And Jones's ploy of alerting the referee to Cutler's vulnerability worked perfectly. The All Blacks were kept off him, allowing Cuts to win a mountain of possession for us, especially in the five-man lineouts. In fact, I couldn't sing his praises higher than after that Test. Cuts absolutely dominated the game, and I tremendously enjoyed my role of minder behind him in the lineouts, which we won 25-16. With all that ball, everything else fell into place and Andrew Slack later described the way Australia played as the most disciplined performance he'd ever been involved in.

Forty-eight hours after that was over a huge controversy erupted

Elation: Topo Rodriguez and Roger Gould after our defeat of the All Blacks in the first Test of the 1984 series in Australia

concerning the selection of the Sydney team to play the All Blacks the following weekend. Eight of us withdrew from the Sydney team—Cox, Ella, Hawker, Poidevin, Reynolds, Williams, Cutler and Rodriguez—so that, with the second Test a week later, we wouldn't have to go in against the All Blacks three times on three weekends. While Jones was publicly quiet on the matter, he was unquestionably the prompter, and Hawker, the Sydney captain, was spokesman for our actions. In our defence, the top players should never have been put in the position of being called upon to face the All Blacks as much as they were, with the possibility of being smashed from pillar to post. It wouldn't happen in any other major Rugby nation, but our officials were more than happy to dish us up as fodder for the All Blacks at every turn. It made me recall 1980 when I played against them six times! It was crazy then and was crazy now. Apart from getting terribly battered playing a team like that, you become mentally stale up against the same opponents over and over again. On the other hand, the Sydney team hadn't been beaten by a touring team since 1974, so the Sydney Rugby Union officials were screaming blue murder at our withdrawal. They threatened never to pick any of us again, and the upset coach Peter Fenton said that 'it has got to the point where to win's the only thing that matters.' Interestingly the Australian Rugby Football Union came out publicly and backed the players, having seen the rationale behind our withdrawal. Peter Crittle, who had coached both the Sydney and NSW teams, also gave us strong support in a letter to *The Sydney Morning Herald*.

As the arguments raged, I found myself very ill at ease with the whole situation. I had captained the Sydney team to Europe early that year and had a lot of laughs and hard times with Fenton while we were away. We'd become good mates. So when Phil Wilkins from *The Australian* newspaper rang me that week I poured my heart out to him and told him I wanted to be back in the team again. I'd play for Sydney if I was allowed. The next morning I winced at the headlines—DEFECTOR WANTS HIS PLACE BACK IN SYDNEY TEAM. The rest of the media picked up the story and ran with it. They were all asking: can't Poidevin make up his mind? Suddenly I wasn't very happy about having gone public on the matter and at the end of the day all my plea did was create many conflicts. The outcome was that my appeal for another chance was too late, the Sydney Rugby Union didn't want me back and I watched from the grandstand with the rest of those who'd pulled out while the All Blacks beat them by 28-3.

On the morning of the match, the eight of us who had withdrawn had a training run together. Although I'd taken a contrary view to them there was no criticism of me whatsoever, which was pleasing.

For the second Test at Ballymore, the All Blacks brought Robbie Deans back into the team at fullback in place of Allan Hewson, who had only kicked two from seven attempts in Sydney. It was very important for them to have that part of their game up to scratch, so at training we tailored our skills around reducing penalties. We were determined Deans wouldn't kick us off the paddock. The night before the Test we all went along to the movies. I made the choice, but Jones wondered what had struck him when he realised the movie was 'Indiana Jones and the Temple of Doom'. Did he whinge! 'What is this stuff you've brought me to, Poidevin!' he demanded, for it definitely wasn't his cup of tea.

The Ballymore hoodoo, which was to intensify so much in future years, thwarted us again. The All Blacks won 19-15 after we'd been ahead

12-0. At the end of the day we'd lost the lineouts 25-12. The reason for that was Cuts being wiped out early by an All Black boot. Take away all the possession that he always provided and we weren't the same outfit. Despite our planning, Robbie Deans also did the job for the All Blacks in goalkicking, because while we scored a try apiece he potted five penalty goals to provide the difference. There were plenty of post-mortems, but basically it was a highly motivated New Zealand team that really pulled itself back from Death Row. And, for some reason, they seemed to like playing at Ballymore, like all touring teams. Why Ballymore? Perhaps it's that it's much more of a Rugby ground than the Sydney Cricket Ground and more like their typical grounds back home. It's a beautiful setting and the crowd's so close to the playing area that they provide much more atmosphere than you get on the vast expanse of the SCG.

After that loss, the criticism of us came thick and fast, but none more pointedly than from Evan Whitton in *The Sydney Morning Herald*, who ripped into all of us and wrote of Hawker being a graduate of that 'pre-eminent joke factory, Sydney University Rugby Football Club.' We never forgot that quote and delightedly threw it right back into the lap of this purveyor of frequent venom and Rugby fantasies over the coming months. What he wrote then was totally unfair and lacked loyalty to the players who had done so much for Australian Rugby.

Despite the second Test loss, the Australian team was unchanged for the deciding Test a fortnight later in Sydney. Again, Jones was into the pre-game hype, getting both the media and referee focusing on the areas he felt needed to be watched more closely for our sake. One newspaper heading read AUSTRALIA READY TO TRADE BLOW FOR BLOW TO WIN TEST MATCH. He warned that if the All Blacks intended turning it into a donnybrook, then we'd match them. 'We've come too far to be intimidated,' he warned. 'There has been a significant catalogue along the way of people being opened up and pulled off the paddock and we're not going to stand for that sort of business. If they want it tough they'll get it tough. If strong-arm stuff is needed to win this Test match then strong-arm stuff it'll be.' Again, he repeated that Cutler wouldn't last for more than two minutes before being taken out of the play. It was vintage Jones leading up to a Test. I'd have found it all very amusing, except that Jonesy would be in the grandstand come kickoff time and we'd be out there facing them.

The build-up for this Test was easily the most intense I'd ever experienced to that time. Behind the scenes many things were happening; the most intriguing was Alan Jones' request that Michael Lynagh play fullback. Lynagh was one of the form players at that time and a magnificent goal kicker. It is a tragedy that he declined the offer because he felt he wouldn't succeed in this highly demanding role. The Australian players were all on a knife-edge with the Bledisloe Cup at stake, as the

THE CALM BEFORE THE STORM—FIJI AND NEW ZEALAND

Mark Ella and myself working as a defensive team against the All Blacks in the second Test at Ballymore, 1984

All Blacks obviously were too. I didn't realise until speaking to Murray Mexted sometime later that the Australian Rugby Football Union had even given them extra ammunition by putting the touring team in what they considered to be sub-standard hotels and then asking them to save on the laundry bills by washing out their undies in their hotel sinks! The reason, as I understand it, for the last direction was because the All Blacks' laundry costs were unusually high. It was suggested that the tourists would get some of their supporters' laundry done in their hotel and then charge them for it, thus making a decent profit for the team funds. Still, the ARFU direction to scrub out their gear in the handbasin every night was great motivational fuel for their wanting to beat us.

As has happened so many times in our nations' Test clashes, there was only one point in the result. It was 25-24 ... their way. Before a massive crowd of almost 50 000, the All Blacks scored two tries to one, including a very easy one conceded by us. There were 26 penalties in the Test, nineteen to Australia, a remarkable statistic. Yet again Deans kicked six goals from seven attempts, which gave them the narrowest of winning margins and also the Cup. We had problems that day in the backline, with Mark Ella calling the shots at five-eighth and Hawker and Slack in the centres. All were senior players, and there was an unblievable amount of talk between them during the game—far too much. Each seemed to have different ideas. I can remember sitting down with Jones outside the old Members Bar after it was all over and bluntly telling him: 'Listen mate, the backline situation today was absolutely ridiculous, because we had so many people out there talking that in the end no-one knew where the ball was going.' The Australian forwards did extremely well, but our backs, with all their talent, simply got themselves into a horrible mess. It was a sad night afterwards in the wind-up dinner at the AJC Centre at Randwick Racecourse. After a heap of beers, Slacky had tears in his eyes when he handed me the All Black tie he had been presented with as Australian captain. 'You have this,' he said poignantly. 'You deserve it. I don't.' He wasn't the only sad one. We were all deeply distressed at losing a series to New Zealand by a single point in the decider, but it certainly strengthened our resolve to succeed on the forthcoming tour of the British Isles. We were really going to make amends over there.

THE GRAND SLAM BEGINS

*T*here was nothing too startling about the names of the thirty players chosen for the eighth Wallaby tour of the British Isles, although there was some diappointment when Peter Lucas didn't make it. Luco stood extremely high in everyone's estimation as a back-row forward, because of his unquenchable commitment to the game. But he wasn't exactly a ten-storey skyscraper and, with guys like me and Chris Roche in the team, there simply wasn't room for another back-rower of average height and lineout ability. With such an emphasis by Jones on lineout ball, Luco probably lost the final back-row spot to David Codey, who was that much taller and potentially a consistent ball-winner for us at the back of the lineout.

Other than that, there was no room for complaint. From the looks of things, we would be fielding the largest set of Test forwards ever seen on a Rugby pitch, averaging more than 101 kilograms per man, the backs had all the firepower you could want in Nick Farr-Jones, Mark Ella, David Campese and Brendan Moon, and having Roger Gould's massive boot at fullback was like having a bazooka against the enemy's peashooter. Given the work Jones would drum into us, his exceptional organisational ability, his uncanny motivational powers and the way any team develops on a long tour, we looked capable of shaking the hell out of anything the four Home Unions had to offer.

I spent the exhausting flight over reading *In God's Name*, losing my money at cards and enjoying the pleasures of economy-class travel while dwelling on the vast amounts of money our team would generate for the Home Unions. It was uncomfortable enough for me at 185 centimetres, but how Cutler and Campbell coped at 200 and 201 centimetres respectively I really don't know. We were welcomed at Heathrow by a host of the usual tweed-coated officials from the Rugby Football Union and our baggage-man for the next two months, Graham Short (the best in the business and destined to become a lifelong friend to many of the Wallabies).

On the bus trip into London I received the shattering news that Stan Pilecki was to be my room-mate. Now sleeping in the same room as the Friendly Pole is like bedding down alongside a foghorn and a chimney stack, because he generally snores all night long, or, if he's not doing that, he sits up in bed smoking his head off.

We were kept waiting interminably at what was to be our city base at the noble St Ermin's Hotel, right across the street from New Scotland Yard, because our rooms weren't ready. We were eventually allowed to change in a few rooms so that we could go to training, a move which baffled the British media after such a long plane flight. And the training session was so intense and so high in skills that those watching on the touchlines were in awe.

We were all so worn out after getting back to the hotel that we hit the sack immediately. I was asleep by 4.30 in the afternoon and didn't stir till the next morning, despite Stan's greatest attempts to weaken the foundations of the hotel with his snoring.

I'd thought a lot on the flight over about the tour and particularly about the likely composition of the Test pack. Chris Roche sought me out soon after our arrival, because he'd obviously been thinking about the same things. Jones had removed the vice-captaincy from Rochey and given it on this tour to Steve Williams, the big second-rower who played in Jones's 1983 Manly premiership-winning side. It was becoming increasingly apparent to us that Jones was nurturing Williams to become Australia's Test captain in the event that Andrew Slack, who wasn't in the best of form, had to vacate his Test centre spot. This was merely another example of what appeared to many of us in the team to be Jones's leaning towards the Manly players. This theory later proved to be totally incorrect. The other conclusion we came to was that, because of his obsession with height, there wasn't going to be a place for both Rochey and I in the Test pack. One of us would have to go. So we made a gentleman's pact to train our insides out, give it all we had and may the better man win.

On our first morning there I did some stretching and went for an early jog to Buckingham Palace and had a look around while Stan, who exerted himself only when absolutely necessary, went for a leisurely walk and a smoke. That night Stan, our team doctor Syd Sugerman and I decided to go to the theatre. At the Globe Theatre we saw 'Daisy Pulls It Off', which we rated about five and a half out of ten. The others had to rely on me to make an assessment of the show, because Syd slept right through the first half and Stan the second.

The next evening we decided on something less cultural, taking in the soccer match between Liverpool and Tottenham Hotspur. A great game, but the crowds and the congestion were unbelievable and we arrived back at the hotel much, much later than the coach would have liked.

During those early days the team was settling in nicely, we were getting to know each other better and the training was coming along fine. Jones had us working our butts off, but we were all revelling in it. It was pretty fierce at times, yet controlled. Until my short fuse went off. I had perceived David Codey as a threat to my Test breakaway position, and when a ruck at one of these early training sessions became fairly willing I just lost control and sank my boot into him. It was one of the silliest things I'd ever done and I felt immediate remorse. It also brought the wrath of the team on me, for which I certainly don't blame them. But given the all-round aggro in the team at the time it was not surprising that someone would crack.

There's always a heavy emphasis on social activities on a British Isles tour. In the first week we attended a welcoming dinner by the Four Home Unions at the snooty East India Club (my co-author was tossed out of there for wearing an expensive leather jacket—'no leathers allowed', he was told), and another day a Sportsmen's Luncheon at the Savoy Hotel. My table at the Sportsmen's Luncheon was very cordial and hosted by Rear Admiral Sir Anthony Miers. He was one of the greatest Allied submariners during World War II, and was awarded the Victoria Cross in 1942. He was a great character. You can meet some stuffed shirts in British Rugby, but you also meet some really fabulous people like him.

Between all the training and socialising, most of us occupied ourselves shopping, sightseeing, catching some more theatre and playing Trivial Pursuit, which was all the rage with the team.

Our opening game was against London Counties at Twickenham on Wednesday, October 17. The famous old ground was in great condition and looked quite a picture. We were very anxious to win this one and did so comfortably, wrapping it up by 22-3.

From the beginning, Jones demonstrated quite a different policy regarding team selections. Previous national coaches would always pick all the players in the first two matches to allow them to find their legs, but Jones did not follow this tradition. When the team to meet South & South West at Exeter was announced Phillip Cox, Tim Lane, James Black and Ross Hanley hadn't made either of our teams.

That second game provided a nail-biting finish. Australia didn't play all that well, and we were fairly lucky to get away with a 12-all draw.

Our next stop was Cardiff. On Rugby tours of Britain you're constantly reminded 'wait until you get to Wales, boyo', because that's where they live and breathe the game and where you generally strike the toughest opposition. Cardiff are one of the great Rugby clubs of the world and to draw them so early in the tour presented us with a huge hurdle. It was all deadly serious stuff during our build-up to that game, except when we all went out one night to hear Roberta Flack in concert at the beautiful Cardiff Theatre. The lead-up act before her was two English comedians, who were hilarious until they started telling jokes against Argentina. It was in pretty poor taste given the Falklands War. They also couldn't have known that Topo Rodriguez was in the audience. He didn't take too kindly to jokes about his homeland, and stood up in the middle of the packed house to roar out, 'I am from Argentina. I will see you after the show.' With terror in their eyes, they immediately switched to Irish jokes. The next day we lost the game to Cardiff by a narrow margin, which meant we had the even balance of a win, a loss and a draw in our opening three games.

The Wallabies beat Combined Services easily in their next game at Aldershot, but in the process lost some players. Topo Rodriguez had his head split open by one of their breakaways, who happened to be a marine who fought in the Falklands War. The irony of it wasn't lost on the rest of us, but it really was accidental. Cameron Lillicrap was also injured, and was going to be out for some time with an ankle injury, and so was Andrew Slack. Because we'd used the maximum two replacements, I finished up on the wing and had the time of my life: I caught a few high balls (and dropped another) and was taken out in the corner by Rory Underwood just as I was about to score. These wingers sure get it easy.

From there back down to Wales, where we were leading Swansea 17-7 in a night game with about twelve minutes remaining when there was a blackout. Nothing could be done to get the lights on again, so the game had to be ended prematurely and awarded to us. Afterwards, the team was on the bus about to head back to our hotel when some of the journalists travelling with us asked if they could hitch a ride. Dr Charles (Chilla) Wilson, our very easy-going manager, readily agreed, but then Evan Whitton from *The Sydney Morning Herald* emerged from the gloom and made towards the bus with the rest of the journos. Whitton had been writing what we reckoned were unfair and excessively critical articles on our early progress, and Chilla told him that he couldn't guarantee Whitton his safety if he boarded the bus. Whitton wisely sought alternative transport after that, but the lingering antagonism between him and the team, particularly Alan Jones, would surface again several more times on tour. Even that night, Jones gave Whitton a verbal lashing at the reception.

The team for the England Test was announced the next morning, with Rochey out of it and me in. I had double reason to celebrate, because it was also my twenty-sixth birthday. Jones had made significant changes to the team that had faced the All Blacks months earlier. Gone was the Manly No 8, Ross Reynolds, replaced by Steve Tuynman. Half-back Phillip Cox, another Manly player, was replaced by Nick Farr-Jones, Michael Hawker by Michael Lynagh, and Chris Roche by David Codey.

The next day the Wallabies were given an official reception at Buckingham Palace in the presence of the Queen and Prince Philip. We had a marvellous time looking at all the Rembrandts and Van Dykes, gawking at the splendour of the palace and speaking quite freely to the Royal couple. It's an experience I'll never forget. Unfortunately there were some red faces when one of the boys sat on the edge of a magnificent antique table and accidentally broke it. I wonder were the Home Unions billed for that?

That evening the British Rugby Writers' Association turned on a cruise for us down the Thames. It was superb drifting down the river looking at all the bright lights, the Houses of Parliament, Big Ben and everything else, while sipping a can of beer. And the British Rugby writers, with a few exceptions, were a pretty decent bunch of guys. The Test team was off-loaded at 9.30 for an early night, while the rest carried on merrily.

By the day of the Test we were well and truly ready. We'd prepared well, Jonesy had us all steamed up and we were anxious to knock over the Poms in what hopefully would be the first leg of the Grand Slam.

Some nasty-looking rain clouds were hovering around on the way to Twickenham, but they didn't amount to much which suited us fine. A tremendous crowd had packed into the games' citadel, the paté and chicken legs were doing the rounds in the car park before the game, and altogether it was a marvellous atmosphere for the first international of the tour. But if we were intent on the Grand Slam it certainly didn't look like it early on. In spite of the wind at our backs, we were only 3-all at half-time against what should have been by far the weakest of the four Home Unions.

But with the second half only just begun, Ella looped around Lynagh, the English defence moved up too fast and he shot through the gap for a try under the posts. From there we gathered momentum. For the last of our three tries I was tailing Campese down the touchline like a faithful sheepdog when he tossed me an overhead pass and over I went to score the Twickenham try every kid dreams of. Even though we were all elated by the 19-3 victory, it was tainted by Brendan Moon breaking his arm. I've got enormous admiration for Benny—he's the best winger I've played with or against—and it was a dreadful shame to see the tour end so tragically for him.

That night the official black-tie dinner was held at the London Hilton Hotel, and as the orchestra of the Coldstream Guards provided somnolent background music we supped on Entrecote Bordelaise, washed down with Beaujolais Villages Duboeuf Domaine de Buillats 1983. Not all that hard to take. Then came the speeches, which were all excellent, port and cigars and a very, very late evening, or rather early morning, out on the town.

FOR LOVE NOT MONEY

At our next stop at Leicester we made the obligatory visit to Rugby School, where William Webb Ellis picked up the ball and ran with it, thus creating the game of Rugby football. Had it not been for Ellis, who went on to become a man of the cloth, none of us would have been there that day. We paid our respects at the plaque commemorating the feat and then trained in very cold conditions on the school grounds.

The night game against Midlands Division will be remembered—for all the wrong reasons—as one of the more illustrious in Australian Rugby history. Rival hookers Mark McBain and Peter Wheeler, the British Lion and immediate past England captain, were both ordered off by the referee Winston Jones. In their absence, Australia had a tremendous 21-18 win against a team laced with English internationals. Tim Lane had a huge game. So did James Black. And the whole forward pack went very well. Two days later in Dublin a disciplinary committee, which included our manager, met. Chilla was in the minority in a 2-1 decision to suspend the hookers up to and including November 19, which meant three matches for McBain and an even harsher penalty for Wheeler, for he copped a mandatory thirty-day suspension from the RFU and was unable to play for England for the rest of the season. What was extraordinary was that evidence at the hearing seemed overwhelmingly to support the view that neither hooker had thrown a punch, for which they were charged, condemned and sentenced. It seemed very much a case of supporting the referee without demur and Jonesy had plenty to say on that matter to the media.

Rochey came into the team for the Test against Ireland, with Jones anticipating the Irish would be very fast around the paddock and thus choosing his own line-up accordingly. Matthew Burke came in for Benny on the wing. We had one of the funniest nights of the tour in Dublin when Slacky, who had played there previously with the Wanderers Club, arranged for some of his former clubmates to take us and some of the journos to the Blue Light Hotel in the hills above Dublin for a singalong, with Slacky plucking his guitar. But the roof was so low and the tiny pub so crowded that Steve Cutler couldn't fit his two metres under the roof and had to spend the whole night squatting on the floor.

The players all loved their first taste of the Irish. They were extremely warm and friendly people, and very humourous. We couldn't understand why they were the butt of so many jokes before a few of the journos told us that they'd asked the way to a ground where we were training and were told by an old woman to 'follow the road and turn left two miles before the church.' Some of the boys went out for a round of golf another day and spotted a sign near the first tee which carried the simple direction 'Do not lean your golf clubs against this sign'. Then we started to understand.

THE GRAND SLAM BEGINS

Lansdowne Road, which was only about five minutes walk from the hotel, was in extremely good order for the Test match. We'd had perfect weather for both Tests, so someone up there was on our side.

Again we won against the very committed Irish, this time by 16-9, although it would have been more had muggins not thrown the most hopeless forward pass to Matthew Burke with the unattended goal-line screaming for a try. It was a blunder of classic proportions. Campo made a sensational midfield break, gave to me and Burke loomed up alongside me with their fullback Hugo MacNeill the only guy to beat. Burke was on my right, my bad passing side, and as I drew MacNeill I somehow threw the ball forward to him. I could only bury my head in my hands with despair. Didn't I feel bad about it, especially as Ireland went on to lead 9-6 for a while, and I imagined my blunder costing us the Test. But when it was all over, we had two wins from two Tests: halfway to the Grand Slam. Yet the surprising thing was we had not played all that well. If and when we hit our straps then look out world. There was much celebrating afterwards when the team came together behind closed doors for the traditional happy hour, which started with me skolling a pint of Guinness quickly followed by another. Staying sober was going to become a problem. The dinner that night at the Shelbourne Hotel was noteworthy for Alan Jones's early departure. He'd also been forced into some over-indulgence at the happy hour when he really wasn't much of a drinker. Those happy hours must have seemed a nightmare at times for Alan Belford Jones.

The following day was our first full free day on tour. The whole team went for a QLD ('Quiet Little Drink') at the Wanderers Club. We didn't realise it was going to turn into a bash for every Wanderers player and ex-player for miles around, all their pals and a host of Australian supporters. There was a singing competition, a constant flow of the black stuff, and the QLD finished up lasting from morning until very late in the evening.

Next we headed north by bus, picked up our police escort at the border at Newry and then settled into the beautiful Culloden Hotel on the outskirts of Belfast. The Irish soccer team was also staying there for their game against Finland, and it was nice to yarn with them and exchange views. A pal of Ross Reynolds came by with a mini-bus one afternoon and offered to take us for a drive around the city, and we jumped at the chance. While it's reasonably quiet there these days, it's still hard to get used to the presence of armoured carriers and seeing heavily-armed British troops wearing flak jackets on patrol around the streets, often with an army helicopter hovering overhead. A very interesting afternoon.

I'm not saying this because I didn't play, but I felt the team wasn't fully tuned into the game against Ulster, and sure enough we lost by 2 points after scoring two tries to nil, our first defeat after five straight wins. From there we were to head south again for Limerick. But when we arrived at Belfast Airport it was found our luggage was way over the limit for the charter aircraft we were catching. So we had an extended stay at the airport while they found another plane large enough to get us off the ground.

During the first night in Limerick we had a fifteenth century banquet at Bunratty Castle, which turned into one of the real highlights of the tour—absolutely tons of fun in this glorious old castle. A huge spread of food and endless supplies of mead and red wine, wenches and servants in medieval dress waiting on the tables, and the musicians playing the most lilting melodies on harps and fiddles. Chilla was appointed lord of the proceedings and immediately tossed McBain into the cells for throwing the punch at Leicester (which he hadn't done). Bread rolls finished up being pelted around the dining room, and altogether it was an evening we shan't forget for a long while.

The following day Jones gave the team a very strong lecture on tour discipline, where the team was going, and the attitude of certain players leading up to the Munster and Llanelli games and the Welsh Test. He said a lot I agreed with. We were halfway through the tour and the toughest part of it was still to come.

A soupy fog had rolled into Limerick the morning of the Munster match and showed no sign of lifting. When we got to the ground you could stand at one end of the playing area and not see the goalposts at the other. It was an eerie experience, but the referee determined that the game would proceed. After two early tries by Munster, we fought back and played extremely well to win 31-19. The forwards' display was probably our best in a non-Test match.

Back to Shannon Airport the next morning for our charter flight to Cardiff and, while we waited, most of us spent any money we had on Waterford Crystal or, in Jonesy's case, a mohair overcoat. I was rested from the Llanelli game, as was virtually the whole Test team, and again we threw this one away by mistakes. We had them on toast, gave them a sniff of victory, and the team that gave credence to Darwin's theories got up by 19-16 to maintain their outstanding international record. One disgusting aspect of the game was the Llanelli supporters who spat on our captain Andrew Slack, a cowardly act that provided further fire for the Test the following Saturday. At the dinner that evening, Michael (Lord) Hawker, who had captained the Wallabies that day, said in his speech that 'when it comes to Saturday this victory by Llanelli won't matter a hoot, because it will be wiped out by Australia beating Wales'.

The Wallabies headed down to the coastal resort of Porthcawl to prepare for the Test against Wales. Nobody ever goes there in the dead of winter, so the old Seabank Hotel right on the water's edge is the ideal spot for peace and quiet while you prepare. Rochey was dropped from the Test line-up for Codey, and Burke went for Peter Grigg on the wing. As the Test approached, the weather closed in and we had to train in some pretty fierce rain and swirling winds. But the team was feeling very strong and confident. No-one much liked the Welsh and, besides that, the prospect of winning the Grand Slam was growing larger by the day.

Rugby wasn't the Wallabies only claim to fame in Porthcawl, as a mate of mine in Limerick had given me a special for the races in England. So Pilecki and I collected money from half the team and headed for one of the local betting shops. I instructed Stan to lay the money for a win and then went out to buy a newspaper. When I came back he'd already laid the money but had got cold feet and backed the horse each-way. The horse romped home, and even with the each-way bet the betting shop couldn't pay us in cash. They had to write us a cheque! If Stan had made it for a win, Porthcawl would never have been the same again.

We had a police escort up to Cardiff on the morning of the Test and, considering the weather of the previous few days, the ground was in remarkably good order. We survived the singing of 'Land of My Fathers' by 67 000 Welsh fans, and went into battle. After only five minutes I knew we were going to beat Wales and beat them well: they just didn't have any answer to the way we were playing. The Welsh players told us afterwards that when they tried to shove the first scrum of the game and were pushed back two metres they immediately knew the writing was on the wall. Yet all the media had focused on in the lead-up to the Test was how the power of the Welsh scrum would prove the Wallabies' downfall.

As Alan Jones said later, for the first 23 minutes of the Test we didn't make a single mistake in our match plan. Everything was flowing our way and the Test was ours long before it was over. The real highlight came 22 minutes into the second half. Australia were leading 13-3. The call of 'Samson' went out from our hooker Tommy Lawton as the two packs went down within the shadow of the Welsh line. It was the call for an eight-man shove. All feet back. Spines ramrod straight. Every muscle tense and ready. The ball came in, we all sank and heaved with everything we had and then like a mountainside disintegrating under gelignite the Welsh scrum began yielding unwillingly. As we slowly drove them back over their own goal-line I watched under my left arm as Steve (Bird) Tuynman released his grasp on the second-rowers and dropped into the tangle. The Bird knew what he was doing, and the referee Mr E E Doyle was perfectly positioned to award what has since become legendary, our pushover try. The stands went into shock. The Arms Park had never seen such humiliation. We went on to a fantastic 28-9 win and had an equally fabulous happy hour afterwards. There was lots of skolling of beer, singing, laughter and tom-foolery. And why not! Three Tests. Three wins. Three-quarters of the way to the Grand Slam. Suddenly it was right within our grasp.

It was understandably a big night. The next morning after a few more quiet drinks at Porthcawl (although night met day very quickly for some of the players) a few of us decided that a dip in the ocean would be just the thing. In the midst of a British winter! Still, we weren't feeling any pain by then so the Wallaby Swimming Club of Williams, Hawker, Codey, Tuynman and I hopped in wearing nothing but hangovers.

After a long bus trip our next stop was Southport, where all the fun parks and tourist shops on the beachfront were closed with winter having rolled in. Jonesy took the opportunity at training there to really rip into some players for their attitude. They seemed to think the victory over Wales meant the end of the tour. Far from it. Our very aggravated coach made it known very forcibly that the toughest part still lay ahead. He really took it out on the whole team and had us train until well after sunset.

Late in the session there was a fierce blow-up between Jonesy and Nick Farr-Jones. Nick was feeling tired and let the coach know. He was promptly told there were other halfbacks around if he didn't feel like continuing. At that point Stan Pilecki piped up and offered to play halfback, which didn't go down at all well and Jonesy jumped right onto the Pole about that. But Stan, who was much the same age as Alan, stood his ground and it developed into a real slanging match. Stan and the coach had about three meetings afterwards to sort out that little altercation, but Stan really spoke up and said he'd gladly go home if that's what Jonesy wanted. It wasn't surprising that they came to words, because Jonesy was very short-tempered at that point because of his chronic back condition which had worsened in recent weeks and was really giving him hell.

The next day he was into us again verbally, talking of the great successes of Rod Laver, Herb Elliott and co., outlining the many pitfalls that still lay ahead on tour and basically getting us right on course for the Grand Slam.

Fortunately, we quelled Jones's annoyance by beating Northern Division by 14-12. This was one of the better teams we'd seen on tour, and included Rob Andrew at five-eighth.

From there, we motored through the Lakes district and into Scotland, a wonderfully picturesque part of Britain. We stayed in a beautiful old inn out in the countryside at Melrose, and the night we arrived ten of us went out poaching with some locals. A very funny experience. It was a para-military-style operation carried out in the dead of night. Our group of Steve Williams, Hawker, Ella, I and three locals, one of whom had just come out of the slammer, headed to one of the nearby streams, jumped out of the car, scrambled down a steep bank and waded into the freezing water in search of the salmon and trout. We headed upstream and promptly heard two men coming from the other direction! Probably the bailiff or police! Imagine the calamity if four Wallabies were arrested for poaching. So we ducked into the bushes before they spotted us and silently watched them go past; silently apart from Steve Williams, who was finding it hard to contain his laughter. But it wasn't the law—only two more poachers! Suddenly one of our hosts called out from the darkness: 'Hold up there. Bailiff here!', and these two shadows took off like startled roos into the night. We fell about laughing, but of course all that din and splashing about wrecked any chance of us ever gaffing any fish. The rendezvous back in Hawick with the other two groups showed that Gould, Reynolds and McIntyre had had much more success and had a whopping ten-kilogram salmon to prove it.

The next day we toured the Pringle factory at Hawick ('as fascinating as watching grass grow,' said Jones) and then investigated the Pringle shop, where many of the team bought jumpers and cardigans; a huge boost to the local economy.

That night I rang my racing contact in Ireland and he declared a 'sure thing' at the races, Sure Row, which had also won the previous weekend. So the next morning, before the game against South of Scotland, Stan and I whipped around the players and collected 700 pounds from them to put on its nose.

I'd had a sore neck for a few days, but with the Scottish Test just around the corner I decided to play that afternoon. We never were in with a strong chance against the South. We hadn't prepared very well, Andy McIntyre was a late withdrawal, I was carrying this injury and wasn't feeling too comfortable, and the ground in Hawick was wet and sloppy. Yet we were up against a team with players like Peter Dods, Keith Robertson, Roger Baird, Roy Laidlaw, Colin Deans, John Jeffrey and Alan Tomes. Scotland's captain of the previous year, Jim Aitken, was only a replacement! We thought we had it won when we were leading 6-3 at halftime, but the tide turned and Peter Dods hooked over two second-half penalties to get the South home by 9-6, even though they hadn't played very well themselves for a team containing so many internationals.

At happy hour that night, Stan didn't help our spirits by relating details of the horse race with Sure Row. It was leading for most of the race, was beaten in the straight, came back again and went to the line in a photo-finish. The camera showed it was beaten by a head. Then a protest went up. Stan thought we had it won, but after 30 minutes the protest was finally dismissed. Had it won, we'd have all been rolling in dough.

The next morning the Wallaby Swimming Club was active again.

FOR LOVE NOT MONEY

Murray Mexted beaten for line out possession at the SCG in 1984

Hawker, McBain, Lillicrap and I—with Tuynman declining the invitation and thus facing likely dismissal from our ranks—headed down to the Tweed River and plunged into the icy depths.

Glasgow hadn't changed when we got there. Still grubby, very industrialised and not very attractive. That night some of us had a few drinks with the journos, who in all their generosity put some money on the bar, and I had some discussion with Frank O'Callaghan of the *Courier-Mail* about the possibility of my moving to Brisbane. I wasn't serious about it but it gave Franko something to write about.

Our team against Glasgow comprised all the non-Test players, the first time we'd not mixed our players. But with the last leg of the Grand Slam now right upon us, Jones wanted to keep all the leading players injury-free. Despite what was theoretically our weakest team, they played magnificently that day, especially James Black at fullback, and their 26-12 win put the whole team in tremendously high spirits for the Test against Scotland. Now there was just one more game that mattered. Beat Scotland four days later and we would create Rugby history.

VICTORS THEN VANQUISHED

Anybody who has been to Edinburgh knows the North British Hotel. It's the venerable establishment at the far end of Princes Street; tall, grey, amply sprinkled with pigeon-droppings and with all kinds of turrets and figurines protruding from it. Inside it's remote and olde worlde, with a huge circular staircase sweeping up from one floor to the next. Directly in front as you walk in the main entrance is the sitting room where hotel guests or the well-heeled locals have afternoon tea of scones and jam with pots of Earl Grey tea. The rooms are as ample as corner playgrounds with large double beds, and each bathroom has one of those massive tubs with rims so high you've almost got to high-jump to get inside. And the bath taps are so big they look like they've been made for King Kong's grip. It mightn't seem the ideal lodging for Rugby footballers, but that's where visiting international teams always stay in the Scottish capital and that's where the Wallabies camped as they prepared for the ultimate game of their careers: the Test against Scotland, the last leg of the Grand Slam.

In the last few days before the Test the feeling we all had was not one of great expectation and excitement, but rather of fear. Unadulterated fear. Fear that we might get beaten. Fear that we'd come all this way, that we were on the point of an historic moment and that we might lose. The game really meant so much to all of us. I imagine those who've made a Wimbledon final, or the FA Cup final at Wembley, or an Olympic final, or any mountaineer who's been within sight of Everest's tip would know what I'm talking about. We worked hard to control the fear, and that's where Jonesy's talents came into play. He kept us thinking positively: that we were going to win and that defeat was never to be considered. How Jonesy coped himself at that time I'll never know, because his back was absolutely killing him. The poor coach couldn't even sit without feeling agony—trying to move around a training paddock must have been excruciating. But he had the greatest job of his coaching career to complete, and although he couldn't move freely it didn't stop his usual barking and squawking.

The training workouts were very intense and competitive. At one session a helicopter turned up and hovered only about 80 metres above us for virtually the whole session. We'd no idea who was in it. Presumably a nosey television crew or press photographer. Or maybe a spy from the

Scottish camp. Whoever it was didn't worry us, but its presence definitely did. It stayed there for nearly an hour, making a terrific din and of course throwing this enormous downdraft onto us. There was nothing we could do to get rid of it and all it did was help increase the tension among the players. I still had a sore neck, and at one stage Stan Pilecki bumped me there and I was so uptight about everything that I swung around and went to belt him. Something stopped me at the last second, but there were actually a few scuffles among other players in that period which went to show the extreme tension we were all feeling.

The press build-up was huge. You couldn't escape from headlines asking whether we could do it; about the big part Mark Ella might play; whether he could score a try as he had in the other three Tests and the increasing speculation that this would be the end of his Test career; whether Scotland's Triple Crown team would deny us victory, even though only eight players from the previous season were still in it because of injuries, retirements, droppings etc. Among those omitted was Jim Aitken, who'd been their captain. I felt this was a serious blunder and it was to our advantage not having him there because he was a fine leader and a good prop. Somewhere I also read that of eighteen major tours to the United Kingdom, only five of the teams had done what we hopefully were about to do and make a clean sweep of all four internationals: Graham Mourie's 1978–79 All Blacks and the Springboks of 1912–13, 1931–32, 1951–52 and 1960–61. They were hard acts to follow.

Obviously there was great interest back home as well. We even received a rare telegram from Prime Minister Hawke. He always went to a lot of cricket Tests, VFL games and Rugby League grand finals, but never had much time for Rugby. His was one of literally hundreds of telegrams we received. When they started being delivered in sugar bags the players began to comprehend just how much this thing meant to everyone back home.

The only thing worrying Jonesy in terms of personnel was who to make Australia's goalkicker. Michael Lynagh's kicking had gone off early in the tour and he kicked only four from fourteen attempts against England and Ireland. Roger Gould had taken over against Wales and landed five out of seven. But in the last training run we had, Lynagh slotted over fifteen out of sixteen in a swirling wind. Jonesy also knew that he'd been making a fair number of calls home to Brisbane, where his dad's a sports psychologist, and this had obviously been beneficial in getting him back on the rails mentally. So the coach was faced with the gamble of calling Lynagh back for the greatest task he'd ever face or else sticking with Roger, who was a cool old head but technically not as good as Noddy. I know Jonesy spoke to my co-author on the Test eve and sought his opinion. Jim suggested he use Lynagh, but not to inform him till the morning of the Test. Jonesy did just that.

I was a great fan of the Irish folk group The Furys, and in the countdown to the Test my roommate Tommy Lawton and I constantly listened to them. On the morning of the Test we were again playing their tape in our room when Ray Gravell, the former great Welsh centre, happened to be walking by, heard their beautiful sound, ducked his head in the door and declared: 'I'll tell you boyo, anyone who listens to The Furys is bound to win.' It sounded like a pretty good omen to me.

While we were lying about listening to The Furys that morning, Jonesy took a secret trip out to Murrayfield with Andrew Slack. He wasn't in uniform and, inside the ground, began talking with one of the old groundsmen who had been there for years. The old Scot told Jonesy everything about the ground, where the prevailing winds came from, what to be wary of and which way a team should run in which half. It proved invaluable information and I often wonder if he'd have been so forthcoming had he known the identity of the curious Aussie with the bad back. Jonesy had also watched an unbelievable number of video tapes of Scotland's matches the previous season, so by the time the Test was due to start there was no stone that we'd left unturned. If we didn't win that afternoon, then it was because we simply weren't good enough.

When we arrived at the ground in the early afternoon it was drizzling, cold and blustery and 65 000 fans were waiting. We changed and then the team went out the back of the dressing-rooms and, as could only happen in Rugby, warmed up in one of Murrayfield's large car parks, ducking and weaving around the Rovers and Jags. People stood around and watched, others made comments about our chances and wished us well, and throughout all this Jonesy kept talking, trying to focus our minds on what we had ahead of us.

But even he couldn't contain all our keenness and anxiety to get stuck into it. The side had too much adrenalin pumping, there was no doubt about that, and early in the Test we did some stupid things, made some unforced errors and gave away far too many penalties. In the opening few minutes even Ella dropped a pass! The man with glue on his fingertips put down his only pass of the entire tour as over-anxiousness also caught up with him.

Our first try came after a quarter of an hour when Ella cut out Lynagh for Gould who came rampaging through like a bull elephant, drew in the defence, and then Slackey threw a mile-long pass to Campese who went for the lick of his life for the line. With Dods and Lynagh exchanging a series of goals it was 12-9 our way at halftime.

Two penalty goals from Lynagh just after halftime eased the

pressure a little and allowed us to settle down and concentrate on really getting on top of the Scots in the forwards.

Then from a ruck, Ella took a pass and gave back inside to Gould, who drifted left before Ella came again on his inside in support play so typical of him and galloped over. He'd done what no man had done before him. He'd scored a try in every Test! Lynagh slotted over his sixth goal from six attempts. We were starting to boil now.

Next, from a two-man lineout where our jumpers were standing well back from the five-metre mark, Tommy Lawton threw a perfect ball to Farr-Jones as he charged through in front of the jumpers. He went one way, then stepped the other to avoid one of their forwards and finally carried their winger across in the corner.

Finally, our fourth try was the most marvellous piece of counter-attacking you'd ever want to see. Griggy intercepted a Scottish pass, flicked it back and off we went until Campese straightened up, gave to Tuynman on the left flank and The Bird then turned it back in for Campo to make a 50-metre dash for the line. Lynagh goaled again and that wrapped it all up 37-12, with Lynagh knocking over eight out of nine attempts in a masterly display.

When the final whistle went we could scarcely believe it. It was all over and, as I described in Chapter One, the Wallabies had set records that would never be equalled.

The official black-tie dinner that night at the North British Hotel was quite a show. We were all in the happiest mood, as you could imagine, and one thing led to another until players from both teams hopped onto the chairs and tables (with Andy McIntyre, Nick Farr-Jones and Steve Tuynman in kilts) and arm-in-arm started singing 'Auld Lang Syne' at the tops of our voices. What a sight. The Scots, God bless 'em, were good losers.

The next morning we all met reasonably early at the front of the hotel for a trip to the home of golf, St Andrews. There were some very sick boys, and I was rather surprised the team management persuaded so many to turn up. But the fresh air did us the world of good and we all had a good laugh as Steve Williams, Steve Tuynman and Bill Calcraft amused passers-by outside the hotel by washing passing cars and buses with mops and buckets they'd borrowed from the hotel staff.

When we came back to Edinburgh later in the day the whole team gathered in a nearby pub and we got into mystery shouts. It's an express route to disaster and led to some yahooing as we made for the local station and the train journey to Wales, where we still had two games remaining. As we were boarding the train, Steve Williams grabbed his Manly clubmate Phillip Cox and dangled the frightened halfback down between the train and platform. Coxy wasn't too impressed and it was a silly thing to do, but with spirits as high as they were it all seemed terribly amusing. By the time the train left Edinburgh station we were quietening down and soon after everyone bedded down for the night. We were all so whacked that a derailment that night wouldn't have woken most of us.

Over the next few days some sections of the British media started lamenting the poor state of British Rugby. But it wasn't that at all. It was simply that the Wallabies were so good. It was easily the best Rugby team I'd ever been associated with. Four years beforehand when we won the Bledisloe Cup we had some fantastic backs, but for a complete team from front to back this outfit was almost faultless. There was nothing they couldn't do. We could play open attacking Rugby, as shown by the record number of tries we scored, or else percentage stuff when we needed to. And our defence throughout the tour was almost impregnable. It was the complete side. We also had Jonesy: the ultimate coach, an absolute workhorse, extremely smart, able to get his message across and with an extraordinary ability to read players' moods and know precisely when to increase or ease the workload. In the background was his assistant Alec Evans, who worked primarily with the forwards and became very close to us all. We all had enormous respect for him, because he'd been through the wars so many times in Queensland's front-row. He inspired great confidence in the forwards. We can't forget Syd Sugerman, our doctor, who was always such a thorough gentleman and who unfortunately passed away not all that long after our return home. And finally there was our manager Charles (Chilla) Wilson, who was the perfect balance for Jones because he was as disorganised as the other fellow was meticulous. A real larrikin in every way, but the blokes had every respect for Chilla and he was more of a friend to all of us than the team boss. Finally, Graham Short, our faithful baggage-man, fixer of everything and friend of all, was an invaluable cog in our machinery.

So down to the grime and slagheaps of Pontypool for our penultimate match. I don't know who dreamt up the itinerary, but forcing us to play the brutal, uncompromising men from the Pontypool coal-face at that stage of the tour was farcical. They were Britain's most successful club side and hadn't been beaten after 22 games. We had beaten them back in 1981, and all the talk when we arrived in town was how they were going to avenge that defeat. What a great incentive they had to beat the side that had just won the Grand Slam. It was going to require an awful amount of effort and guts on our part to beat them, but because we were the Grand Slam winners we were determined not to sully that image and to remain unbeaten till we hit Australian shores once more.

A massive fog moved into the valleys on the day of the game. The hill that's such a feature of the ground might have been laden with people, but we couldn't see most of them. Underfoot it was like a quagmire. It was going to be trench warfare. Jonesy determined that we wouldn't even try running the ball. Just put it up all day and cream them. Then score from the scraps. We lost Nigel Holt during the game with an injured arm and he went off to hospital for x-rays. When they told The Shredder that it wasn't broken he almost cried with disappointment, because he knew the ribbing he'd get from the rest of us. We all accused The Shredder, who fancied himself as the toughest guy in the team, of being scared of the big, rough Pontypool second-rower John Perkins. Gregg (Flounder) Burrow also came on as a replacement, and this late tour replacement did a remarkable job against the mighty Pontypool front-row including the legendary Graham Price. When it was all over we had tossed them by 24-18. One game to go.

From there to Cardiff for the last fling against the Barbarians, the mix of players from all over the United Kingdom and France that traditionally winds up international tours. It's like a fifth Test, but with the Baa-Baas always committed to letting the ball fly. In another strategic move, Jonesy eased right off on the training at this stage. He thought we'd respond better to that than if he continued to drive us hard. But as the game drew closer, we became concerned and realised we had to win this last game, despite much talk that it was going to be very free-flowing and not too intense. It was very amusing at this time to see Mark Ella's room. Cans of Fosters and XXXX were lined up on the ledge outside his window and our champion five-eighth enjoyed immensely what was going to be his last ever week with the Australian Rugby team.

The ABC commentator Gordon Bray went along to the Baa-Baas training and came back with a tape recording of what was said to the players by the manager and captain. He let Jonesy listen to it. Forget the casual approach. They were planning fire and brimstone. They were out to salvage the pride of British Rugby by belting these Wallabies. Thanks to Gordon, we had all the motivational dope we needed to get our guys revved up. At our last-ever training run together as a team, Jonesy asked all the players to work out tap moves that we might use in the game. Some of the most intricate moves imaginable were suggested. Then it was Stan Pilecki's turn. So what move did the Pole suggest? 'Kick the bloody thing out!'

After the first few minutes of the game all our planned tap moves went clean out the window when we realised that the Barbarians really were deadly serious. It was on for young and old. Jonesy had changed our team around for this game and swung in some of the older players who'd not played in all the Tests but had helped so much in getting us where we were: Stan, Chris Roche, Phillip Cox and Michael Hawker. For all of them bar Rochey, who'd played against Ireland, this was their one and only chance to prove themselves and they gave it everything they had.

It was a fantastic game to play in, especially as I bagged a couple of tries. Towards the end the Baa-Baas got close to us before we kicked away again. It was a gutsy win, one of the gutsiest I've played in. We won 37-30 and I don't think I've ever been more exhausted after any game. I almost crawled off the ground and could barely climb the grandstand stairs for an interview with Gordon Bray. Later in the dressing-room I just fell into one of the Roman bathtubs filled with piping hot water and guzzled champagne like the rest of the team. It was the most relaxing, fantastic feeling I've experienced. We'd done well.

The Wallabies arrived back in Australia to much celebration and back-slapping and also incessant media talk over whether Mark Ella was going to retire. He had stayed behind in London for a while and, despite the many overseas phone calls that passed between Mark and Jonesy, he finally decided to pull the pin. As soon as Mark's retirement was announced a series of ghosted newspaper articles appeared under his name making all kinds of accusations about Jones, including that he wouldn't accept the view of the majority and had been much too dogmatic in his approach to everything. It upset Jonesy enormously and it was to his credit that he swallowed his hurt and agreed to be photographed with Mark when the formal and very lavish dinner for 600 people honouring the Eighth Wallabies was held on April 12 at Sydney's Sheraton-Wentworth Hotel. But those articles really were the beginning of the end for their relationship.

With Andrew Slack also retiring, there was much speculation in the media as to who was going to be Australia's captain in the 1985 season when we had the Canadians making a tour, another one-off Test against New Zealand in New Zealand, then the Fijians coming. I was sure Steve Williams had a mortgage on the job and I was right.

The Canadians turned up in June like meek little lambs being led to the slaughter. They were very inexperienced and really not in the same class as Australia. But we had to whip them to keep our image intact and their whole build-up was based around the fact that they were determined not to lose by the same 46-point margin that their keenest rivals, the United States, had two years before. In the first Test we romped past them 59-3 and in the second by 43-15, so they achieved their goal the second time around. Australia copped a fair amount of criticism for their play, but this really was unnecessary because you couldn't have asked for a more disciplined performance than our first Test win.

A week later we headed off to New Zealand and faced the most unusual build-up because of the impending tour of South Africa by the Cavaliers. Anti-tour demonstrators were out in force. Every entrance to our hotel was guarded by police and we trained behind barbed wire a few times.

There was tremendous interest in the Test, with New Zealand still rated the world's number one team and us having won the Grand Slam. It really was the original High Noon shootout. The clash of the titans. While our Grand Slam pack was still intact, with Ella and Slack retired and Campese injured it meant an inexperienced centre pairing of James Black and Tim Lane with Matthew Burke on the wing.

Unfortunately, the All Blacks again won by a point, 10-9. The referee David Burnett awarded 25 penalties, which meant the Test never flowed. You felt paralysed, you just couldn't do anything. It was also a game where there was so much at stake that neither team was prepared to take any risks. Again the Australian forwards played extremely well. The All Black captain Andy Dalton later paid us the compliment of saying it was the hardest pack he'd ever played against. That's a very big rap. The scoring was low because the kickers were both off-target. Crowley missed six from eight attempts and Lynagh five from seven. The move which finally sank us was one they called the Bombay Duck. It really caught us napping.

I was an angry young man taking the ball up to the vicious Fijians in the 1985 domestic series.

We were leading at the time, when they took a tap-kick 70 metres from our line, halfback David Kirk went the blindside and linked up with a few more before left-winger Craig Green dashed 35 metres for the match-winning try. Our cover defence wasn't in the right position and we never had any hope of stopping them. We did remarkably well up front but missed several golden opportunities to pull the Test out of the fire. Tommy Lawton and Andy McIntyre both dropped balls close to the line. The one-point difference at the end was the second successive Test they'd won by that narrowest of margins, as the third Test in 1984 went New Zealand's way 25-24.

A little over a month later the smiling, happy-go-lucky Fijians arrived for their tour and before long were showing that they left all their charm and good manners in the dressing-room. They quickly ran into allegations of testicle-twisting and head-kicking, and their management replied by saying that Australian players should release the ball on the ground and not hang onto it. Stop that, they intimated, and there wouldn't be any more nonsense. The Australians got so churned up about it that it looked like there could be some real fireworks in the two Tests.

Australia careered away with the first Test by a massive 52-28, with David Knox at five-eighth for the injured Lynagh contributing 21 points in his Test debut. The Fijians improved markedly for the second Test, cutting our winning margin to 31-9. A very nasty incident occurred during this Test at the SCG. Alan Jones had brought Mark McBain and Cameron Lillicrap into the team to give them an opportunity to play in a domestic Test. Unfortunately McBain, alias 'George the Animal', sometimes gets a little over excited during any game of Rugby. As play moved down to the Members' end McBain gave a couple of Fijians a good rucking which immediately sent the whole Fijian pack into a murderous frenzy. I thought to myself at the time that the next Australian on the ground would be a dead man. Speculation became reality as in the very next ruck I found myself pinned on the Fijian side and the three-inch scar down the side of my face is an unwanted souvenir of two Fijians trying to kick my head into the Members Stand.

But when all was said and done, the Australian public hadn't received much value for money that season. They'd not had the chance at firsthand to see the Grand Slam Wallabies at full throttle, and in this regard the Australian Rugby Football Union had done a woeful marketing job of the team. They could have made a fortune ditching us in against better opposition than that. Instead, the ARFU faced a six-figure loss on these nothing tours by Canada and the extremely disappointing Fijian team.

THE PINNACLE

I might easily have missed the 1986 season. In fact, I might well have closed my appointment book for good because of something that happened off Coogee Beach during the preceding summer months.

To keep fit in the offseason I used to occasionally swim a lap or two of the beach between the headlands. Even though it's a long haul and you're a fair distance out at sea, I found it relaxing, it gave me time to think and kept the muscles nicely toned.

I took advantage of daylight saving late one afternoon, dived in off the headland near the Coogee Surf Club and an hour or so later climbed out at the same spot, having crossed the bay a few times. When I went back into the clubhouse some of the members asked where I'd been. When I told them they went into fits of laughter, because the beach had been closed much of the afternoon after a shark had been spotted. It seems I'd either been swimming further out in the bay than the shark or else we'd crossed paths somewhere along the way, but fortunately hadn't met.

The 1986 season was the first in a long while when there wasn't an overseas tour either immediately behind or in front of us, but there was enough on our plate domestically to keep Rugby ratbags like me happy. It was an unbelievably packed representative program.

One thing on my mind as the season approached was the Australian captaincy, as Steve Williams had retired to concentrate on his stockbroking career. But Andrew Slack, who had led us so well on the Grand Slam tour, was making a comeback and had charge of Queensland on a European tour. Alan Jones got hold of me for a chat about the captaincy and told me he'd also spoken to Slacky, who was keen to get back into international Rugby. He asked for my thoughts and, to be honest, this caused me a great dilemma. I certainly didn't lack ambition to captain Australia, but Slacky had been such a tremendous captain that my initial feelings were that if he wanted the job again then he should have it although this effectively put a hold on my own captaincy aspirations for another season.

At the start of that season the NSW Rugby Union had its grand reopening of Sydney's Concord Oval, which included an extravagant $50 000 launch at the Hyatt Kingsgate Hotel with more razzle-dazzle, balloons and curvy females than you'd see in the grand parade at the circus. This turned out to be a sort of Last Supper for the NSW Rugby

Union because it subsequently learned when its debts went sky-high that you simply cannot maintain heavy spending like that if you don't generate the income to sustain it.

About this time Australia managed to push through the International Rugby Board changes to the amateur regulations which allowed the various Unions to compensate players for financial hardship. It was of great credit to the ARFU and the two delegates, Ross Turnbull and Roger Vanderfield, that these changes were made. Over the years it has been quite remarkable just what Australia has pushed through in the decision-making processes of the game.

In March I played in the World Sevens at Concord Oval. We were expected to do pretty well, but were comprehensively thrashed 32-0 by New Zealand in the final. It was a tremendously physical game and was marred by Glen Ella being elbowed in the head by Wayne Shelford. It was the first time I'd come up against this character and to say I didn't like his approach was putting it mildly. I was sickened by what he did to my Randwick clubmate and simply couldn't contain myself. Within a minute of his clobbering Glen I got into a stoush with him and we finished up rolling around on the ground in front of the packed main grandstand, not only in front of Premier Neville Wran but in front of a far more important person—my mother. While we were grappling I thought to myself 'we really shouldn't be doing this', but my blood was boiling after the Ella incident.

We went from there to the Hong Kong Sevens but didn't get to play the New Zealanders again because we were knocked out in the semi-final by the French Barbarians in a game in which I thought my own play was diabolical. They scored a couple of easy tries early on through what I felt was my lax defence. I was pretty chopped up after that loss, particularly as I'd been very keen to make the final so that I could have another crack at the New Zealanders.

The performances by New Zealand, who won that final as well, were a great personal triumph for their coach Bryce Rope, who'd worked so hard to lift their sevens football, and under him they'd become equally as good at the compressed form of the game as they were at the XV-a-side variety. This was the beginning of an enormous rejuvenation in the backline play of the All Blacks. We've seen any number of very good players come out of that particular seven-a-side team, for which Bryce Rope can take much of the credit.

Something which stuck in my mind at that time was the generous praise by Alan Jones of David Campese. At one point he dubbed him 'a Bradman' and said that he had a very special quality and that no-one in Rugby was more talented. Two years down the track in New Zealand when Campo's form left something to be desired, I often chuckled over

FOR LOVE NOT MONEY

those descriptions.

About a week later I headed off to the UK with Andrew Slack, Steve Cutler, Nick Farr-Jones, Tommy Lawton, Roger Gould, Steve Tuynman, Michael Lynagh and Topo Rodriguez for two matches celebrating the centenary of the International Rugby Board. We went over on the same flight as the All Blacks who'd been chosen for the invitation side and, to our pleasant surprise, were all booked in business-class. Having travelled steerage my entire Rugby career, it was nice seeing what the front-end of a Jumbo looked like at long last. Not much fraternising went on between the Australians and New Zealanders in the first few hours of the flight, but as the beers flowed we started getting together with Andy Haden, Gary Knight, Murray Mexted, Mark (Cowboy) Shaw and Dave Loveridge and getting to understand each other a bit better. In London, we met up at our hotel with the South Africans in our team, including Flippie van der Merwe who was the biggest prop I've ever laid eyes on. He was more than 133 kilograms, which makes even Artie Beetson look like he has been to Weight Watchers. Given all the nonsense and hypocrisy that tumbles forth when official or rebel tours to South Africa are mentioned in Australia, there wasn't a beep from the Federal Government at the time about us playing with the Springboks. Does distance absolve responsibility? Or maybe there's just no political mileage in a bunch of Aussies playing Rugby on the other side of the world.

Throw in Serge Blanco and a couple of his French pals and we had an international mix of class players who looked like they could beat any team on earth. Added to this great stable of players were two of the world's leading coaches, Brian Lochore and Jacques Fouroux. I don't know that I've ever looked forward to a game as much as the first between us (we were tagged The Rest) and the British Lions at Cardiff Arms Park. I was in the back-row with All Blacks Mexted and Shaw, and beforehand I told them it was going to be a real pleasure playing alongside them. I also suggested that after belting each other so often, 'how about we go out and really belt some other guys for a change.' They agreed.

The day before the game we had team photographs taken and I was joking around with Blanco about how I could picture us combining for this really spectacular try. 'Serge, tomorrow this try will happen. It will be Blanco to Poidevin, Poidevin to Blanco, Blanco to Poidevin and he scores in the corner.' Blow me down if we didn't win the game 15-7 and I scored virtually a repeat of this imaginary try. The French fullback hit the line going like an express train, tossed the ball to Patrick Esteve, then it came back to Blanco and he tossed it inside for me to score. The pair of us could hardly stop laughing walking back to the halfway line for the restart of play.

After the way this United Nations team had beaten the Lions on the flimsiest of preparations, the French players didn't want to leave us, but they had to. The game at Twickenham three days later was between Overseas and the Five Nations, which included the froggies.

We fielded probably the biggest set of forwards that has ever graced a football pitch: Rodriguez, Dalton, Knight, Cutler, Haden, me, Shaw and Tuynman. In the backs we had loads of talent in Loveridge, Botha, de Plessis, Taylor, Gerber, Kirwan and Gould. The whole team went out intent on showing the northern hemisphere just how good the southern hemisphere was when it came to playing Rugby. We were going to show that the globe was top-heavy Down Under with class. And that's just what we did. After ten minutes we'd sorted out the Five Nations forwards with some awesome power and then just annihilated them by 32-13 to wind up a magnificent trip. John Mason, of the *Daily Telegraph* in London, had this to say about that final performance: 'Here was a forthright exercise of deeply-rooted skills of an uncanny mix of athleticism and aggression which permitted the overseas unions of the southern hemisphere to thrash the Five Nations of the northern hemisphere in a manner as stylish as it was merciless.' That typified the comments.

The nicest thing of all to come out of those centenary matches was that we were able to get to know the All Blacks so much better. For many years unscalable barriers had built up between the Australian and New Zealand players because of the constant competition, and you never got to know them as people. I knew Cowboy Shaw as my hardest opponent, but not as one of the funniest blokes you'd ever want to meet. Gary Knight the same. Dave Loveridge ... another lovely guy. And you wouldn't want to meet a nicer person than Mex. Finally, there was our coach Brian Lochore, a fantastic bloke, a thorough gentleman, quiet and unassuming, a very keen thinker on the game and a man for whom I developed the utmost respect and friendship. Here we'd been thrown together for the same cause, all the barriers were quickly broken down and we started to appreciate each other as individuals rather than All Blacks and Wallabies.

The Springboks were equally terrific and there were some fantastic footballers among them. One guy I'd been anxious to watch at first-hand was their five-eighth Naas Botha, who's something of a demi-god in South Africa because he's such a marvellous attacking player and can kick goals with his eyes closed. But he wouldn't tackle to save his life. In one of the games an attacker went straight at him from the end of a lineout and Botha neatly stepped aside and simply let him past. I had to take off and cover the tackle for him. Botha just doesn't want to know anything at all about tackling or getting himself in the position where he might get hurt. He has obviously been cotton-woolled in South African Rugby, but in international Rugby his extraordinary weakness in defence would be exploited by every team he came up against.

During our time together in the UK, the New Zealanders kept sending out some unusual currents. They'd be talking among themselves but when you approached they'd quickly change the subject. It was obviously nothing to do with the rest of us in a personal sense, because as I said they were as friendly as pie. They were also training extremely hard and even going off on early morning runs by themselves, as if they were striving for super-fitness.

The rest of us didn't catch on to what was happening until the Saturday night of our final game when, amid all the yahooing and drinking, it slipped out that they were all heading out from London the next day bound for South Africa on a rebel tour. The whole Rugby world was thrown into turmoil when the news finally leaked out that the All Blacks, under the guise of the Cavaliers, had decided to do what they had been denied through official channels—do battle with the Springboks.

And I almost became one of them. Their breakaway Jock Hobbs had suffered concussion and was a doubtful starter for the tour. Andy Haden and Murray Mexted approached me before leaving London and asked would I be willing to join them in South Africa as a member of the Cavaliers if Hobbs had to withdraw. I gave them my telex and phone numbers in Sydney, they gave me all the tour details, and I headed home with the rest of the Wallabies wondering if the invitation to join them would come. What an experience it would have been! I chuckled a few times imagining myself not just playing alongside four or five All Blacks but being one-out in the whole All Black team. Alas, the invitation never arrived, and I watched the wild brawling and intensely furious Rugby battles from the comfort of my lounge room.

Not that I had much time to think about the Cavaliers. No sooner was I back than I took over the captaincy of NSW in the South Pacific championship matches and led them to a 50-10 romp over Fiji in which the current League players Brett Papworth, James Grant and Andrew Leeds scored 42 points between them, with Pappy emerging as a goal-kicker of some note with eight from ten attempts. The following week we wiped Queensland by 18-12 at Concord Oval, with Pappy getting another five from seven. To come back from such a marvellous time in the UK followed by these two wins put me in tremendous spirits, and made me feel that I might be a chance to lead the Wallabies to New Zealand despite my earlier conversation with Jonesy when I'd supported Andrew Slack.

About this time we saw the unbelievable headline RUGBY BANS MARK ELLA. He'd been dumped from the Australian Barbarians team to play in Townsville because he was no longer considered an amateur after the newspaper articles he had written. This sort of treatment, especially to someone like Mark who'd done so much for Rugby at every level, just left the rest of us players dumbfounded and was a tremendous indictment of the game's administrators and its immediate future.

Invitations arrived about then for the Wallabies to tour South Africa the following year. Although it never eventuated, the first seed was sown for us to make a tour there either officially or unofficially. With the agitation and interest caused by these invitations, Jonesy became extremely keen for us to tackle the Springboks in a Test series and so were all the players.

When the Australian team was chosen for the Test against Italy at Ballymore—the first of seven Tests we were going to play in fourteen jam-packed weeks—Slacky was again captain. At that stage I very much regretted having scuttled my own captaincy chances in my conversation with Jones earlier in the season. Had I been more ambitious and shown more eagerness when Jonesy had first asked me then perhaps it would have been me at the helm. What made it worse was that I had really enjoyed the leadership of both Sydney and NSW in the previous weeks. Slacky had even made the observation in a newspaper article that I'd come on 'in leaps and bounds' as far as leadership was concerned and that he wouldn't be surprised if I was made Australian captain. Still, it was not to be, and under Slacky we beat the very determined Italians by 39-18.

NSW were beaten in the return interstate game at Ballymore, and the following day I agreed to stand-by as a reserve when Randwick played Parramatta out at Death Valley, Granville Park. Near the end that great campaigner John Maxwell came off injured, I ran on as his replacement and 30 seconds later was off again, with my forehead looking like it had been worked over with a can-opener. Parramatta had nothing to do with it. I'd had a sickening head-on collision with one of my own centres, Brett Dooley—I thought I'd killed him we hit so hard, but fortunately hadn't. While I was lying half-unconscious on the ground I cupped my hands over the wound and came away with a handful of blood. After being helped off the field, I had a queezy look at myself in a mirror and told reporters present that 'it looks as though I've been attacked by Jimmie Blacksmith.' I told our club doctor, Joe Casamento, that I'd buy him a bottle of Scotch for Christmas if he could repair it perfectly. But as Rugby injuries go, it was easily the worst I've had, and has left me with a long scar which I'll carry to my grave. But Joe got his bottle of Scotch all the same.

The French arrived in June on a brief stopover on their global three-nation tour of Argentina, Australia and New Zealand. As brief as their stay was, everyone here had been waiting for them for ages. We'd won the

Grand Slam two years before and now France were here as equal Five Nations champions; beat them and we'd have cleaned up everything the northern hemisphere had to offer. The froggies were running hot after two Tests against the Pumas in Buenos Aires, and immediately blitzed Queensland by 48-9 in a magnificent display of open Rugby to show that we were really going to have a struggle on our hands in the only Test. It was a huge challenge for Australia: beat France and we'd not only have taken the most prized scalp north of the Equator but would then be primed for the forthcoming Bledisloe Cup tour of New Zealand. Beat France and then New Zealand and we'd be right on top of world Rugby.

We knew we had to shut France right out of the Test and not give them a sniff of latitude, otherwise Denis Charvet and Philippe Sella, who were unquestionably the world's best centres, and my old mate Serge Blanco would take to us like the guillotine in the Revolution. We had to control the lineouts through Cutler, Campbell, Tuynman and Codey and get on top of them in the scrums. And we did just that in one of the most devastating performances by an Australian forward pack. Our domination of territory and possession kept them right out of the Test. Even though France scored three tries to one, we kept so much pressure on them that they kept making mistakes and Lynagh just kept popping over goals. He finished with a 100 per cent score, seven from seven. With a field goal into the bargain he collected 23 points, equalling his record in a Test, this time against an International Board country. The final scoreline was 27-14, giving us another fantastic notch to put on our belts after the Grand Slam, and high hopes for New Zealand.

Later there was criticism of us for playing ten-man Rugby against France, but Test matches are all about winning for your team and your country and absolutely nothing else. Over the years we'd learned that the hard way. You can play great Test matches, be very entertaining and, at the end of the day, lose. And you'll be remembered as losers. We wanted to be remembered as winners. This Test was a classic example: we knew the razzle-dazzle Frenchmen had the ability to run in tries against any team in the world, but all that shows for them in the history books that day is a big fat L for loss, with nothing about how attractively they played. Sure, at times we played percentage football against them, but it was far more important for us to win than to throw the ball about like they were doing and lose. And Jacques Fouroux would be the first to support this sentiment.

No sooner had France departed than Argentina arrived, but when NSW and Queensland amassed 89 points between them in whacking the Pumas, and their genius Hugo Porta suffered a serious groin injury, it was pretty obvious they weren't going to be a patch on their 1983 team. With Slacky missing from this series, words can't describe how happy I was when I was made Australian captain for the opening Test. I was absolutely overjoyed. It's a responsibility that deep down I'd always wanted; I felt that I'd served my apprenticeship for it and that my time had come. I'd have liked to earn the honour against more formidable opposition than the Pumas, but to lead Australia in any Test match had always been my big dream, so there was no prouder person in the world than me on July 6, 1986 when I led the boys onto Ballymore. At that same moment our prop Topo Rodriguez was feeling very different emotions. The cornerstone of the Pumas' scrum in 1983, here he was three years later playing against many of his old mates. When the two national anthems were played before kickoff, Topo sang both of them, but when the whistle went he only saw the crowd opposite him as the enemy and he gave it everything he had, just as always. Topo's heart and dedication were as big as he was and if ever I had to go out of the trenches and onto the battlefields, I'd want Topo beside me.

As expected the Pumas weren't all that flash and we thrashed them 39-19 in that first Test, with Lynagh collecting another 23 points from goals, and then even easier by 26-0 in a fairly spiteful second Test in Sydney, when I was again captain.

Ahead lay the tour of New Zealand. The unavailability of Andy McIntyre, Cameron Lillicrap, Tim Lane, Brendan Moon, David Codey, Roger Gould and Dwayne Vignes was going to make it very hard. It meant taking many relatively inexperienced players on what's traditionally the toughest Rugby tour of all. Ten new Wallabies in fact. There was intense speculation beforehand on whether the Queensland ferret Jeff Miller or the tough Sydney cookie Steve Lidbury would get the last back-row spot, but I'd had a talk with Jonesy and so I wasn't surprised when Miller got the nod. His Test career since has wholly vindicated that selection.

The Wallabies gathered in Sydney for a few days training before leaving and Jonesy drove us unmercifully as he worked on our skills and physical fitness. My sister-in-law was researching for her PhD at the time at Sydney University. She told me she could always tell when the Wallabies were training at University Oval. She could hear Jonesy shouting profanities from several hundred metres away, usually at our new prop Mick Murray: 'Murray you'd better f.... get up here with the rest of these players or you won't get to f.... New Zealand or anywhere else for that matter.' Towards the end we were all counting the hours until we boarded the plane, just so we could escape the training ground.

When we arrived in Auckland, Jonesy took the huge media contingent head-on, tieing them up in a coil of expansive vocabulary, strong predictions and heady optimism. Obviously they'd never struck anything like him before, and most reckoned that at first meeting he seemed much more suited to the debating table than Rugby coaching. Then straight

Steve Cutler playing the clown on the Stock Exchange Floor with Bill Campbell, Roger Gould, Andy McIntyre and myself looking on

on the bus up to Hamilton and, typical of Jonesy wanting to make an impression first-up, within fifteen minutes of our checking into the hotel we were out under lights on the training paddock for a brutally tough run in extreme cold to show the whole of New Zealand that we really meant business.

During the first few days the team had two tracksuits stolen and a good quantity of beer taken from our team fridge. A week or so later Joey, the big wallaby mascot we took with us everywhere, who sat on the touchline during the games, was also nicked from the team bus. Nice place, New Zealand.

We drew the first game against Waikato using a novice team, which included five new Wallabies and a few others who hadn't played for a while after injury. Down 21-12, we drew up to 21-all with our rookie fullback Andrew Leeds kicking some sensational goals for us. During the game another of the new boys, Jim McInerney, suffered the worst Rugby wound I've ever seen. I went over for a look when it happened and a huge chunk of flesh was hanging from his leg. One could only wonder how an ordinary football stud could cause such an horrific injury. It really ruined the whole tour for Jim. Soon afterwards we had a meeting with representatives of the New Zealand Rugby Football Union and it was agreed that before every subsequent tour game the boots of players on both teams would be checked not only in the dressing-rooms but also in the tunnel before going onto the field.

Later it emerged that referee Bob Francis had repeatedly sworn at our front-row during that first game. Jonesy had plenty to say about that, and our team management submitted an official complaint to the NZRFU. About this time the All Black captain Graham Mourie told a newspaper that Australia's wins against France and Argentina didn't really amount to anything and implied that the Wallabies were about to face some real class. The crusade was really starting to hot up.

The Wallabies started to get their act together on the field after that and despite much mud and slop beat Manawatu (even though Topo took a tap-kick at 6-all within kicking range late in the game, only to be saved by a Lynagh goal a few minutes later), Wairarapa-Bush, Counties and Wanganui in succession. We were getting better all the time and our scrummaging improved markedly when the elaborate and highly beneficial Powerhouse scrum machine, which Jonesy freighted across to New Zealand at his own expense, arrived. Two wonderfully-generous farmers fron Pukekohe, Paul and King Reynolds, thereafter carted it around New Zealand for us on the back of a truck and trailer. Off the field we spent as much time as we could watching on satellite television Australia's many gold medal-winning performances at the Edinburgh Commonwealth Games, as distinct from the very biased local coverage which only seemed to show Kiwis coming sixth in the discus or plodding home ninth in the 5000 metres.

All in all, the Wallabies were in tremendous spirits when we flew into the windy capital for the first Test against the All Blacks, who had been badly weakened with the 31 Cavaliers under suspension for having gone to South Africa. They were even being called the Baby Blacks. We were really in a no-win situation, because if we won we wouldn't get much credit and if we lost it would have been a diabolical loss of face for Australia.

We ran into controversy as soon as we arrived. The Waterloo Hotel simply wasn't good enough for an international touring team and Jonesy told everyone. He said of his own room: 'I think those cats that are still alive have not been swung around in my room or they would have received a resounding crack on the skull on several occasions.' He was immediately labelled a whinger and one Sunday newspaper advised him to PUT A SOCK IN IT OCKER. But in the room I shared with Ross Reynolds there wasn't enough room for two of us to stand between the single beds. We had to take turns dressing. As one of the boys said: 'I had to go outside to change my mind.' Because NZRFU was going to make an absolute king's ransom out of our tour we had every reason to whinge.

Australia won the Test, only just, by 13-12 on a wet and windy Athletic Park. Another one-point margin. We had it won more comfortably than it looked until David Campese, who was at fullback, made a mistake towards the end of the game. Standing in a tackle, he flicked the ball back infield where it was snapped up by All Black centre Joe Stanley who then popped up a pass as he was being tackled to breakaway Mark Brooke-Cowden for a try beside the posts. The easiest of conversions made it one point the difference, and in the dozen minutes remaining we had to tackle like mad dogs in the fierce wind and pelting rain to keep them out. We were tremendously relieved at fulltime, but couldn't help thinking that if these were the Baby Blacks, just how tough would they be if those who had been away with the Cavaliers were allowed back for either of the remaining Tests. Former All Black Bernie Fraser spoke out on that topic, saying that 'the NZ Rugby rebels have the ability to blast the Australian pack off the paddock'.

We took those words with us as we headed for the peace and isolation of ruggedly-beautiful Westport on the South Island's west coast where we mounted the biggest winning margin (62-0) by an Australian team on a New Zealand tour since 1905. There we also had our variety night, which was one of the funniest nights I've ever had on tour. We all came in fancy dress and had to perform an act, with Jonesy heading the bill when he came dressed as Al Jolson and gave a remarkably professional rendition of 'Swanee'. Peter Grigg staggered in as a drunken Kiwi dairy-farmer wearing the obligatory lumber-jacket, abusing 'you Aussie jokers'. World championship wrestling also came to town that night with such stars as Sergeant Slaughter (Rod McCall, the Queensland policeman), the Ginger Bees (me and Jeff Miller) and George 'The Animal' McBain.

During our few days there the small matter of Julian Gardner had to be attended to. The Queensland back-rower wasn't responding to Jonesy's discipline and I was made to room with him in Westport in the hope of trying to straighten him out. I did my best, but he wasn't going to attend the variety night. That was it. Jonesy told him to front up or ship out for Australia the next day. He came along.

The relaxation and fun of Westport were quickly lost in a 30-10 thrashing by Grizz Wylie's very tough Canterbury outfit at the ever-so-English Christchurch. We took a grave risk in omitting six of our Test players from this match, because Jonesy didn't want to see it develop into an unofficial fourth Test, and we paid the price with our first tour loss. Very late that night Grizz turned up at our hotel after a skinful of beer, went to Jonesy's room and invited himself in for a talk about Rugby. He wanted to give Jonesy a better understanding of forward play. Those two are as alike as chalk and cheese and I'd have loved to have been a fly on the wall to hear what went on.

At our next stop at Timaru, where we beat South Canterbury, a few of us took a joyride in a light plane over 3764-metre Mt Cook, which was wonderfully spectacular. As we were winging over the snow-clad peaks and glaciers of New Zealand's Southern Alps, Bill Calcraft asked the pilot if he could do any tricks. He refused, saying there were other people in the plane who weren't in our group. So Bill asked them would they mind and when they said 'no' the pilot immediately launched into a series of hair-raising dives and turns as if he was being hunted by a Spitfire. After 30 seconds we were screaming for him to stop. It turned out that he was a crop-dusting pilot and could really handle a plane.

From there down to Dunedin for the second Test at Carisbrook Park, where Australia hadn't won since 1903. The NZRFU caused an enormous stir by rushing nine of the Cavaliers straight into the lineup—Gary Knight, Hika Reid, Steve McDowell, Murray Pierce, Gary Whetton, Jock Hobbs, Allan Whetton, Warwick Taylor and Craig Green. With that lot included, the Baby Blacks suddenly became adults and, with their full firepower restored, they beat us 13-12. Exactly the same score as the first Test, only reversed. Another one-point margin. It was a game I enjoyed immensely; a very good contest in heavy going. We didn't play well, but at the same time there were some very gutsy efforts by our boys. Everybody thought we were going to be blasted by the All Blacks, but that wasn't the case—in fact we should have won. Steve Tuynman scored a perfectly fair try that was disallowed by Welsh referee Derek Bevan, who wasn't in the ideal position to see what happened and said there were too many hands on the ball as the Bird forced it underneath him. Most of the All Blacks even thought it was a try. It would not only have given us the Test but would have wrapped up the Bledisloe Cup. Jonesy had lots to say about that to Bevan afterwards, and whether it was a try or not became the focus of the whole of New Zealand for the next 24 hours.

Tales of Jonesy screaming at Campese in the dressing-room immediately after the game for the poor way he played that afternoon was absolute nonsense. Nothing at all was said by anyone for nearly three-quarters of an hour, and the only noise I can recall was that of tough men openly sobbing from disappointment. We'd really wanted to wrap up the series there, and to go as close as we did and then have that try disallowed was hard to take.

That night we attended a dinner for the two teams. As I said earlier in the chapter, I'd become very friendly with Brian Lochore and the All Blacks who'd been with us in the UK four months before and some of us had a few drinks with them. Well, the reaction from Alan Jones had to be seen to be believed. He interpreted our actions as showing disloyalty to both him and Australia. It was nothing of the kind. In the case of Lochore and Poidevin it was a matter of cementing further a strong friendship that had developed during the IRB centenary celebrations and remains till this day.

When we arrived at our next stop at Invercargill, the last stop before Antarctica, Jonesy pulled a few of us into his room and had another crack at us over our fraternising with the All Blacks. He again said we were being disloyal, but I was adamant that it was nothing more than friends getting together and got pretty annoyed about his accusations. The upshot was an air of bitterness and tension through the whole team. The next morning at training, Jonesy singled out the Test players once again. We were expecting a mad-dog run or another tongue-lashing, but he ordered us all to go and play golf and forget all about what had taken place on tour to that point. He told us he didn't want to see us for the whole day, to try to hit as many trees as we could and swear as much as we liked; get it all out of our systems and cleanse our minds and bodies of the previous five weeks.

As far as the Wallabies were concerned, we were about to start a fresh tour beginning against Southland on the weekend. Jonesy wanted us to refocus our attention on the third and final Test, and each provincial match before that would be crucial in that build-up. So we had our crazy game of golf and then took aim at the All Blacks.

We couldn't have had a better start to our campaign than walloping Southland by 55-0. The boys played fantastically well. We were on a roll. Bay of Plenty fell to us next at Rotorua by 41-13, with Lynagh kicking 18 points. Then up to Thames to play Thames Valley in the last game before the big one. We inadvertently walked onto a minefield. We arrived after dusk and found that the team was split between two hotels, which didn't make us at all happy. One half moved into its hotel and the other half into the Brian Boru Hotel. But the rooms at the Brian Boru were just totally unsatisfactory. They were so small that players like Steve Cutler and Bill Campbell simply couldn't fit. And if I remember correctly, in some cases there were four rooms of players sharing one bathroom. Jonesy hit the roof, both literally and figuratively. There was a council of war between Jonesy, Slacky, me, the liaison officers and hotel manager, and the very next morning the Wallabies moved to Pukekohe 70 kilometres away. After our walkout the national newspapers didn't have to worry about what was going to be on their front pages for the next week.

Nobody liked us in Thames after that. One of the journalists, Greg Growden, went to cash a travellers' cheque at a bank. When the teller found he was Australian she immediately closed up and said 'I'm going to lunch.' The feeling in the town was really running high and the game itself was very spiteful because of what had happened. We won 31-7, but some of the Thames Valley players undoubtedly should have been sent off for their exceptionally dirty play.

The confidence of the Wallabies at training leading up to the Test was extremely good. I had a gut feeling that we might just pull it off. And off the field Jonesy was doing all the stirring. He was accused of being 'the master of psyching rhetoric and media manipulation'—which wasn't totally wrong of course. And in the background the Thames Valley walkout wouldn't die down.

My biggest fear, as in Britain in 1984, was that we had come so far and gone so close in Dunedin that to lose this Test match would have meant the end of the world for me. Just thinking of it made me cringe.

The Eden Park Test was stunning. From the word go the All Blacks threw the ball around in madcap fashion. I couldn't believe their totally uncharacteristic tactics. I'd never seen them playing the game so openly. As we chased and tackled from one side of the field to the other it crossed my mind how grateful I was for all the gruelling training Jonesy had put into us early in the tour. But the All Blacks had an epidemic of dropped passes in their abnormal approach, often when our defences were stretched paper-thin, and we took every advantage of that. When it was all over we had achieved a 22-9 victory, which to me was more satisfying and even greater than the Grand Slam success in Britain.

Year in and year out the All Blacks have been our most difficult opponents. I've been trampled by the best of them. New Zealanders are parochial about their teams and have every right to be proud of them. The French in France are extremely difficult to beat, but the All Blacks are totally uncompromising and the whole nation lives the game religiously. The game itself over there is not dirty, just extremely hard. They're mostly big strapping country boys who won't take any nonsense from anyone, and week after week they play some of the hardest provincial Rugby in the world. Rucking is the lifeblood of their play. If you wind up on the wrong side of a ruck, you'll finish the game bloodied or with your shorts, jerseys or socks peeled from your limbs by a hundred studs. Maybe I'm a masochist, but I somehow enjoy playing them. They are the greatest Rugby team in the world, and to beat the All Blacks in New Zealand in a series as we did in 1986 is the ultimate in Rugby.

The aircraft home rocked to Waltzing Matilda and Advance Australia Fair. We had really reached the pinnacle. We'd taken the Grand Slam in 1984, and now had knocked over the Five Nations champions, France, and finally the All Blacks. Who the hell was there left in Rugby for us to beat?

Only South Africa.

WORLD CUP DESPAIR

*1*987 might have been among the Hunter Valley's best-ever vintages for chardonnays, but it certainly wasn't a good year for me. It started badly, ended badly and much of what happened in between can be happily forgotten. Yet I'd worked extra hard to get myself in the best knick possible, with the initial World Cup coming up in Australia and New Zealand.

As early as February, coach Alan Jones began getting together the Sydney members of his World Cup squad for regular pre-season training at University Oval. As I have mentioned, Jonesy was once a very successful coach of schoolboy runners, and he used that ability in preparing his Rugby teams. Not only did he work us consistently hard, but he improved our running techniques and hence our speed to the point where all of us were running much faster than ever before. The following month when I went along to Randwick's training, Bob Dwyer, our club coach, simply couldn't get over my speed. We all enjoyed that early work with Jonesy, and in those sessions together you could feel the spirit and expectations starting to build for the World Cup.

Then came the season's first big disappointment: the Australian Rugby Football Union's announcement that all games scheduled for Sydney in the World Cup would be played at the refurbished Concord Oval and not the Sydney Cricket Ground. It was the strongest show of support possible for the NSW Rugby Union in its efforts to develop the suburban ground as headquarters of Rugby in Sydney.

But the decision broke the players' hearts and eventually had a very significant effect on our World Cup performances. The Rugby officials involved in making this decision weren't nearly as recognisable to the public as were players such as me, and we took the brunt of what built into enormous public opposition towards the use of Concord Oval over the traditional SCG. It was pressure we could well have done without immediately before the largest and most imaginative showpiece that Rugby had ever attempted.

And like the public, we wanted the matches at the SCG. Playing there meant a lot to Australian teams, and in a Test match I reckon it was worth five to ten points seeing those packed stands and feeling the extraordinary atmosphere and sense of history that the whole place generated. Here was where Bradman excited the cricketing world, Churchill took those brutes of Pommy forwards so courageously around the ankles, and giants of our own game like Towers, Phelps, Catchpole, Hawthorne, Lenehan, Hipwell, Loane and Moon had thrilled so many people. Just thinking of all that history in the dressing-room before a Test used to make my skin tingle, and not once did I get that same feeling playing on the patch of ground opposite Burwood bus depot.

When all the criticism erupted, Ken Elphick, who was then executive director of the NSW Rugby Union, conceded that Concord Oval didn't have any tradition, but kept saying that tradition had to begin somewhere. Fine, but had the ARFU really wanted us to become world champions they should have kept the games at the SCG, as the players and public wanted, and gradually moved to Concord Oval over subsequent years.

More bad news followed in April. I was in Hong Kong at the time, playing in the sevens tournament, when a telex message arrived at the Hilton Hotel from a Sydney radio station advising me that I'd been dumped as NSW captain in favour of Nick Farr-Jones. Telephone communications between Sydney and Hong Kong were still working as far as I was aware, but no Rugby official bothered to ring me. I accept that the NSW Rugby Union, the new coach Paul Dalton and his co-selectors could do what they liked and had no official responsibility to inform me that I was no longer in the job, but morally I felt they had a very strong obligation to advise me of the decision and explain why. I'd led NSW the previous season when we'd done exceptionally well in beating Argentina, Fiji and Queensland and I'd thoroughly enjoyed the responsibility. I'd also led Australia in both Tests against Argentina, which we'd won handsomely. So to say that I was pretty upset about getting the heave-ho as NSW captain was putting it mildly. And it was not the reasons the selectors had for sacking me (the ones they touted publicly seemed awfully flimsy) that bothered me—my disappointment related more to the manner in which the news was broken to me.

To make matters worse we were beaten in the semi-finals of the Hong Kong Sevens by Fiji, who blasted out of the blocks and scored three sensational tries to lead 14-0 after five minutes, and finished up eliminating us by 14-8.

All in all, that was a real humdinger of a trip. Jonesy had made David Campese captain of our sevens team because his morale needed boosting and frankly it didn't work out at all. Campo didn't fully appreciate the honour, and while we were in Hong Kong a great deal of tension developed between him and Jonesy. We finished with both of them coaching, Campo on the field and Jonesy from the touchline. Eventually Jonesy pulled him into his hotel room and gave him a decent old carpeting about anything and everything.

When we arrived home, my sacking as NSW captain was still a big issue and very much on the boil. Some of the senior State players like Steve Cutler and Topo Rodriguez had taken grave exception to the treatment dished out to me, so a council of war was arranged one evening at Concord Bowling Club between the players, Dalton and some other officials. In the run-up to the meeting there were rumours that Nick Farr-Jones was going to refuse to accept the captaincy. Dalton opened proceedings by asking what the problem was. I gave a full rundown on my feelings and finished by saying that I felt the team had a great deal of confidence in me as captain. Much supportive talk by the players followed, although no-one actually stood up and said they wanted me back as captain. The upshot at the end of the meeting was that Nick was NSW captain and I was last season's model.

During the drive home from the meeting I pulled over to the kerb at a telephone box with a handful of coins in my hand ready to ring the Concord Bowling Club. I was going to tell Dalton that he could stick it, and that I wasn't interested in playing for NSW at all that season. I don't really know why I didn't go ahead and do it, but I left the telephone box and continued the drive home. I guess it would have been nothing more than sour grapes, so I swallowed my pride and decided to get on with the job of playing under Nick.

The NSW Sevens at Concord Oval started the representative season, and Australia really had something to prove. New Zealand had won both the Concord Oval and Hong Kong Sevens the previous season, and in the Hong Kong Sevens just past we hadn't even reached the final. We were empty-handed.

We started the tournament smartly enough, beating Western Samoa, Korea and The Netherlands on the first day, then Tonga (when we had cans hurled at us from parts of the crowd) and Korea in the semi-finals. Our opponents in the final? New Zealand of course.

I had plenty to say to the boys in the precious half-hour before we went out for the final. So did Jonesy. He called on us to reproduce the spirit of Eden Park the previous season. But I didn't need much stirring. I so wanted to avenge those other sevens losses, and that very morning I had picked up the *Sunday Telegraph* to find Mark Ella—a mate of mine, I thought—writing that I wasn't fast enough for sevens and that David Codey should have been picked ahead of me. Yet an old Clydesdale like him didn't make a bad sevens player. Whatever Mark's reasoning, his stinging words were all the inspiration I needed, and the driving urge to beat New Zealand was also enough to ensure that the whole team turned on a big performance.

Just before we left the sanctuary of our dressing-room I reminded the team that they'd all seen plenty of Rugby League and to do just what the League boys do in defence: smash them. And that's exactly what we did from the word go. It was full-on big hits on the New Zealanders and you only had to see the shocked looks on the faces of Wayne Shelford, Zinzan Brooke and Mark Brooke-Cowden to appreciate the effectiveness of our methods. These blokes had also come through a bruising semi-final against Fiji and so were more vulnerable than they might otherwise have been. We also had Troy Coker in our forwards. He'd been brought in for his injured fellow Queenslander Jeff Miller and his 118 kilograms gave us far more muscle than normal. In fact, he even finished up in a wild stoush with Zinzan Brooke. The whole atmosphere was fantastic, we took on New Zealand in the tough stuff and came out ahead, and also scored three sensational tries to lead 16-0, finally winning by 22-12. Later I told the media that 'the nightmare's finally over', and I'll always regard that victory as one of the most satisfying and gutsy that I've been associated with in an Australian team.

I played through the South Pacific championship matches under Paul Dalton as coach and Nick Farr-Jones as captain and played extremely well, which proved to me that I'd been able to overcome the enormous disappointment that I'd felt over losing the captaincy. Playing under Dalton was a new experience entirely. I don't think I've ever heard anything like his halftime talk, or rather blast, to us against Fiji in Suva. Admittedly we hadn't played well, but he screamed and swore at us so loudly that the big crowd of Fijians could hear every word and started laughing and sniggering at his performance. Among everything else, he threatened never to pick any of the backs for NSW again if they kicked the ball in the second half. In the first few minutes after halftime, Andrew Leeds caught the ball at fullback in a position where he'd normally have kicked for touch. But with Dalton's word ringing in his ears he clung onto it and was absolutely flattened by a wild herd of Fijian forwards. Despite Dalton's negative psychology we came back to win the game, but there's no way I could play for long periods copping all the abuse he dishes out to his players.

One of Australia's problems for the World Cup would be not having the proper environment to prepare for this ultimate Rugby challenge. Our greatest successes over the past few seasons had come when we went on tour and had gradually warmed to the task. As we developed unity as a team our football improved accordingly. So playing in Australia, where we weren't in a touring environment, was going to be very difficult.

When we eventually came together in Sydney the local players went off to work or to their studies when not training, which meant we never had that essential unity. Another factor that didn't help was that Alan Jones continued to do his morning program on 2UE, a contract he couldn't get out of. This meant players had to sit around in the mornings and wait until the afternoon for training, when traditionally we always trained in the mornings. We also had heaps of problems at our near-city motel. I had my room broken into and all my best clothes stolen, Nick Farr-Jones had three suits swiped from his car in the car park and Mark Hartill suffered more than anyone when he had his car pinched. The team also spent much of the time eating out at restaurants because we didn't feel the food in the hotel was good enough.

In contrast, England, Ireland, Wales, Scotland and France came straight from the Five Nations championship, all primed and ready to go. At one point England even went off to Hamilton Island for a relaxing break between matches. The New Zealanders made a huge commitment to the World Cup. They stopped their players from working and took them to hotels out in the country for training so that they would be single-minded in their pursuit of the World Cup.

And people want to know why we weren't too flash. I call tell you, it's pretty hard winning a race with the sort of handicap we had. In my work as a stockbroker we were also in the midst of a bull market, and it was virtually impossible for me to be dealing with this for five hours every morning and then simply switch off and be fully tuned in to the World Cup in the afternoon.

Australia's playing preparations before the Cup were restricted to a single Test against Korea. They weren't exactly the world's strongest opponents, but they were very gutsy players and gave us a decent workout even though we won easily by 65-18.

We had some mad-dog training runs the following week as we prepared for our opening match against England at Concord Oval, which followed Jonesy's pattern of driving us very hard physically at the onset of every campaign. On Thursday, he promised that he was going to ease off but the English media unexpectedly turned up en masse at training and that was the end of that. To make the big impression, he drove us harder than ever before.

The next day I took Steve Cutler, Bill Campbell, Andy McIntyre and Roger Gould to see the Sydney Stock Exchange operating, and trading was suddenly suspended for a few minutes when Cuts and Campbell walked in. The operators just looked in amazement at seeing the two-metre tall giants.

Jonesy had made a controversial selection when he chose Troy Coker at number eight against England and put our established Test number eight Steve Tuynman in the unfamiliar position of breakaway. Admittedly, Coker did have an exceptional game for Queensland against NSW, but it was still hard to understand the Bird being moved out of his natural position.

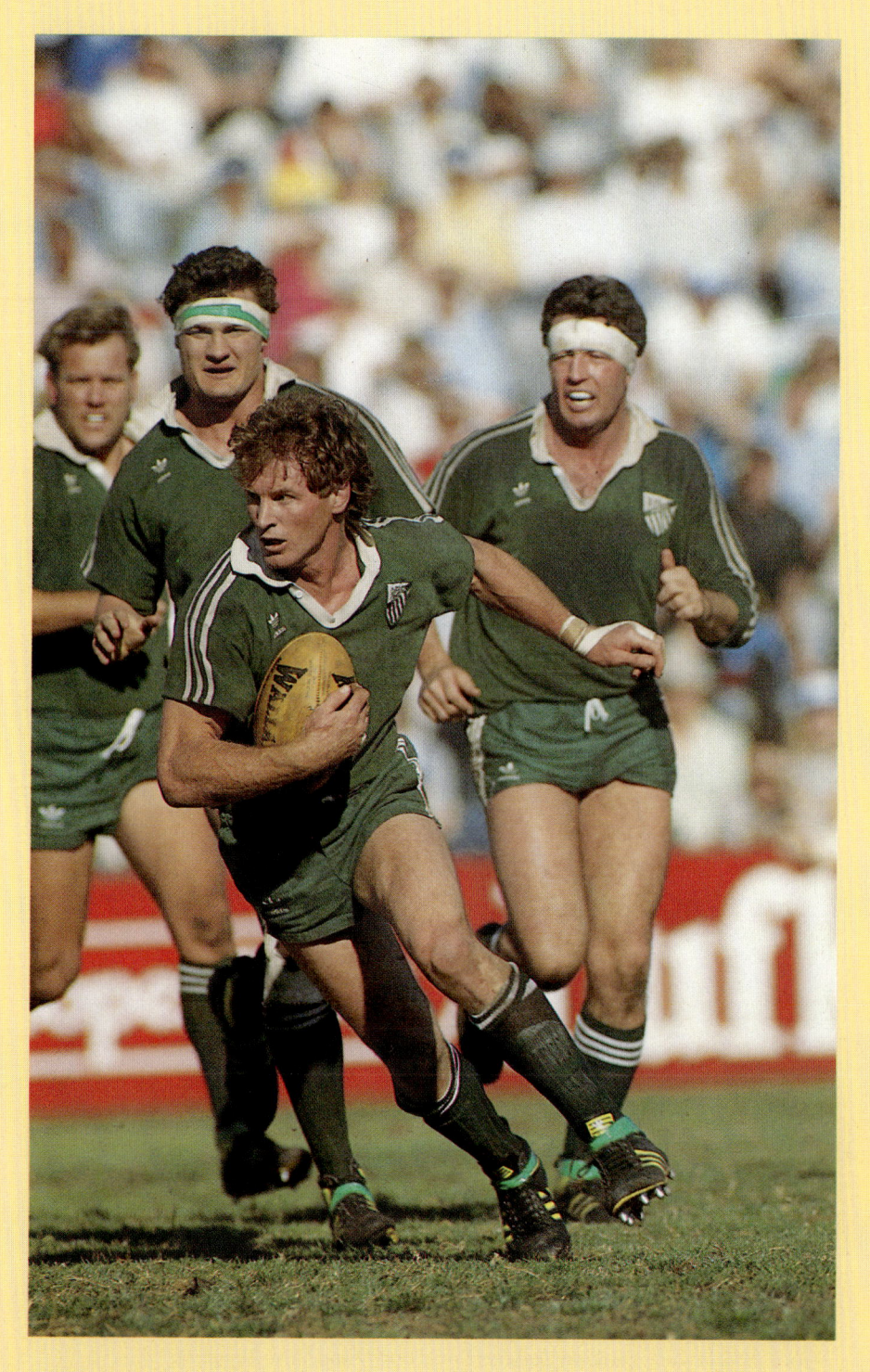

1989 Grand Final: heavyweight support from Mick Murray, Tim Kava and Gary Logan

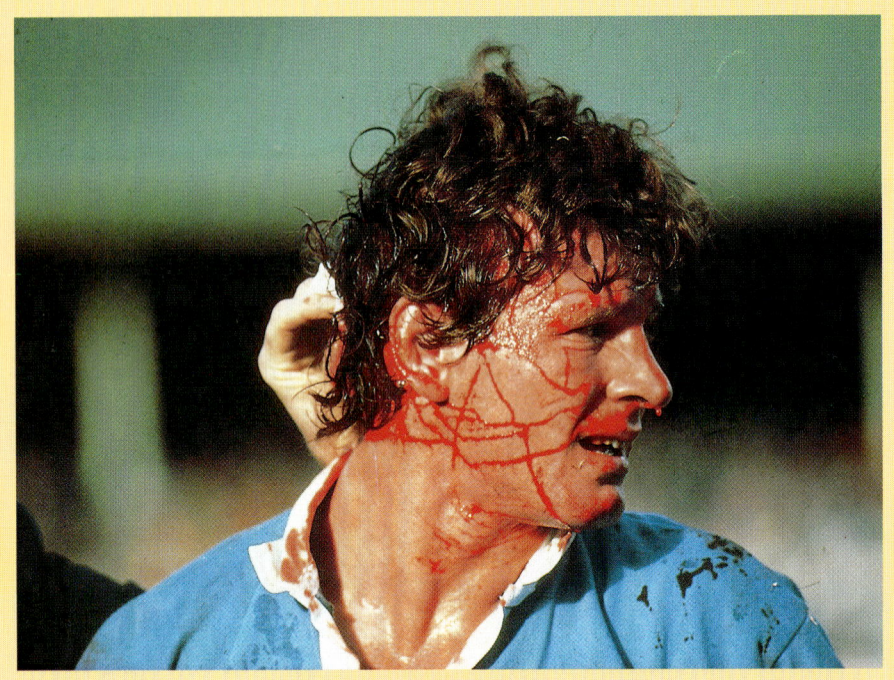

Which way did that All Black go?

France 1986: ecstatic backrow buddies David Codey and Steve Tuynman (**Action Graphics**)

Everyone was expecting more of Australia in this opening match than we were ourselves. We weren't nearly ready for an England team fresh from the Five Nations. We were more a rusty hulk than a cruise ship at that stage, even though we still got home by 19-6 in a very frustrating performance. My only satisfaction came from scoring a try on the occasion when I equalled Peter Johnson's record of 42 Test match appearances for Australia.

Over the next few days I tackled Jonesy about his treatment of Tuynman. Indications were that my partner in the back-row was going to be pushed out of the Test team by Coker when the finals came around, which I didn't feel warranted. Despite my call for an explanation of what was going on, I couldn't get a satisfactory answer out of the coach and was told not to be so emotional. But I'd played an awful lot of Test matches alongside the Bird and when the chips were down he was the one player I wanted playing number eight for Australia. At least I'd let Jonesy know how I felt.

I didn't play in the next game, against the United States in Brisbane, which we won by 47-12. Jonesy used the approach on the team that Mike Tyson fought just as hard whoever his opponents were and Australia had to do the same against the Rugby minnows. While we were up there Jonesy informed the team in private that our team manager Ken Grayling had cancer and was growing weaker every day. We had all suspected something was seriously wrong with Ken, but hadn't realised it was as bad as that. He was always a jolly soul and a thorough gentleman and, although Ken lived way out of the Rugby mainstream in Adelaide, he loved the game intensely and would do anything to help the team. News of that was weighing heavily on us when we returned to Sydney to be confronted by Farr-Jones losing his clothes and Hartill his car. (Ken Grayling passed away less than four months later on September 19.)

In a very warm gesture, Slacky wanted me to captain Australia against Japan in the next game as it was my 43rd Test, which meant that I would become the outright Australian record-holder for the most Tests played. The ARFU also wanted to make a presentation to me. I usually shy away from such publicity before a Test match—afterwards it doesn't matter—but it was a nice thought on the part of both Slacky and the ARFU and I proudly led Australia out that Wednesday afternoon at Concord Oval. The Japanese tackled like madmen and made us struggle for our 42-23 victory.

About this time New Zealand coach Brian Lochore went into print saying that he thought it would be a France v New Zealand final, which made The Jones Boy really see red. He almost gave himself laryngitis with everything he had to say about that forecast.

Ireland were our next opponents in the quarter-finals. On Thursday before the game, Jonesy called Slacky and me into his room to discuss the team generally and our prop Topo Rodriguez in particular. He was worried about Topo's form, more so as the younger Cameron Lillicrap was undoubtedly eventually going to replace him and right then was begging to be given a chance. So Jonesy dropped Topo, which must have been among the hardest selection decisions he has ever made. The Argentinean had been the cornerstone of our scrum right through the Grand Slam and Bledisloe Cup successes, and he took his dropping after 22 Test appearances for his adopted country very hard indeed. Yet he told the media: 'That's selection . . . that's life. But Cameron's good and he's going to get even better. I've just got to work harder now and bounce back. In the meantime, I'm going to give him all my support but I'll try to beat him out of the position next time.' That was typical of Topo: mature, sensible, level-headed and with a great ability to communicate with people. Everyone in the Australian team was uplifted by Topo's attitude to his sacking, as nobody else would have taken it as graciously as he did.

The day before Australia met the Irish, we watched on television the quarter-final between Scotland and the All Blacks from Christchurch and were very impressed with the way the Scots forced them all the way. There was a lesson here for us. It wasn't going to be easy: the Irish would give everything they had and we'd have to follow the example of the All Blacks and maintain our standards if we wanted to wear the Paddies down.

I didn't entirely trust our success to my teammates. On the morning of the match I went to Mass at the church across the road from our motel and whispered a few words to the Almighty, asking if He wouldn't mind filling in as an extra man.

Before going out our assistant coach Alex Evans had a quiet talk to me about the game and what was required of me in this sudden-death contest. He's a great mate, but apart from that he has the ability to remove all the superficial nonsense you sometimes get in Rugby, and what he said then really inspired me. I also believe that Australia will really fire if tears appear during the playing of Advance Australia Fair, and there were plenty of watery eyes that afternoon out in the centre of Concord Oval when we began singing the anthem. As it happened, the Irish also provided us with some unplanned inspiration of their own when their breakaway Phil Mathews clobbered our halfback Nick Farr-Jones in the opening minute. Nick went off and Brian Smith came on. Smithy said later that when he got on the field all his teammates were 'going nuts'. We sure were. The team was really wound up even before the incident, but that made us turn the blowtorch up even more. Greg Campbell wrote in The Australian at the time that the incident 'sparked one of Australia's best, well-controlled and most-dominant opening 25 minutes of Rugby ever seen'. We went on to give a sensational performance to win 33-15 after leading 24-0 at halftime. The team was well and truly back on the rails again. This was the way we played well into the UK and New Zealand tours. Now we'd give that theory of France v New Zealand final some curry!

But the following weekend we had to beat France in the semi-finals at Concord Oval. Win that and we were into the final at Eden Park in Auckland for Rugby's greatest prize; lose, and we were committed to the erupting geysers and sulphur fumes of Rotorua for the playoff for third and fourth positions.

Selections were really under the microscope for the game against France, but Jonesy resisted making any changes other than the one forced upon us when Steve Tuynman couldn't play. So Coker found his way into the team without too much controversy, although I'd have leaned towards David Codey because of his great experience and proven ability. At the same time, I would never doubt Coker's commitment to any team.

During the lead-up to the game we had problems when the scrum machine at Trinity Grammar School, where we were training, kept breaking down and we simply couldn't put in the many hours that scrummaging demands.

In the UK and New Zealand we'd had our own machines with us all the time and sometimes on those tours we worked till we dropped while developing that part of our game. Many people don't realise the vast importance of being able to dominate a rival team in the scrum. Not only is that the springboard for so much of your play, but it gives the forwards in particular an immense psychological lift if they know they're physically superior in this critical area and are wearing out their rivals.

The absence of Rodriguez's experience during the scrummaging sessions also greatly worried me. If hooker Tommy Lawton was the engine-driver of our scrum, then Topo had always been the stoker. He used to keep Tommy's mind on the job and push him along incessantly. But now Topo spent his time at the far end of the paddock, kicking a football around with the other reserves. With hindsight it's clear he should never have been dropped. Later the mistake was emphasised when the astute French coach Jacques Fouroux told us that when he saw Topo wasn't playing he felt confident of victory because France's scrum would be able to take control of the Australian pack.

In the opening scrum of the semi-final, we noticed a marked difference. The French front-row was Pascal Ondarts, their captain Daniel Dubroca, and the experienced Jean Pierre Garuet, who looks like your friendly Lourdes greengrocer with his droopy moustache and warm smile, but is about as gentle as a mating rhinoceros. Ondarts and Garuet hadn't toured the year before, when their scrum was considered excellent, and their presence this time improved it even more. No sooner did the packs come together for that first scrum than we felt this huge surge of power coming through on us. Hang on, what's this? Our scrum hadn't been moved for three years. What's the story here? Psychologically, the French immediately had the upper hand on us.

That semi-final has been described as one of the finest games in the history of Rugby football. It had everything. Power, aggression, skills, finesse, speed, atmosphere and reams of excitement. Australia had peeped ahead 9-6 at halftime, but then the lead was flicked and tossed from one team to the other in the second half until it seemed the 24-all deadlock would not be broken. But France came with one final charge and, after eleven players had handled, their brilliant fullback Serge Blanco speared for the corner to break the deadlock. Winger Didler Camberabero converted and they had won 30-24. That the French lock Laurent Rodriguez knocked-on just before the try went undetected by the Scottish referee Brian Anderson, whose excitement was probably boiling like everyone else's.

Exit Australia from the World Cup. From our point of view, it was a huge blow losing our zip-zip centre Brett Papworth and lineout stepladder Bill Campbell inside the first seventeen minutes, both with medial ligament damage. But basically the team didn't perform well, and I felt that had we played to our potential we'd have quite easily overcome the French on the day. A couple of milestones went almost undetected in the sad aftermath. David Campese went over for his 25th try, making him the most prolific try-scorer in the history of Test Rugby, and Lynagh took his Test aggregate to 269 points, nine more than the previous record for an Australian held by Paul McLean.

Afterwards, I'd never seen Jonesy more devastated by a loss, not that too many of the players were jumping over the moon. I was as affected as anybody. I'd held great hopes and dreams for this World Cup and getting into the final in New Zealand. Codey, who'd come on for Campbell, took me aside back at the team motel and comforted me. 'I know you're very upset mate, but it's not the end of the world,' he said, but what had disappointed me so much was that we hadn't played as well as we could. Had we played our best and lost it would have been so much easier to accept. But we hadn't. I felt deeply disappointed in myself and disappointed in the team.

So first and second prizes had gone. New Zealand and France would be shooting for those on June 20 at Eden Park. Two days beforehand we'd be fighting with Wales for third and fourth prizes at Rotorua.

At the first training run after our defeat by France, Jonesy's pre-training talk was very tough on Campese, Farr-Jones and Coker. He just didn't think they'd performed well enough and said so emphatically. We had a team dinner that night at a restaurant, where everyone got up and spoke. Some very warm words were said, but it was interesting to hear the comments from some players once we got home that night. The superficial words soon disappeared and it was obvious some had said things in the team environment which they didn't really mean. Had they been more honest, it would have been far better for the team in the long run.

So across to New Zealand. On the flight over, Jonesy came and spoke to me in private. He speculated on the possibility of the Wallabies making an officially-sanctioned tour of South Africa and wanted me to play a principal role in getting a feel from the players on what their attitudes might be. Jonesy had visited South Africa the year before and was really gung-ho about us going there. Despite our not having won the World Cup, we still had the Grand Slam and Bledisloe Cup successes behind us and our places in Rugby history would be secured for all time if we could add the Springboks to that list.

The South African Rugby Board had invited the Wallabies to make an official tour but the issue had now been on hold for more than twelve months as talks dragged on between the ARFU and the Federal Government, which vehemently opposed sporting contacts with the republic. Some members of the ARFU executive had apparently given veiled promises about still getting official approval for the tour in the form of the issuing and approving of individual invitations. So the whole scheme for a South African tour was hatched on that plane flight. While fascinated by the idea, what did surprise me was that Jonesy conducted this supposedly confidential conversation in the presence of Brian Smith, who was one of the youngest and least experienced Wallabies. Smithy treated Jonesy very much as a father figure, so Jonesy didn't seem to see anything wrong with being very open in front of him. The other thing was that any team going to South Africa would naturally involve older players like me and younger ones like Smithy, and he saw him as representative of them and their thoughts. So Smithy was involved from the word go.

From Auckland we went by bus down to smelly Rotorua, arriving late at night. The next morning we had our first training session for the playoff match against Wales but, rather surprisingly, Jonesy wasn't there. Alec Evans took the team. We all wondered what was going on, but our coach simply never turned up for what I considered an enormously important training session. To this day Jonesy has never offered an explanation for his absence. Yet I wonder what his reaction would have been had any of the players decided not to attend a pre-Test training session for no apparent reason?

FOR LOVE NOT MONEY

The International Stadium in Rotorua is a magnificent natural amphitheatre. The Romans would have used it for baiting the Christians. The New Zealanders used it for baiting us. Never have I played in front of a crowd so hostile towards Australia. You expect it when it's New Zealand v Australia, but our whole team was absolutely bowled over by the open hatred towards us and the desire for Wales to win. I'm not sure whether it's jealousy and envy of Big Brother across the Tasman, anger at our Rugby prowess, annoyance at underarm bowling or a combination of the lot. But there was plenty of hatred around that day at Rotorua.

The game was fire and brimstone from the opening whistle, and before we knew it our breakaway David Codey was cautioned for an elbow or late charge on one of the Welshmen. With smoke still coming out of our ears, Codes climbed into another ruck pretty strenuously in the fourth minute, and without hesitation the English referee Fred Howard ordered him off. We were stunned. Wander into any Rugby ground in New Zealand any Saturday afternoon and you'd see the same thing attract not the slightest attention. But nothing could be done about it and, as leader of the forwards, I appealed to my mates to quickly adjust to being a man short and accept the immense challenge of trying to beat Wales with only fourteen men. But as the game progressed I realised just how much harder it is at international level to cover scrums and lineouts with only seven forwards. The Welsh five-eighth Jonathan Davies enjoyed giving us plenty of lip over our difficulties and I did everything I could to shut him up.

Remarkably, Australia led 15-13 at halftime, and we had them beaten until they scored near fulltime and their fullback Paul Thorburn put over the goal from out on touch to make it 22-21. But we still weren't finished, and in the closing minute Matthew Burke very nearly scored for us again.

When the whistle finally went, I ran off the ground. I wanted to get away from that cauldron of hatred and smell of defeat. It was one of my biggest Rugby disappointments. The other players felt much the same way, because we burst into the locked dressing-room and then didn't even wait to have showers (the water was cold anyway). We grabbed our clothes and caught the team bus straight back to the hotel.

No sooner were we back at the hotel than the pow-wows started over Codey's dismissal. Jonesy was incensed and quickly took up the running, just as he had done over Mark McBain's dismissal in the UK three years earlier. During the disciplinary committee hearing of Codey's case he went right off the deep end and called one of the committee members, Dick Littlejohn, a 'turd'. Finally the NZRFU told him to mind his own business and keep right out of it.

That night Jonesy and I had a long talk about the whole World Cup and that game in particular, and the drinks that accompanied it became an escape from the reality of the whole nightmare. The next morning I thought I was in a bad way until I saw our assistant coach Alec Evans with an arm in plaster. Our prop Cameron Lillicrap had some fuel aboard during the post-match revelry and had apparently become too playful.

The bus trip back to Auckland was very subdued and we found the NZRFU had booked us into a motel way out of town near the airport. Fourth placegetters and second-class citizens. On the Saturday morning of the World Cup final between New Zealand and France we picked up teams and had a State of Origin Rugby League game on a patch of mud near the hotel. Before long we had twenty or 30 people incredulously watching some of Rugby's biggest names playing the other code. That afternoon only two or three of the Wallabies, including me, bothered going to the final, in which New Zealand blitzed the froggies by 29-9 to claim Rugby's first world title. The rest of the team were too cheesed off with everything to go. And at the official World Cup dinner that night, not only were there nine speeches, but we were made to sit next to the Welsh players, which was all we needed. It just hadn't been our year.

When we returned home, NSW was to play Queensland at Concord Oval in what turned out to be a very significant game because of the radical team Paul Dalton selected. I kept my jersey, but Steve Cutler was chopped, which was the equivalent of hoisting Wally Lewis from the Queensland State-of-Origin line-up. He chose a small, very mobile set of forwards and his gamble paid off—we won 21-19. The intensity that Dalton put into that game gave me another telling insight into his character. At one training session I wasn't listening to his rhetoric but rather to the number of times he used the word 'I'. After reaching the half-century I stopped counting. The fact that I hardly ever listened to what he said was an indication of what I thought of him, although I can never take it away from the bloke. His record with Parramatta was very, very impressive and shows that his approach works very effectively with some people. He also called for us once (I must have been listening at the time) to die for NSW. Not even frequenters of rucks are silly enough to go out and die for NSW or Australia in a sporting fixture, and certainly not at Concord Oval in front of only 5291 fans. Resorting to those sorts of foolish rhetorical extremes never got real commitment from anybody.

I had a feeling at the time that my presence in the Australian team for one of the regular one-off Tests against the All Blacks in July was in jeopardy. I was also aware after a conversation with Wally Lewis, of all people, that David Campese was putting the knife into me and telling various people just who should be in and out of the team. I took grave offence at that. Of all blokes, Campese shouldn't have been mouthing off.

Then a few days before the team was selected, I received an ominous summons to Alan Jones's Newtown bunker where he confirmed that my feelings were accurate. A foul wind was blowing. When the team was announced, Slacky and I were dropped; captain and vice-captain one minute and antique pieces the next. It was extremely disappointing. Michael Hawker was resurrected in the centres and I was chopped in favour of my Queensland mate Jeff (Ginger) Miller, with David Codey the new captain. While Australia had fiddled with its tried combination, the All Blacks naturally kept intact the team that had won the World Cup. For posterity's sake, it's worth recording the line-up, for when I'm talking Rugby with my grandkids 40 years from now I will more than likely suggest that this was the finest national Rugby team of my time:

John Gallagher, John Kirwan, Joe Stanley, Warwick Taylor, Craig Green, Grant Fox, David Kirk (c), Wayne Shelford, Michael Jones, Alan Whetton, Gary Whetton, Murray Pierce, John Drake, Sean Fitzpatrick and Steve McDowall.

This was a truly great team, immensely powerful in set pieces and at the ruck and maul, with Grant Fox one of the deadliest goalkickers in the game's history, and a backline with much more incisiveness than the All Blacks had ever had before. Thank goodness New Zealand took until the mid-eighties to realise the value of moving the ball about, or we'd have seldom pinched any Tests from them before that. But with Bryce Rope developing their backline play through sevens football, and Brian

Randwick/Parramatta Grand Finals were no place for the faint-hearted

WORLD CUP DESPAIR

The intensity of the Ireland v Australia quarter-final in the World Cup. l to r: Steve Tuynman, myself, Ireland's Phil Matthews and Andrew Slack

Lochore implementing it in the normal game, the All Blacks suddenly became a superbly balanced, all-round Rugby team and not one top-heavy with forward machinery. And this particular team that won the inaugural World Cup simply couldn't be faulted on any count. It came as near to Rugby perfection as anything I've seen and, had they ever needed a pretty intense, boisterous breakaway, I'd have been honoured to have pulled on the number six jersey for them.

There was much talk beforehand that if Australia could beat them they'd have redeemed themselves and become pseudo world champions. I was doing some commentary on the Test for the ABC and went down to our dressing-room beforehand. I smelt the familiar linament and felt the electricity, and shook the hand of each and every one of my mates. As I walked out, I had a very empty feeling.

Australia held them that afternoon at Concord Oval for over an hour, which was as well as any team could have done, but then the yard gates were gradually forced open and the All Blacks went thundering over them in the last ten minutes in an awesome display of fitness, commitment and artistry. Being able to lift their game an extra cog has become a feature of their play in recent years. The final score was 30-16. Australia could probably count itself lucky that it had kept them to a 14-point margin, which was six points better than what France had managed in the World Cup final. Yet the wolves immediately began baying for Alan Jones.

SOUTH AFRICA, ARGENTINA AND THE EMPIRE SLIDES

In my whole Rugby career, the one issue which has infuriated me more than anything is South Africa. Each time Rugby contacts with the republic are mentioned, media bosses immediately determine that it's a major news item, politicians start bleating their sorrowful hearts out and every anti-apartheid campaigner climbs out from under a rock and starts complaining.

While I have never been to South Africa, let me make my position on the matter infinitely clear: I abhor apartheid and everything it stands for. It's the most denigrating, selective and obnoxious practice ever conceived, falling not far short of what Adolf Hitler and Idi Amin implemented.

If the Federal Government determined that this country should have nothing at all to do with South Africa, in an attempt to impress upon it the global revulsion that's felt, then I would be the first to agree. But it's the rampant hypocrisy that angers me and my fellow Rugby players so much.

Why just pick on us and cricketers? Why allow tennis players, surfers, golfers and any number of other sports persons to compete there and not us? Why trade with South Africa, as still openly happens, and not allow us to play there? Why allow Soviet and Chinese interchanges on social, economic and sporting grounds? Did the occupation of Afghanistan not occur? And maybe they were shop-window dummies who were butchered in Tiananmen Square?

Whether it be a Labor or Liberal Government in office, the only thing which will satisfy us as Rugby players will be an all-or-nothing attitude. If the Government oversees a complete outlawing of South Africa in trade, social and sporting terms, then we'll all willingly abide by that. But it's the selective morality of successive Governments that infuriates players, and it made the likelihood of a Rugby tour of South Africa such a major issue in this country in mid-1987.

As I said in the previous chapter, Australia was officially invited by the South African Rugby Board to send the Wallabies there on a major tour in 1987, but because of unflinching Government opposition the invitation was not taken up and eventually lapsed in the middle of that year. Then the SARB appealed to the ARFU to allow players to tour as individuals. It wanted any number of them, but the ARFU said that any players undertaking a rebel tour would be banned for life. Yet in the background, the players were being given veiled assurances by the national coach Alan Jones that an official tour might still be sanctioned if only we would have patience. The SARB president Dr Danie Craven gave credence to this by saying publicly that he had met an ARFU official (not Jones) at the Hong Kong Sevens back in March and had been promised a tour by an Australian team.

About the end of July, the ABC's Sunday afternoon program Sports Arena crossed to South Africa where a statement was read from Andrew Slack saying that Australian players were willing and prepared to go to South Africa regardless of whether official blessing was forthcoming or not. In other words, if South Africa wanted a rebel tour by the Wallabies, then they could have one. Reading between the lines, it was abundantly clear that much behind-the-scenes organising by Slacky had already been done and a rebel tour by then was obviously up and running, although who was behind it at the South African end was unclear.

The existence of plans for a rebel tour was confirmed when Slacky contacted me and other players and gave us some scant information. But from the outset I didn't have any close involvement with the venture and wasn't party to details regarding the length of the tour, number of matches, opposition etc, although the undeniable fact was that an Australian team was being assembled.

Why did the Wallabies want to go to South Africa at all? Well, our team had been together for several years at that stage and after the success we'd had it was only natural that we'd talked about South Africa and wanting to tour there. None of the players had been, except Topo Rodriguez who was there with South America in 1982, and yet it was one of the world's most beautiful and fascinating countries as well as being among the great Rugby strongholds. The World Cup was over, there were a blank few weeks on the Rugby calendar—it was the ideal time to tour there if ever we were going to.

When the official tour died the rebel tour gained momentum. Slacky took up all the front-running and only later did David Codey come onto the scene as his co-organiser and eventually the more prominent spokesman. A small committee headed by these two started to make plans for the tour. At no stage was my close involvement encouraged because of my strong friendship with Alan Jones, who was still vigorously campaigning for an official tour and hoping that the issue was not completely dead. He'd often said that when he went to South Africa he wanted 'to go through the front door'.

But Slacky and Codey soon began to experience difficulties. I could only think that Codey was the unnamed Test player who made these media comments on July 31: 'Three weeks ago the tour was 90 per cent on. Now it's 50-50. Time's running out. We've got no air tickets, no itinerary and nobody has applied for visas. It's up to the people in South Africa if they want us. I, for one, have a bag packed.' I was very concerned when I read this. I was wanting to go, but was staggered that the whole thing was so wishy-washy and that no firm arrangements had been made. When the New Zealand Cavaliers toured South Africa the previous year everything was mounted like a secret military operation. The players leaving from New Zealand were in Hong Kong before anybody knew they were gone and those few who were with us at the centenary matches in the UK didn't let the cat out of the bag until the night before they flew to South Africa. Everything had been meticulously planned and executed. They had avoided all the media flak, yet the whole issue of the Australian rebel tour seemed as if it was being conducted in the media. If you're going to have a tour like this then you've got to keep it extremely close to the chest and then suddenly disappear. The emotional pressures on the players when something like this becomes public are substantial and can easily cause them to get cold feet.

Finally the wishy-washy talk, which was really all we'd had till then, was replaced by some firm action when Slacky and Codey flew out for South Africa on August 4 to attend a meeting of provincial unions organised by the Natal Rugby Union official, Roger Gardner. At last we knew who was behind it. Claims then that 30 leading Australian players were waiting to make the rebel tour were simply not accurate. Certainly there were at least twenty Wallabies who were ready and willing to go, and any number who hadn't played any high-profile Rugby who would step into the shoes of the internationals who declined to go.

By this time, Jonesy and Dr Craven had washed their hands of getting an official tour off the ground and Slacky and Codey were desperately trying to get their tour up and running under the direction of the South African provincial unions, although not having Dr Craven's support was very damaging to their cause. As he's the godfather of South African Rugby, mounting a tour without his help was going to be very difficult. At the time I found it hard to get a feel for whether he was genuinely taking the official line in dissociating himself from the rebel tour or whether he was foxing and underneath it all really wanted to see international Rugby played in South Africa, no matter who organised it. Applying pressure to him in the background were the money-hungry entrepreneurs who had done so very well financially from the Cavaliers tour and desperately wanted us over there. To give an idea of the attention such a tour would attract, the New Zealand Herald's Rugby writer, D J Cameron, who covered the Cavaliers' tour for his newspaper, recalls: 'It was big news there, really big. The tour seemed to dominate everything throughout the country—TV, newspapers, the lot.' There were capacity crowds, sometimes as big as 70 000 at many grounds, and near-capacity crowds elsewhere.

Jonesy then started to show concern about the consequences of a badly-arranged rebel tour and the banning from future Rugby in Australia of any younger players who went away. His chicks would all be lost and his future coaching success made all the more difficult. The Federal Government was also speaking out again, with the Minister for Sport, Recreation and Tourism, John Brown, issuing a strong statement and warning that any player touring South Africa placed the international future of the code in jeopardy and threatened the international futures of other Australians who wanted to compete in the Olympic Games. That boring rhetoric was nothing new. We'd heard it all before and we've heard it since.

For personal and business reasons, I announced on August 9 that I wouldn't be going to South Africa no matter what, although I was still very supportive of Slacky and Codey and what they were doing. They were trying to put some sanity into the argument about sport and politics and I've always been the first bloke to get into the Government over their hypocritical approach to the matter.

A lingering concern of mine was that the Cavaliers had in all probability received large sums of money, and you'd be very naive to imagine the Australians going to South Africa for nothing whatsoever. Besides, there would be every justification for compensation being paid to Australian players on a rebel tour because of the sacrifices necessary to undertake it.

To this day, nobody has been able to prove definitely whether the Cavaliers were paid, although they were reputed to have got as much as $100 000 each for their four-Test tour. But the whole matter of payment to the Australians hadn't been properly addressed, which worried the players.

It was amusing to see the agitation of the ARFU while all this was going on. John Dedrick, the ARFU executive director and its chief spokesman, wasn't particularly well-liked by the players, even though he was an enormously hard worker, and some of his comments at the time didn't help the strained relationship.

When Slacky and Codey returned home, the ARFU summoned them to a meeting in Sydney for talks to 'acquaint them with the facts and dispel some misconceptions of the Union's role'. They were told they couldn't go off organising tours of their own but, at the same time, the ARFU recognised that the pair had apparently received covert encouragement from several high-ranking officials.

A succession of important meetings followed. The Sydney players met the two Test captains at a Double Bay hotel to review the situation. I was invited, even though at that stage I was torn between turning my back on the tour and, on the other hand, missing out on what would be one of the great Rugby experiences any international player could hope for. Certainly the thought of not being with my mates from all those campaigns weighed very heavily on my mind. Codey wanted me along, because he felt my presence and support would help influence those players who were undecided about going. Slacky's attitude was very different. I clearly recall the hatred in his eyes when he saw me. He obviously considered me a Judas, who would immediately go and report everything to Jones. That couldn't be further from the truth. I was always very loyal to my teammates, and if the tour was well-organised then I would give them every support I could.

After that, Jones called a further meeting at his home. Several hours beforehand, Michael Hawker and I met him at the Quay Apartments to discuss what might be said and done. At the main meeting, the Sydney players gave their views on the whole situation. When it was my turn I told the gathering that I felt the tour was going to be badly organised by the South Africans, and tried to alert them to the subsequent dangers.

Hanging over the players' heads were threats of life bans by the ARFU and even from playing in the Sydney premiership. This was really going over the top and giving very little consideration to how much time and effort had been put in by the players concerned for the good of Australia, NSW and their clubs.

Eventually, the rebel tour died in the backside. I believe its collapse came from within South Africa, and that Dr Craven finally showed his hand and stopped the provincial unions from proceeding any further. To this day many of the players involved, particularly the Queenslanders, believe Alan Jones exerted a lot of influence to have the tour stopped. Because he had strong traditional links with the South African Rugby Board, especially Dr Craven, I can understand those suspicions, but they are over-estimating his power to think he could have stopped such a tour. At the end of the day, I feel Dr Craven wanted the SARB to remain a member of the International Board, and their position would have been seriously jeopardised by another rebel tour taking place. And the fact that players like me, Hawker and Steve Tuynman had said we wouldn't be going had also influenced his thinking, for it would not have been worth risking his country's entire international Rugby future on a sub-standard touring team.

The final chapter was the ARFU slapping a twelve months' ban on Slack and Codey for their part in organising the aborted tour. This ban was instigated by the Queensland delegates to the ARFU—Joe French and Norbert Byrne—and was so hypocritical it was laughable. In 1986 and 1987 we had played against the All Blacks who had been to South Africa, and yet here was the ARFU banning our pair for simply going there and talking quite openly and frankly about a tour. Ironically, Alan Jones was the author of a submission by the NSW Rugby Union to the ARFU pleading for the ban to be dropped because of the contributions the pair had made to Australian Rugby. In the face of enormous media pressure and having felt it had made its point, the ARFU finally reduced it to a nominal ban of just a few weeks. Effectively, that's where the whole rebel tour issue died. We didn't tour, either officially or unofficially, and my one regret in Rugby is that I've never locked horns with the Springboks.

Finally, let me just say that on Rugby and South Africa I've never encountered so much uninformed bullshit as that which has been said and written about this subject. Whenever it has surfaced, I've constantly had to take telephone calls from imbeciles in the media who know nothing about Rugby as a whole, South Africa as a nation, or what's being done over there to at least try to integrate Rugby. All they're chasing is controversy. The best was when some character rang my office wanting some comments from Steve Poidevin. My reply to this ignorant dope was as short as his knowledge of Rugby.

Later in that 1987 season I was named captain of the Wallabies for the tour of Argentina and Paraguay. That tour suddenly brought a breath of fresh air into my Rugby after all the nonsense that had gone on. That I was made captain was unbelievably satisfying, and I took offence at some opinions that it was because of my loyalty to Jones throughout the South African issue. My concern with the rebel tour to South Africa extended way beyond any loyalty to Alan Jones. I believed that if we were going to go to South Africa, we should go on our terms and not those of the South African organisers.

The biggest task I had as captain was to reunify the Wallabies. Firstly we had failed to win the World Cup, and secondly the South African issue had proved very divisive, with a number of players who had wanted to go and a few who were strenuously opposed to it. It was a challenge for me to smooth over those divisions.

The most interesting tour selection was Warringah breakaway Steve Lidbury, a tough nut by any standards, who had never played for Australia previously because of the abundance of good back-rowers we always seemed to have. But I couldn't have been happier than to see Libo among the 26 players picked. A serious omission to my mind was Ricky Stuart, the halfback or five-eighth from Canberra, who was one of the best players I'd seen for many, many years. As it happened, halfback Nick Farr-Jones was injured in the tour opener and Stuart flew over as a replacement, but he should have been there right from the outset.

When the Wallabies assembled in Sydney before leaving, Jonesy had us out for training one morning at 6 a.m. Why, I don't know. I could be wrong, but I suspect that we're the only touring football team that has ever trained at that uncouth hour. At that same session Jonesy asked me to explain to my half-asleep players what I expected of them. I told them that South Africa was to be put behind them and here was the chance to put Australia back on the rails again. We had a good team and were about to embark on one of the most fascinating Rugby tours imaginable.

Our impressions of Argentina were formed as soon as we left our Aerolineas Argentinas jet in Buenos Aires after our Trans-Polar flight. The international airport terminal had obviously been a magnificent structure, but was now dilapidated, which about summed up the nation as a whole. When we arrived at the Sheraton Hotel, Jonesy delivered a detailed historical treatise to the team on Argentina, which was very informative and helped us to understand everything about the country a whole lot better. The only immediate problem we found was that the locals don't like going to bed early, and every night it was just as noisy out in the streets after midnight as it was before.

At our media conference on the first day, the Argentinian media guys seemed to take offence at our attitude that this tour was one to rebuild the Australian team and that we were determined to win every game. Later that day some of us went out for a few drinks and it became apparent from what was said that this was going to be a more difficult tour than I'd imagined. Some significant wounds regarding the South African issue, and even Jonesy's coaching, had to be healed if this was to become a happy, co-ordinated outfit.

We drew our opening game against the champion Buenos Aires club, San Asidra, but the most important thing to come out of it was the refereeing. It was disgraceful, with the referee particularly penalising our scrum. Certainly our scrum was under significant pressure, which was going to be a pattern for the tour, because we didn't have a scrum machine or a live pack to scrum against. But the referee was unrelenting in his attack on the Wallabies and afterwards Jonesy really climbed into him publicly, perhaps pushing the issue altogether too far. This was a pattern that increased in frequency as the tour progressed.

The reception that night at the San Asidra Club was the most enjoyable after-match function I've ever been to. They had some gauchos cooking the barbecue at this magnificent old clubhouse in the middle of Buenos Aires, and while they were working their horses were tethered nearby. After a few pots of beer I asked could we borrow their horses for a while. They agreed and so Michael Hawker, Alan Jones and I climbed aboard and went for a ride around the oval on these magnificent beasts.

The golden era brains trust—Chilla Wilson, Alan Jones and Andrew Slack (**Nick Jacomas**)

Experience plus—Bob Dwyer and Bob Templeton, with some helpful advice from Dr John Moulton (**Nick Jacomas**)

Wales at Cardiff Arms Park, 1981: the hunt is on with Greg Cornelsen and Tony Shaw (**Nick Jacomas**)

Brendan Moon—one of Australia's greatest wingers (**Action Graphics**)

All the team members were hoping Jonesy would come off and make a fool of himself, but he'd done plenty of riding in his youth on the Darling Downs and there was no risk of that. About three o'clock in the morning, by which time we all had plenty of idiot juice aboard, Queensland prop Cameron Lillicrap decided that he wanted a ride too. He insisted to the gauchos that he'd grown up with horses and they let him climb aboard one. He was immediately catapulted off, but got up and climbed back on. The horse gave a few more bucks and he was off again, only this time Crappers badly hurt his AC joint when he hit the turf, so here was one of our most promising Test hopefuls suddenly out of action for a few weeks. To his credit, he went to Jonesy later that morning and explained that his injury hadn't occurred during the game but because of what had happened during the buckjumping exhibition. Farr-Jones also hurt a medial ligament during that opening game, which brought Stuart winging across to join us.

Two days after that first game, we at last had some scrummaging practice against some local juniors and were amazed at how extraordinarily strong their scrum was. Obviously the scrum is given top priority in Argentina from the earliest levels and is their most powerful weapon, which we learned so forcefully in 1983 against the Pumas. Scrummaging against these youngsters only confirmed our fears that the scrum was going to be a real problem area for us on tour. So we worked extremely hard on that and, with Jonesy driving us elsewhere in our training, things started to look better. We beat a Provincial Selection at Neuquen in the south-west by 47-0, then flew up to Mendoza at the foot of the Andes, where Topo was appointed captain of the Wallabies against Cuyo Selection in a well-deserved honour, and led Australia to a 40-3 victory. The happy hour that night, however, degenerated into a full-scale drinking bout, some things were said that shouldn't have been, and finally Jonesy got up and let both barrels fly over behavioural standards.

Monday, October 19, 1987 was unimpressive for us, involving little more than a quick flight from Buenos Aires to Santa Fe, but the world will remember it better as the day the stockmarkets crashed. Being in the stockbroking business, I was rather more pleased to be in this cowboy-type town in South America than in Bond Street in Sydney. At one o'clock in the morning my girlfriend Kim rang to give me more details, and then I rang my office in Sydney to get the full implications of this world-shattering news. I was then so restless that I got dressed, went downstairs and tried to explain the disaster to the hotel's night manager and a couple of hotel workers, but they were as interested as if I was telling them tomorrow was Tuesday. Because of the horrific state of the Argentinian economy it didn't make any impression on them at all, because they were only earning about $US70 a month. They shook their heads and nodded off to sleep again. From there I wandered into the team room and found the inevitable card game in progress. I broke the news to the punters involved and Tommy Lawton's reaction was most amusing, as he had bought on margin some speculative gold shares before leaving Australia. He asked in all honesty what a 500-point fall in the All Ordinaries Index would mean to his net worth and I replied: 'You'd better start winning a few hands of poker, real quick.' In what was left of the night I didn't sleep a wink.

The next day we beat Santa Fe Selection by 37-18. Again, the most dominant individual in the game was the referee, who was appalling, and he was again roundly criticised by Jonesy. At the official dinner that night the referee dished out some abuse in return when he was receiving the Australian Rugby tie that we traditionally present to each of them on tour. An unusual aspect of this dinner was that because of the game's extremely late kickoff time, the speeches were taking place at 2 am!

Then back to the capital, where we defeated an Invitation XV by 36-15, but at the same time encountered the worst and most dishonest referee we'd yet had. By this time, however, we realised that criticism of the refereeing was only becoming counter-productive. Our team manager Andy Conway, Jonesy and I made an agreement between ourselves that we wouldn't comment on them further.

From there we flew north to Asuncion in Paraguay, where the Australian Rugby team had never played before. The accommodation was the best we had experienced on tour and the silence in the streets after the noise of Buenos Aires was a tremendous relief. The following morning I was up early in anticipation of our adventure into Brazil to visit the Iguassu Falls. About twenty of us flew to the border of Paraguay and then boarded a bus for the rest of the journey to the falls. They were magnificent—250 thundering cathedrals of water that make up the largest falls in the world, located where the boundaries of Brazil, Argentina and Paraguay come together. We could only afford about an hour there taking photographs before we headed back along the border to the airfield and the plane flight home among gathering storm clouds. That's when the fun began. The flight was so turbulent that half the players were joking about it and the other half either praying or throwing up. However, when an alarm went off in the open cockpit everyone on board was gripped with terror, the pilot quickly descended to a very narrow corridor of safety between the raging storm and the ground below and fortunately got us home in one piece. This experience was worse than the most horrific Alan Jones training run.

The next day we beat the Paraguay Selection by 44-9 and then headed back into Argentina for the two-Test series.

Missing from our Test line-up when it was announced were three of our key members in recent years, Nick Farr-Jones, Steve Tuynman and Andy McIntyre, who were replaced by Brian Smith, Steve Lidbury and Mark Hartill respectively. I was particularly concerned about McIntyre's omission, but Alan Jones and Alec Evans convinced me that Hartill's scrummaging technique had accelerated ahead of the vastly experienced McIntyre. We would see. The team had a fresh, new look about it but I knew we'd do it tough against the Pumas, because of our scrum problems and the fact that they are always so much better playing at home than abroad. But at least we had a neutral referee, Keith Lawrence from New Zealand, and not some local cheat.

The 19-all result in the Test was a reflection of Australian Rugby that year. That we were ahead 19-12 with only five minutes remaining and couldn't hold on was another familiar tragedy. I always felt that we were set to win. But the Pumas applied the pressure in the second half and we found that you can't score points when you're camped in your own 22-metre zone. Our five-eighth Stephen James lost his composure as the game went on, and I felt that we had many opportunities out wide that went begging. Outside-centre Brett (The Stepper) Papworth only handled about three times and yet he was the player who could really cut any defence to ribbons. As well as seeing the Test thrown away I hurt my hand in the 65th minute and had to be replaced. X-rays later showed that I had a fracture in the metacarpal and would have less than a 50-50 chance of playing in the second Test.

With Steve Tuynman in the second-row and Mark McBain in the equally unfamiliar position of breakaway, we defeated a Rosario Selection next by 35-15. On the morning of that game I was ruled out of the coming weekend's Test because of my hand. Then it was back down to Buenos Aires by bus to prepare for the Test.

Jonesy announced that Australia's new captain would be Michael Lynagh, and that Farr-Jones, Tuynman and McIntyre were all back in the lineup—a chance to see if the older guys could do better—with Julian Gardner taking my place.

The feeling within the team before this final Test was excellent and, when we quickly went ahead 13-3, it looked as if we were on our way to a resounding win. The first ten minutes of the second half were critical, with Argentina's kicking genius Hugo Porta being given far too many opportunities by both us and the referee. The Pumas crept up to 13-12. We were in the danger zone. We had to turn them around then, or else. But we didn't, and all the time Porta kept piloting over one goal after another. I wrote in my diary at the time that 'his performance was again freakish and he must go down as one of the game's all-time best players . The emotional drain I felt watching the Test slipping away from us from the grandstand was incredible. I'd never have believed I could have felt as washed out as I did. When the whistle finally went, Argentina had won 27-19 and Porta had contributed five penalty goals and two dropped goals on his own for a huge 21 points.

The dressing-room was the all-too-familiar sight we'd seen throughout 1987. Bowed heads. Silence. Lack of people. Beer instead of champagne. The stench of defeat. Later at the traditional press conference, I had the unenviable task of announcing that Topo Rodriguez had played his last game for Australia. He was retiring. Topo had been a big part of the Australian team's soul over the years 1984–1987 and to suddenly realise that he would no longer be with us was very sad. It was of immense credit to Topo that he played as well as ever during the Argentinian tour at the age of 35. He had also done a huge amount for us in the way of being translator, guide and general helper to everybody and I thanked him for that. That started him crying. Then I became very emotional too, and the pair of us left the stadium leaning on each other and shot to pieces.

I had only very fond memories of Argentina. It had been my most enjoyable tour ever, the South African rupture had been partly repaired, we had scored a huge number of tries and the team had been an extremely happy one.

Argentina had also provided a valuable lesson in social studies for the young Australians on that tour. To see such a beautiful country on its knees economically, and to experience the total lack of hope of Argentinian youth in the future of their country left a permanent impression on my mind and the minds of the other players.

CONTROVERSY, CONTROVERSY, CONTROVERSY

The vultures were circling well before we arrived back in Sydney from the tour of Argentina in 1987, waiting to pick our bones for having lost the series to the Pumas. Alan Jones would obviously be the first attacked, despite Australia having won nineteen, drawn one, and lost only seven of the 27 Tests in which he was coach. He had made a heap of enemies during his four years of unrivalled success. In his uncompromising pursuit of excellence he'd criticised, condemned and rebuked many people who stood in his way or maligned his players, and now our series defeat was the chance for all those who'd fallen foul of him to even the score.

The get-squares started at the media conference at the airport. How could we draw a Test and lose another against a Rugby nation as unobtrusive as Argentina, which was known mostly for its gauchos, superb wine, beautiful women and the Pampas? What went wrong? Who was to blame?

All I could emphasise to the media was the imposing international record of the Pumas in recent years and the enormous spirit they generate when playing at home, especially in Buenos Aires. Jonesy said that he was prepared to accept the entire blame if a scapegoat had to be found.

It appeared also that an open secret in Sydney was that Brett Papworth and Matthew Burke were going to immediately turn to Rugby League. The question was asked: how could the Australian Rugby Football Union pick them for such a tour when they were morally, if not legally, bound beforehand to the professional game?

In reply, I said I couldn't see why they shouldn't have been picked. I knew in all probability they were going to League, but I fully supported their selection. Both had done much in their own way in the short time they had been in the Australian Rugby team and selectors should always take on tour the best available team. And as they hadn't signed any contracts as far as anyone was aware, they hadn't breached any of the amateur laws.

I'd hardly unpacked from the tour before I made an appointment with Dr Bruce Conolly, the Macquarie Street hand surgeon who had operated on my finger after the 1984 Sydney tour of Europe. This time I wanted him to check my left hand and the damage that I'd suffered during the first Test against the Pumas. When x-rays were taken immediately after the game, the staff at the Buenos Aires hospital told me there was no break. Later an orthopaedic surgeon told me there was indeed a very bad break. Given the totally opposite views, it didn't exactly send you into raptures over the Argentinian medical system and its doctors.

Dr Conolly confirmed that my hand was badly broken and, after hoping without results that physiotherapy might help the mending process, he decided in December to operate.

When I came out of the operating theatre, he had some illuminating news for me. He said the joint was so badly smashed that he had no hope of repairing it. Had it been operated on in Buenos Aires immediately after the Test, there might have been a chance of saving it. But he had no choice when I was on the operating table other than to replace it with a plastic joint. That cleared my head of the anaesthetic fairly smartly. Would I be able to play again? Dr Conolly said these joints were normally used to replace arthritic joints in elderly people and I was very much a guinea pig in getting one while still playing such a physical sport. Only time would tell.

It has been a great compliment to Dr Conolly's skill that since then the hand has stood up to some pretty harsh treatment and never worried me in the slightest.

Before and after the operation I became very much embroiled in the bitter war over Alan Jones's position as Australian coach, as the position came up for re-election the following February. I was not given to rushing off letters to newspaper editors or ringing up individual commentators and taking them to task over remarks they might have made, but I simply couldn't let the baseless and totally unfair criticism go unchallenged. John Swords wrote in the *Sunday Telegraph* that 'the coaching career of Alan Jones has been more useful in its wit and literacy rather than its football'. He contended that Jones inherited such a great team that even he (Swords) could have coached the Wallabies to the 1984 Grand Slam! In rebuffing his assertions, I labelled it uninformed drivel. Toby Jones made a similar attack in the now defunct Times on Sunday, when he said that Jones had 'severe limitations' as a coach, and I was so incensed that I even spent Christmas Day at my parents' farm at Goulburn writing a reply to him. The gist of both my attacks was that Jones didn't just fall upon a magnificent team. Steve Cutler was on the scrap-heap after the 1983 French tour. Bill Campbell wasn't even a reserve for Queensland. Nick Farr-Jones was plucked from the obscurity of second division. And David Codey's selection was controversial to everyone but the players and selectors. Yet Jones recognised their individual talents and then nurtured them. I also pointed out very clearly that under Jones the

Wallabies had achieved the two most notable achievements in the history of Australian Rugby—the 1984 Grand Slam and the 1986 Bledisloe Cup victory in New Zealand. To the credit of both newspapers, they published my letters.

I wasn't entering into the debate of who should be the next national coach—Jones, Bob Dwyer, Bob Templeton or Paul Dalton, all of whom looked like they'd have their hats in the ring come election day. I just wanted to see the truth written and justice done to Jonesy. My public utterances were merely about giving him a fair go and I'd do the same for anyone else in the same position.

The criticism that hurt most was from Mark Ella. It was unrelenting. I still don't know why Mark did it. Jones and he had been great friends before bad feeling developed between them, but his constant harping in the media really became very hard to take.

Dalton had his say too. He accused Jones—who almost certainly had a big hand in his getting the NSW coaching job in the first place—of putting pressure on him to choose the players he wanted. I could never imagine that happening. Dalton also issued this monumental challenge: 'Give me Andrew Leeds and Nick Farr-Jones and he (Jones) can pick any Australian side he wants. I'll have second pick and beat him . . . flog him.' The arrogance of the bloke was unbelievable. I just wish that match had eventuated because I'd have had no greater pleasure than playing for Jones and beating and smashing Dalton's team into absolute submission.

About that time a Brisbane newspaper conducted a poll among Australian players to see who they wanted as Australia's next national coach. This took the prize for being about the most destructive, senseless and divisive exercise anyone could have dreamed up, and I wouldn't have a bar of it. All it was going to do was split the Wallabies clean down the middle. Why any of my teammates took part I can't imagine, but the poll reportedly showed that only ten of the 31 players canvassed wanted Jones retained as coach.

On several occasions leading up to to February election date, I had talks with Jonesy over the issue. Topo Rodriguez and Steve Cutler were in on a few of these meetings. I told him that if he was basing his desire for the coaching job purely on emotion, then he should push ahead with it, he shouldn't allow the criticism to affect him. (I knew, though, that deep down he was bitterly hurt by it, not so much the general media harping, but Ella's barbs in particular. And David Campese was lobbying for Dwyer as well. Jonesy was angry at having two players whom he had supported so strongly turn against him.) On the other hand, I said that if he used logic, he should pull out of the race. He'd done more than any other Australian coach had ever done and his record would stand. He could walk away there and then with great honour. I thought for a while that he would follow this second course, but in the end the NSW Rugby Union mafia and his own pride pushed him into seeking the job. My public stance was that Jones and Dwyer were both very good candidates with excellent qualities and I wouldn't openly campaign for either man. I'd just been annoyed that Jonesy's coaching record hadn't been more clearly stated and appreciated.

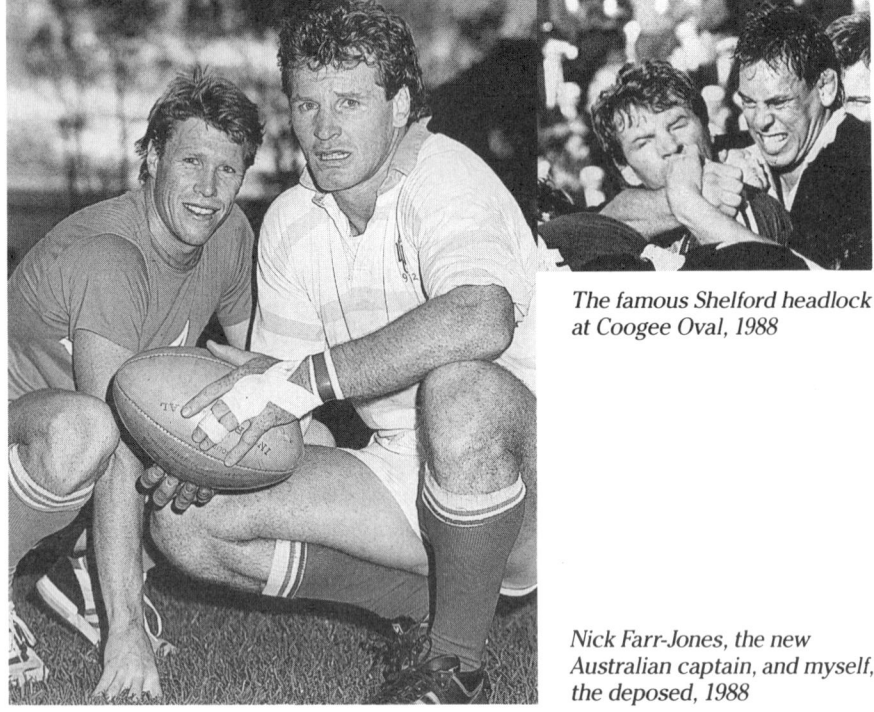

The famous Shelford headlock at Coogee Oval, 1988

Nick Farr-Jones, the new Australian captain, and myself, the deposed, 1988

By the time of the election, Dwyer reportedly had the support of the southern states and Jones of the NSW delegates. The balance of power apparently lay with the Queensland delegates and where they'd cast their votes when their own State coach Templeton was eliminated. But individuals don't always fill in ballot papers like they publicly say they will, and Dwyer won. In spite of Australia having won 89 of its 102 matches with Jones as coach, including three single-point losses to the All Blacks and another to Wales with only fourteen men, he had been unceremoniously dumped.

Asked my opinion on the election, I went into print as saying: 'What saddens me about the decision is that in the last two weeks there has

CONTROVERSY, CONTROVERSY, CONTROVERSY

been a campaign of mud-slinging directed at Alan Jones through various outlets of the media. And that has been done without any regard for the result he has achieved in Australian Rugby. I find the whole matter disgusting, with some of the things being written being so far from the truth it's not funny. It has been a cruel thing and I view it with some disbelief. People are going to get the wrong perspective of Jones's achievements as coach because of what has been written and said.'

On reflection, because of all the mud-slinging beforehand, Jonesy was better off out of it. He'd run his race. Besides, there was no doubt that by then there were significant divisions among the players about Jones, generated largely by the failed rebel tour of South Africa the previous year. Some players still held the view that Jones had plotted the abandonment of that tour because of his strong ties with certain administrators within the South African Rugby Board.

So Dwyer was given charge of the Australian Rugby team and Jonesy went about withdrawing from the scene completely. In fact, I don't remember having seen him at a game of Rugby since.

The earliest debate after Dwyer's election was who was going to be the Australian captain? Nick Farr-Jones, Michael Lynagh, or me?

A savage blow early in Dwyer's reign was the signing of young Ricky Stuart by the Canberra Raiders. I regarded him as the most exciting Australian Rugby player I'd seen since Michael O'Connor. The League contract, he tells me, was simply too good to refuse. I've got enormous time for Steamboat, he was fantastic in Argentina, and I was very sad when he turned pro, although I always felt with him that it was inevitable. His skills were very adaptable to League and it was gratifying to see him become a Wallaby before he switched.

On April 5, Australian Rugby lost one of its legends when Tony (Slaggy) Miller died suddenly, aged 59. A fantastic bloke. One of the best. Apart from Jeff Sayle, I've never met anyone who has given as much of his life to the game. He played 345 first-grade games for Manly and appeared in 41 Tests over an incredible fifteen years. That's some record. He was a tough man—among the very toughest I've ever encountered—and he never asked for or gave quarter. It was a very sad day when he went. In fact, I wouldn't believe it for a while. I simply couldn't accept that anyone as tough as Slaggy would die. I'll bet he has made himself captain and tight-head prop of the Heavenly XV and is now waiting for some old mates like Alan (Smacker) Cameron, Eddie Stapleton, John Thornett, Peter Johnson, Rob Heming, Ken Catchpole, Sayley and all the rest so he can get a game going.

I played in all the South Pacific championship matches in 1988, until the last of them between NSW and Queensland. Then I disappeared. I wasn't dropped or hurt for the big match of the domestic representative

Taking the ball up for Randwick with Tim Kava in support

season, but took a leave pass in order to play in the Monaco sevens on the French Riviera. My priorities might have seemed wrong, but I'd been playing interstate Rugby for nine or ten years and felt I'd had my share. I also spoke to the national selectors before going away to see if my Test selection would be jeopardised and they said it wouldn't. Given half a chance, they said, they'd be going themselves. I'd heard about this tournament the previous year from Bill Calcraft. He absolutely raved about it, so I actually rang the organisers and said if they were interested in having me, then I was interested in participating. An invitation came back for me to play for Monaco itself. Nick Farr-Jones was also going, to play with the Bahrain Warblers.

It was an incredible tournament. Eight teams, among them the French national team with the likes of Lagisquet, Blanco, Rodriguez and Camberabero. Our Monaco team contained French second division players, an American who was playing in France at the time and me. We were booked into a beautiful hotel on the waterfront at Monte Carlo, and at our first training run I made a stunning discovery. Not one of my teammates had ever played sevens football before! So I immediately tried to explain how, wondering meantime what the hell I'd let myself in for.

Farr-Jones was watching my dilemma from the touchline and laughing his head off.

The official dinner was held the night before the tournament at the Hotel de Paris in the presence of Prince Albert and, as we were the Monaco representatives, we had the privilege of spending some time during the night with him. It was quite an evening—the classiest dinner I've ever attended. And at one point some players from another team rushed up excitedly and called me outside to have a look at who was in one of the bars. It was Ringo Starr, although by then he was moving to the beat of a different drum and even having trouble staying on his bar stool. Dave Allen was also at his witty best as a face in the crowd at the dinner.

Those aware of the Monaco team's total lack of experience didn't give us any hope at all in the one-day tournament, but the local population didn't know that and they turned up expecting us to be a pretty starry outfit. When it got started, we somehow won our opening game and then, miracle of miracles, the second game as well. And then the third game. Our team manager was a massive French madam, and with each win she got more and more emotional and teary. So by this time she was virtually out of control. We were into the major semi-final and had to play the French national team! Prince Albert came over and told us that he couldn't wait for the game, but would come back to watch us in the final. 'Fat chance, mate, of that happening,' I thought. So out we went, our team of spare parts, to play against seven of France's famous Rugby internationals. As you might expect they were immediately all over us. But by now my mob had started to understand the principles of sevens football and our young froggies were pretty keen to show the Test players that they weren't entirely hopeless. Slowly we started to climb back at them, eventually took the lead and, blow me down, if we didn't win. The whole place was stunned. Our manager was an emotional wreck. For the final, not only was Prince Albert there, but he'd brought dad back with him too, Prince Rainier, and they sat together in the Royal box. We were the heroes of the principality. In the final we were up against Nick's team, the Bahrain Warblers, which also contained the likes of Murray Mexted and Jamie Salmon. But we'd given so much to the semi-final that we were very much a spent force and were well beaten. But it was a fantastic effort by our side and had stunned everybody. At the presentations later, I apologised to the two princes for not being able to win the tournament for them and then gave Prince Albert an Australian Rugby jersey as a memento. So if ever you're over there and see a handsome young guy walking around the Riviera in one of our jerseys, you'll know who it is.

That night I rang coach Bob Dwyer in Sydney. I was anxious to know the situation with the match between Australia and a World XV at

Concord Oval on 15 May. If there was a chance of my not making the team, then I'd stay in Monaco for a few days and do some work. He told me candidly that I wasn't included and David Carter was in my place. And the new Australian captain was Nick Farr-Jones. I couldn't believe it. Australian captain one season and nothing the next. It was the quickest roller-coaster ride I'd ever been on. When I hung up I was shocked and furious. I headed back down to where many of the tournament players were having a drink and they wanted to know why I'd been axed. I realised Dwyer hadn't given me an explanation, so I went back to my room and rang again. By this stage I'd regained my senses and really climbed into him. He tried to explain the reasons. Basically, he thought my form wasn't as good as it could have been. After the call I headed off to a local nightclub with a great mate of mine, Greg Przybylski, who lives over there maintaining the yachts of the world's millionaires. It didn't take long to experience a new shock when the bill came and we found we'd been charged $US30 for a can of beer! After thinking twice about decking the barman, I headed for the famous Casino to try to win some roulette money to offset the cost of the drinks, which I succeeded in doing. Then we went off to another nightclub, became involved with the French national team and a bottle of Scotch, and I finally staggered home about six in the morning. I was so pissed off with everything at that stage that I'd given up the idea of working there for a few days and just wanted to get home. When I got to my room, my American teammate woke to tell me Dwyer had rung me and that I was back in the side, but as vice-captain and not captain. I immediately rang Dwyer's office and left a message that I had received his news, but was now unavailable. Then I packed my gear, Przybylski and I jumped in the BMW that he had hired and somehow safely negotiated the winding road down to Nice. There we said farewell, and I caught a flight home via New York.

On the Continental Airlines flight to New York, I decided to retire from Test Rugby and actually scribbled down on some airline notepaper the options I faced when I got home. Did I stick to my intention to retire and explain why? If my unavailability was not accepted, do I play in the match on Sunday and then retire? Or if it's not accepted, do I just retire there and then? In New York, I rang Alan Jones to see what was in the media about the Test team. He had the surprising information that I was still in the team as vice-captain and the newspaper headlines were 'Poidevin Gets Axe As Aussie Skipper'. Dwyer was quoted as saying: 'He (Poidevin) didn't express any disappointment whatsoever and said he wanted to cement his place in the Australian team and that the captaincy was very much the lesser of his worries.' That's simply not true at all and I don't know how Dwyer ever got that impression. I told Jonesy the full story and, as someone who's always wanting truth and justice, he said he

One of the hardest days of my life: announcing my retirement from international Rugby, 16 May 1988

wasn't going to let it slip and would tell the full story on his 2UE program that very morning. I objected strongly to his doing this, but he wouldn't be deterred.

By the time I arrived home the selection fiasco and my fury was all over the media. The Australian selectors found the blow torch being applied to them by every Tom, Dick and Harry in sympathy with me for having being dumped altogether and then resurrected as vice-captian. I was upset by all the publicity, but Nick Farr-Jones told the media: 'If he didn't want this in the press then he made a bit of a blue mentioning this to a friend of his.' I certainly hadn't rung Jonesy with the intention of having it splashed everywhere and was pissed off that the story emerged the way it did. At the same time I felt sorry for Bob Dwyer, who was trying to prepare a Test team and all this wasn't making his job any easier.

All this time I still hadn't said anything publicly about my decision to retire. That would occur after Sunday's match.

In the dressing-room before the match I've never been so emotional. This was it. My last game for Australia after 47 Test appearances. I was sad, extremely angry and very determined to go out with full glory. I really got stuck into the World XV boys and thoroughly enjoyed a fantastic game, which we won 42-38. Brian Smith gave a remarkable exhibition with seven goals from seven shots, two drop goals and a try for 26 points on his own. In the last few minutes they weren't beads of perspiration in the corners of my eyes. I was terribly sad to think it was my last game, and at home that night the hardest thing was taking off my Australian blazer and thinking that I'd never wear it again.

The next morning I organised for my PR mate John Fordham to call a press conference at my office at Grosvenor Place in the city and informed the media of my decision to retire. I said my personal goal had been to retain the captaincy in the series against England and New Zealand that season. 'But in view of the recent selection of the Australian team, which included losing the captaincy, I reassessed the situation and decided that I should control my own destiny at this stage of my career. Hence my decision to retire forthwith from the Test arena. I still thought I had a great deal to offer, particularly against the All Blacks as I had played against them so many times.' I emphasised that my retirement wasn't 'sour grapes', but I'd simply had enough after a fantastic run. What I didn't say was that the phone calls from Monaco had shown me that my Test position was under grave threat. One thing I never wanted to do was finish on the reserves' bench, as happened with former Australian skipper Tony Shaw and All Black captain Andy Dalton.

So the curtains came down on my Test career, though not my Rugby. I captained NSW to a 23-12 win over England and was simply amazed at the weakness of England in the forwards. There was a decent old dust-up at the final whistle between Peter Kay and their prop Gareth Chilcott, and had there been video evidence the Pom would have been cooling his heels for weeks to come. I was nothing more than an interested onlooker when Australia defeated England 22-16 in the first Test at Ballymore and then tied up the series with a much more convincing 28-8 victory at Concord Oval. I was a television commentator for the second Test, but this new challenge didn't bring the same satisfaction as being out there, giving and taking punishment.

It was interesting to see David Campese on the wing in both Tests when he hadn't played domestically at all that season. He had been playing in Italy, but just one phone call to him from this end and he came running back. What of the other players who had battled throughout the South Pacific championship and then found him walking in? It stunk, and was simply not fair. The selectors should not allow Campese or anybody else to walk in and out of the Test team at will. The non-selection of prop Peter Kay in the first Test was also disappointing. He'd done everything to justify being picked, but I felt that he was being punished for some minor transgressions early in his career.

Randwick had an Australian club championship match against Brothers in Brisbane early that season and it just happened to correspond with the opening State of Origin match. Not that there was anything wrong with that, except that the miserable hotel Brothers put us in was just up the road from Lang Park, where the match was in progress when we arrived. We had four players jammed into our room, there were no curtains on the windows, no restaurant, no telephone and we lay awake all night listening to every drunken League bum in creation yahooing outside our bedroom windows. It was an unbelievable experience, but gave us all the motivation we needed for the match, which we duly won 27-9.

I was back up there again soon afterwards as NSW captain for the second interstate game against Queensland. We had won the first 37-15 at Concord Oval and we won that second game as well by 27-18—the first time since 1971 we'd won both games. But I remember thinking the dressing-room later was like a morgue. Our State coach Dick Laffan took his Rugby very seriously and, while someone like Jeff Sayle would have been performing and laughing his head off, Dick was as sombre as a parish priest.

I had come off towards the end of the interstate match with a strained medial ligament, which left me in grave doubt for the mid-week game between Randwick and the All Blacks. Having the premiers play a touring team was something completely new, and I had my heart really set on this particular game at Coogee Oval. Here was my own club team facing the greatest Rugby machine in the world—they'd picked virtually their Test outfit—and I wasn't going to miss being a part of it. Deep down I couldn't see how we could get within a bull's roar of them but that really didn't matter.

The atmosphere at Coogee Oval that day was marvellous. It seemed every Rugby supporter in Sydney had turned up to see if Randwick could at least dent the All Black armour. There was a mixture of curiosity and genuine support for us. Six minutes before kickoff they had to shut the gates with 9250 people inside and no room for another person.

At the kickoff our pack swept forward and climbed into the All Blacks and, right there and then, I thought 'fantastic'. I knew my mates were going to give it everything they had and you could immediately see the shock in the eyes of the All Blacks. When Lloyd Walker scored our first try out wide early in the game the whole crowd went berserk. I thought I

After another tough encounter

was dreaming. But then Grant Fox knocked over a field goal and some penalty goals and the All Blacks slowly pushed ahead. Yet we were really frustrating and angering them, and that was never more evident than when I infiltrated their side of a maul and grabbed the ball. Well, their skipper Wayne Shelford went berserk, grabbed me in a vicious headlock and tried to reef my head off while my arms were pinned. He held on for so long that I lost my breath and almost passed out. When the maul finally broke up I'd even temporarily lost my voice, but neither the referee nor either of the touch judges took even the slightest notice. Afterwards, Shelford and I had a laugh about it, but there was no question that he should have been penalised. In the end we were beaten 25-9 but it was one of the most courageous contests I've been associated with in my whole Rugby career. A team of virtual unknowns challenging the All Blacks and taking them right to the wire. When it was all over, I'd enjoyed the game so much that I found I had a real taste for wanting to play these New Zealanders again. Instinct seemed to indicate that the All Blacks still had

CONTROVERSY, CONTROVERSY, CONTROVERSY

a healthy respect for me, which stirred my ambition. I also thought that if Randwick could be so competitive against them, then so could Australia in the three Test matches. But what the heck, I was retired.

The following Sunday night I was at home getting stirred up as I watched a video of this match against the All Blacks when I was interrupted by the phone ringing. It was Bob Dwyer. Steve Lidbury and Jeff Miller were both injured and would I come out of retirement and play in the first Test against the All Blacks? I thought about it for the best part of ... ten seconds. Of course I would. I hadn't realised how much I'd miss the playing atmosphere until forced to sit through the England Tests. International Rugby was more a part of my life than I'd realised.

So the next day the media was back at my office at Grosvenor Place hearing all about my comeback, 42 days after listening to my emotional farewell to the game. I spoke of my delight at being 'back among the family'. I was looking forward to being back with my mates and, with them, facing the challenge of the All Blacks.

From the theatrics of my return, it was back to reality very quickly when the All Blacks flogged us 32-7 in the first Test at Concord Oval. They were simply much better than us on the day. The selectors made a number of changes for the second Test. Andrew Leeds was dropped and David Campese moved to fullback, outside-centre Gary Ella and lock David Carter were also dumped, while Julian Gardner was switched to the unfamiliar lock position. They weren't the most logical decisions, especially with Campo. He may be one of the great wingers of the world, but he's no Test fullback. Leedsy was always a much more gutsy, reliable player and I preferred him any day.

Then when we assembled in Brisbane, Gardner was ill and Bob Dwyer wanted to reinstate Carter. But I stepped in. I told him the player who really should be there was Tim Gavin. He had a few centimetres on Carter in the lineouts and Carter had found it very hard in the first Test to adjust to playing against the All Blacks. He had got lost in action a bit. Dwyer took the advice of me and some of the other senior forwards, and so the Eastern Suburbs forward won his first Test cap. I also said how worried I was about Campo at fullback, and when Michael Lynagh withdrew with injury, all the backs moved in one, Campo went back to wing and Leedsy returned to fullback. The confidence of the whole side was lifted by the inclusion of Gavin and Leeds and was reflected in the way we played.

It remains one of the great Test matches I've been part of. Australia went berserk in the first half and took the All Blacks by surprise. It was not until right near the end that our discipline and fitness were found wanting. The All Blacks had to unleash a huge effort to scrounge a 19-all draw.

Stung by that draw, the All Blacks took it out on the badly weakened NSW team the following weekend. In a game of aggression and violence, they hammered us well and truly 42-6.

In the third and final Test, it was amazing stuff. Whenever you're playing the All Blacks, if your scoreboard is intact after twelve or fifteen minutes then you'll more than likely go on to win the game. If you can weather that early storm and maintain composure then you've always got a good chance. But after that danger period we were down 12-0, and in that position it becomes almost impossible to compete against them. There was no doubt that the very questionable try scored by Bruce Deans in that critical period was an immense body-blow to our chances. Right from the outset, the pace of the All Blacks was unbelievable. We found ourselves running from bushfire to bushfire simply trying to contain them. They went on to win 30-9 and I don't think I've ever been so tired after a game.

Work commitments prevented me from going on the Wallaby tour of England, Scotland and Italy at the end of the season, when the team had very mixed fortunes. Typically, the Wallabies showed them how to play the running game, scoring 438 points on the 15-match tour with only 236 against. But they didn't always put it together at the important times, as shown when they were as wobbly as jelly against England. As the tour progressed so did the team's play improve. They won all four matches in Scotland, including a 32-13 win in the international at Murrayfield which was described by many, including Bob Dwyer, as probably the best display on the tour. Watching that game back home on television made me very proud to be an Australian. It was no coincidence that the improved performances coincided with the late arrival as a replacement of Michael Lynagh, who gave the inside backs far more experience and composure.

NEVER SAY DIE

I'd made a strong commitment to myself to spend the whole of the 1989 season playing with Randwick—for a change. I'd spent most of my years with the club in an absentee role while tied up with representative teams, and before I retired I wanted to have at least one full season wearing the myrtle green jersey. Yet because I still had a yearning for the big time I made myself available to play for Australia, though not NSW. I know Dick Laffan wanted me to play for the State team, but I didn't want to get involved with all the representative matches in the South Pacific championship and the training out at Concord Oval which that would necessitate.

I was more than happy to spend my training nights with the Randwick boys out at Latham Park, with some Test appearances thrown in if the selectors wanted me. It might have seemed pretentious making myself available only for Australia but, at 30 years of age and with 50 Tests behind me, if people didn't know by then how I played then they'd never know.

Another factor which influenced me to want a more stable season was that the stock market was extremely quiet, brokers were doing it hard, and it was necessary for me to devote as much time as possible to McNall & Hordern Limited, the stockbroking company in which I was a director and equity-holder.

I had also been approached in the second half of 1988 about becoming chairman of a new sports scholarship foundation at my old University of NSW, a position that was to demand much more time than was ever suggested. Initially I was pencilled in for the role of figure-head, requiring a few hours each week, but once involved it was easy to see that the professional fund-raisers were failing in every way. So they were quickly given their marching orders and Bruce Bland, Bruce Miller, Peter Harrison and I worked our butts off to get the whole show on a strong footing, culminating in a highly successful fund-raising dinner for 700 people one Friday night in February at the University. At the end of it all we had the Ben Lexcen Sports Scholarship Foundation.

We thought long and hard about a name for the scholarships and when Ben Lexcen's name was mentioned it was a unanimous choice by the committee provided the Lexcen family agreed to his name being used. Ben Lexcen was not only a great yacht-designer and sportsman (many would not know that he represented Australia at the 1972 Munich Olympics), but successfully combined these skills with academic brilliance. And a huge tribute to the man is that much of the theory he needed for his designs was self-taught. Our view was that if the scholarships could produce just one more Ben Lexcen then our ideals would be fulfilled.

My involvement with the scholarships was strongly motivated by my own experiences at the University of NSW, where I learnt to appreciate the tremendous pressures placed upon any student striving to succeed in a chosen sport and an academic discipline. It's a great pity that a significant percentage of our extremely talented school sportsmen and women discontinue very promising sporting careers when they reach university, because they don't have the financial and moral support to do both.

My work with the scholarships also taught me a valuable lesson: while Australians have a richer love for sporting success than many other nationalities, when it comes to putting their hands in their pockets to provide support then in many cases they are found wanting.

Nowadays when I see the terrific young people being awarded these scholarships, all the hard work that went into getting them established seems worthwhile. But it hasn't stopped there by a long shot and we've still got to raise a large amount of money to support these gifted young Australians.

Co-incidentally the big fund-raising dinner to launch the foundation was held the night before the Kiama Sevens tournament. So without much sleep, I had to drive down the South Coast the next morning and turn out for Randwick in what is traditionally the last tournament the selectors watch before choosing the Australian Sevens team. What happened was that I'd have a game, then curl up somewhere for a snooze, have another game, then another snooze. Our coach Bob Dwyer wanted to know what the hell was wrong with me that I couldn't keep my eyes open between games. Nevertheless I played well enough to make the Australian team and thought what a great buzz it was to begin the year with that honour. Some people might have thought I was getting too long in the tooth for sevens, but I wasn't a selector and my Rip Van Winkle performance at Kiama obviously hadn't affected my form too much.

We bombed out of the International Sevens at Concord Oval in March, when we played very poorly, and then headed off to the Hong Kong Sevens. I've always loved playing in the annual sevens event over in the colony, because it generates one of the greatest atmospheres you can ever experience in Rugby. Even though we lifted our game tremendously from Sydney, we again lost the final 22-10 to the superb New Zealand team.

Then it was back to club Rugby. I was really looking forward to playing regularly with the club and being coached by Jeff Sayle. He's a fantastic bloke and I feel tremendous loyalty to him. I wouldn't think twice about walking over hot coals for Jeffrey Leonard Sayle. The other nice thing was having Mark Ella back with the club after a four-year retirement. He was taking a big risk coming back after so long and carrying the extra weight that he had put on. There were many watching for him to fall. But it didn't take long for all of us at the club to realise that nothing had changed—except the size of his waistline.

In the past Mark and I had been captain and vice-captain of Australia for a number of seasons and, during that period, had enjoyed some fantastic highs and difficult lows. Yet in his retirement Mark had at times written a lot of tripe as a newspaper columnist which loomed as a barrier to our friendship and to our playing together. But I thought about it a lot when he resumed playing and determined not to let anything come between us. He had been a great friend and a truly great player. So I acted as if the years 1985–1988 had simply never happened, and on that basis the legendary Mark Ella and I went on to have a marvellous last fling together at club Rugby.

He wasn't the only Ella in the news at the start of the 1989 season, because his twin Glen stunned everyone by announcing that he was changing clubs and going to Manly. Within Randwick that was seen in the same context as Andrew Peacock suddenly turning to socialism or Paul Keating discovering humility. They couldn't believe it. I'm still not sure why Glen left the club he'd been with all his career, but there sure were plenty of rumours floating about at the time.

I still wanted to play against the British Lions on their approaching tour, because I'd never played against them. But whether the selectors would want me was another story entirely. I hadn't been on the tour of England, Scotland and Italy at the end of the previous season—the first time since 1980 that I'd not been part of an Australian touring side—and for a change I was very much on the periphery of the international scene. I was determined to concentrate on playing for Randwick and just let things happen as far as being chosen for Australia was concerned.

In May, Sayley asked me to captain Sydney against Country, because he was coach, and I did. It was great fun and we absolutely flogged them. A month later NSW ran into injury problems before the game against the Lions at North Sydney Oval and again I was asked would I play. Again, I jumped at it. It was a fantastic place to play Rugby (why didn't the NSW Rugby Union make more use of this beautiful ground instead of redeveloping Concord Oval which is nowhere near the centre of Rugby interest in Sydney?), and the atmosphere was absolutely magic. I enjoyed the game immensely even though the Lions pipped us on the post by 23-21. It was a great challenge for me, because I was out to show that I'd earned my run in the State team, which I think I did judging from all reports, and at the end of the day it also gave me a real desire to play these blokes again. But young Scott Gourley had played extremely well in the UK and was the logical partner for (Ginger) Miller and (The Bird) Tuynman in the Australian back-row for the first Test at the Sydney Football Stadium.

Still, I did play that day—for Randwick in the curtain-raiser against Eastern Suburbs—in a match which just about tore our club apart. When the Australian Rugby Football Union decided that the two leading Sydney clubs should play before the Test match, the players were tremendously excited. Then I walked into training one night and was told the club committee had decided against it. It thought that if we played the curtain-raiser then the club would miss out on its takings at Coogee Oval for that particular game. It was also worried that players in our other grades wouldn't be able to get into the Sydney Football Stadium to see the game. I immediately spoke up on behalf of the players and told Sayley that we wanted a say on the matter. The players were called together, the fors and againsts explained, and then we voted almost unanimously to play at the stadium. The decision was relayed to the committee, which didn't take too kindly at all to what was effectively a players' revolt. It didn't have any option other than to accept the decision, but was my name mud! Hell, all I saw was it being a fantastic chance to play Easts in a local derby before a huge crowd, a great chance to promote club Rugby and to give those players who might never play in such an atmosphere that once-in-a-lifetime chance. As it happened, the game was a marvellous experience for everyone concerned and we ended up beating Easts.

After Australia won that first Test very impressively I naturally wasn't mentioned as a selection possibility, but after the Lions dished it up to us 19-12 in the fiery second Test in Brisbane there were calls for me to be included for the third Test. I thought the selectors might have recalled me, and I really wanted to play for Australia at the Sydney Football Stadium before a packed house. But it wasn't to be, and when I wasn't chosen I was bitterly disappointed. On the day it was terribly hard being among the 39401 spectators and watching Australia beaten in the deciding Test by a much more convincing margin than the 19-18 scoreline indicated. Something was well and truly missing from our game and it was very sad to watch.

The Lions finished their tour a week later with a game against the Anzac XV in Brisbane, with Australia and New Zealand supposedly combining for what potentially would be a finale rivalling the Barbarians' game at the end of a British Isles tour. But as the game approached so too did the temperamental New Zealanders begin withdrawing for any number of reasons. It could have been a fantastic experience for all if we'd had the best players from both nations involved. If the New Zealanders ever do come to the party and fully support this marvellous idea, then these games should become a regular feature of the itinerary of touring teams to this country.

Having lost the Lions series, the next milestone for Australia was the Bledisloe Cup Test against the All Blacks in Auckland in early August. Again, calls went out for my recall and this time when the Test team was announced I was included. It was absolutely fantastic. Having started the season intent on remaining a club player it was extraordinary to think I would be up against my old foes at Eden Park. But what a challenge, given the team that had been chosen! Phil Kearns, our reserve-grade hooker at Randwick, and Tony Daly, the prop who had been plucked from nowhere at Gordon, were also included, which was really radical stuff by the selectors. I was going to have to provide a fair amount of inspiration and guidance for these youngsters, because they were being tossed in at the deep end with rocks around their necks.

All the Rugby happenings at that time helped take my mind off a very unhappy work situation. McNall & Hordern Limited was put up for sale because of the collapse of the Spedley Group, with its losses of more than half a billion dollars. To witness at close hand the unbelievable dishonesty and deception by certain people associated with that group destroyed my trust in human nature for a while. To see a lot of people's lives dislocated by the greed of others was a real lesson in life and Rugby gave me an outlet in this very stressful situation. Asked then what was the greatest remedy for stress I would honestly have said it was getting out to training on Tuesday and Thursday nights at Latham Park with Super Coach Sayle and all the players. That way I forgot my problems for a few hours. It confirmed my view that you can readily mix sport and business and one can feed off the other. I can't understand why some people cut themselves off from competitive sport once they begin to rise in the business world, as I've constantly found that mixing the two has given me a better balance in life.

When we arrived in Auckland I asked specifically if I could room with Phil Kearns so I could help him. The first day we trained in lashing wind and intermittent rain in the middle of a racecourse and, for a while, I wondered what the hell I was doing back in all that. But I soon got back into the rhythm and had dismissed any doubts by the next day when we trained in an opposed session with John Quick's Australian under-21 team.

By the morning of the Test match I sensed that our new prop Tony Daly was finding the whole thing very difficult. He was very strong physically, but to throw him and Kearns in against the All Blacks in the front-row was obviously playing on his mind. So I called Daly and Kearns to my room for a little talk. Just the three of us. I told them: 'Listen fellas. Forget all this superficial bullshit, boasting that you're all ready to go and that it won't worry you a bit. Dales ... Kearnsy ... you're shitting yourselves and, to tell you the truth, so am I! This is your first Test cap and it's my 51st and I'm just as nervous as you are. You've just got to remember that it's only 80 minutes. There's life afterwards. Sure, it's going to be tough while it's on but these Kiwis aren't supermen in black. There's six mates to help you in the scrums and lineouts and thirteen of us in the whole team who are going to help you fight this battle all the way. And remember, we're all going to be doing it for Australia.' When they walked out I could sense them saying to themselves, 'Imagine Poido feeling that way too ... it doesn't make me feel so bad after all.' It was one of the special moments in my Rugby career to be able to help those young colts that way.

I wasn't kidding them. I'd come back from virtual club Rugby to play this international and some people probably doubted my ability to perform. Half an hour before the Test, as we sat in the claustrophobic dressing-room at Eden Park, it occurred to me that 'I've got better things to do with my life than this ... what am I doing here?' But I immediately dismissed these negative thoughts and told myself that I really wanted to be there and had fought hard all year to get this chance in one more Test match.

When the team stood in the middle of Eden Park in a circle, with our arms around each other, and we started singing 'Australians all let us rejoice ...' I gained tremendous inner strength. It really switched me on. When the whistle went the old blood was pumping at a thousand litres a minute and I relished the fact that I was back on the battleground I knew so well.

It was to be one of the best Test matches I'd experienced. The young Australian players were under enormous pressure early, but as the game progressed they started to come good and the whole team responded to it. The feeling was fantastic. We were down only 6-3 at halftime and the players could smell victory. We could see cracks appearing in the invincible All Black armour. As the second half wore on we became more and more enthusiastic, our scrum was starting to make life very difficult for the opposition and it became a Test where a draw would have been a very fair result. But in the end, New Zealand did what they've always done over the past five years and finished very, very strongly. They lifted the tempo, created a last, magnificent rolling maul, prop Richard Loe scored under the posts and they won 24-12. On reflection, I think Nick Farr-Jones and Michael Lynagh should have run the ball more than they did and given us the chance to score more tries. Nevertheless it was a great game, very enjoyable, and it proved to me that I could still mix it with the best of them. Above all else, the fact was that I had enjoyed it immensely. So I decided there and then that I was going to keep my options open in 1990 as far as Test Rugby was concerned. Just because I was 30 and had played 51 Tests didn't have to mean the end of the road. It's probably one of the problems with Australian Rugby. Players such as me should be encouraged to keep playing, not discouraged. The country's got such a lack of depth of top players that it can't afford to lose prematurely those of us who do have a lot of experience.

Back home, I finished off what was probably the most enjoyable club season I've ever had. I obviously played pretty well, because I finished up figuring in all the awards going. I shared *The Sydney Morning Herald* best-and-fairest competition with my Randwick teammate Brad Burke, but then came the biggest reward of all when I won the Rothmans Medal, which had been resurrected after a two-year absence. It was a magnificent feeling in the week of the grand final hearing my name read out before that huge black-tie crowd at the Sydney Hilton International as the outright winner. I polled 24 points, beating Sydney University second-rower David Dix (21 points) for the solid gold medal, which is held in trust until I retire.

Victory is sweet and the smiles tell the story after Randwick's 1989 grand final win. l to r: Myself, Brad Burke and the reborn Mark Ella

The season finished with us winning another premiership when we beat Eastwood 19-6 in the grand final at Concord Oval. The Woods had never won a first-grade premiership and 95 per cent of Rugby fans wanted them to get up. But they played their grand final when they whacked us in the major semi-final. On the only day that counted, we had the right mental attitude, we tore their scrum apart and once again they went home empty-handed. For Randwick, it was our third successive premiership and our ninth in twelve years. And it was our thirteenth straight grand final. Some record!

While on the subject of Randwick, I'm often asked what it is that makes it Australia's most successful Rugby club and one which stands comparison with other great clubs like Cardiff, Swansea, Llanelli, Richmond, Petone and Stellenbosch University. In fact, we dominate one of the world's strongest competitions. Just look at what happened in the 1989 Sydney competition. We scored 1168 points in winning the club championship. Who was second? Daylight. Third was Warringah with 910 points.

I've been in the situation of having played against the Galloping Greens when I was with the University of NSW, and subsequently with them. At Wales, we had all the spirit in the world but not enough technical skills, and our visits to Coogee Oval were never very happy. I could never get over how Randwick were always so confident and cocky. I generally found myself opposing this tough nut named John Maxwell who kept belting me all afternoon, which I hadn't been used to. And the unruly mob down there would hang over the fence like a herd of Cyclopses and cast all kinds of aspersions about your parents, your wives and girlfriends, your being a student, (in my case) the colour of your hair, and any other physical traits you might have. They also branded every referee a flaming cheat and reckoned every game would be better off without him.

Then I joined them, and seeing the Galloping Greens from the inside provided another perspective altogether.

While Randwick might be admired and respected by other clubs for all our success, it's obvious that there's a lot of jealousy towards us, and even intense dislike. Let me try to explain why we're so successful and at the same time so unpopular.

Throughout our grades we have pretty much the same ability as clubs like Warringah, Manly and Eastwood. But the critical factor is that all teams, from first-grade right through to seventh-grade and the Colts, are indoctrinated with the club's famous attacking style of play, which basically means running flat and close-passing. Everybody has it drilled into him, which means that players can move freely from grade to grade without any problems of fitting in. Another important factor is that every player has the will to win constantly thumped into him by the coaches. Every Randwick team runs onto the field wanting and expecting victory. I've often played against teams more physically gifted than Randwick, but our players are so hypnotised by the winning drive that more often than not it pulls us through and creates a confidence, even an arrogance, in the way we play.

The club also has a marvellous administration. Training is very well organised and all the officials, whether they be team managers, gear stewards, trainers, the club doctor, physiotherapists or the old diggers who run the barbecue on training nights, do their job super-efficiently. The administration therefore contributes to the tremendous club spirit, and the enthusiasm within the club is second to none. It's a pleasure to play there. I actually love going to training. I'll finish a hard day at the office, but find myself uplifted by the attitude of everybody at training. It has honestly been a real plus in my life being part of Randwick Rugby Club.

Often we're branded as bad losers at Randwick. Maybe we are, but that's simply because losing's not a word in our vocabulary. We hate to run second and obviously show it. Plenty of people also reckon we're unsociable, that we don't fraternise nearly enough with the opposition after a game or visit their licensed clubs in large numbers like most clubs do. Again, I don't deny that. But Randwick's not a social Rugby club. Players join us to play Rugby and win premierships. At other clubs the social side of the game generally takes a higher priority, which can affect a player's attitude. Win a premiership at Randwick and we have a huge night at the licensed club on Saturday night and a few drinks on Sunday and then that's it. Yet when Manly won the premiership in 1983 the celebrations went on for several months. The difference is that we expect to win grand finals, so when they're over the euphoria dies down very quickly.

Of all the characters I've bumped into on my Rugby odyssey, none compares with Jeff Sayle, who has been with the club in a playing or working capacity for 40 years. He started playing with Randwick at under-sevens and went on to play 379 grade games, including 179 in first-grade, and represented Australia at breakaway. In 1964 he also became the licensed club's assistant manager and in 1985 the secretary-manager. He has also coached at every level in the club. He lives and breathes Randwick Rugby like no-one else, and even wears what he calls his lucky underpants in the club's myrtle green colours every time we play in a grand final! Sayley's not only a great lover of Rugby, but a great lover of people. You wouldn't meet a nicer, funnier or more generous person—he's undoubtedly one of the very special Rugby people in this world.

Some of the stories concerning Sayley have become part of the game's folklore. Back in his early twenties, the legendary Randwick coach Wally Meagher advised him to gargle a mouthful of sherry before every game to help increase his saliva. Except that young Sayle liked the taste so much that he started swallowing the mouthful until eventually it reached the stage where he had a middy of sherry before every game!

He was once asked for some help by the coach of a schoolboy team, which had all the talent in the world but some disruptive rascals in the front-row who constantly distracted the other players. Sayley went along to training and found the front-rowers misbehaving as usual. So he called one of them over and the kid asked: 'What do you want?' This, said Sayle, who then reached into his coat pocket, pulled out an egg, and smashed it on the kid's forehead. His cheeky mates came over and started laughing their heads off, at which Sayle produced two more eggs and did the same thing. They didn't cause problems again that night, but two days later when he went back to help them again the whole team turned up with eggs and pelted Sayley until he eventually looked like a giant omelette.

Once he had his car nicked and it was found by the police outside Matraville High, the school which produced the Ella brothers but which is in a notoriously tough neighbourhood. Next time he was refereeing the school he stopped play in the opening minutes just as one of the Matraville High boys made a break and was flying for the goal-line and awarded a penalty to the opposition. The Matraville High kids began screaming blue murder because there was no apparent infringement. When the captain raced up and demanded to know what the penalty was for, Sayley coolly replied: 'For pinching my car.' Since then he leaves his car at the school unlocked.

Another time he was coaching Navy against a team from some visiting Japanese warships. At halftime Navy was ahead 36-0 and an aide came across to him and said, at the Admiral's request, could he tell his team to slow down as the score was becoming embarrassing. Sayley said to tell the Admiral to go play with his sailing boats in his bathtub, or words to that effect, and Navy proceeded to double the score in the second half.

Then there was the occasion when he returned from an overseas trip and was told by the Customs officer that he couldn't bring into Australia the two bottles of Scotch he was carrying. One litre was the limit. So he opened one of the 750 ml bottles, drank the lot and walked through. The Customs officer just watched in amazement.

The players love playing jokes on Sayley. Once he received a note saying he was wanted for an appearance on Ron Casey's Sunday morning television program. So he dolled himself up in a clean shirt, club tie and blazer, and drove all the way to the studios. He got Casey out of the makeup room, told him he was all ready for the show and Casey informed him that he'd never heard of him, let alone want him for the show. Even before the last grand final, he walked over to the forwards on the Thursday night to help and was told to scram. 'That's funny,' he said, 'because the backs just told me to come over here ...'

John Maxwell's another unique Randwick character. He was playing when Ben Hur was whipping his chariot around the Colisseum and is still going strong. He was an inspiration to me when I joined the club and still is. I've never seen anyone in my life who can equal his enthusiasm at training or during a game. Even on the wettest, coldest and windiest nights at Latham Park he's full of fire, he's full of enthusiasm, he's full of support for the players around him. And I'm sure everyone within the club draws strength from John Maxwell. Behind that oft-mended face is something very special.

Like Sayley and Maxey, I too have been in Rugby now for a long while. Once, I almost turned my back on it. It was at the end of 1983. I was doing it pretty tough financially. I had just finished university and didn't have a bob in my pocket. Rugby League's the high-profile football code in Sydney and there's not a Rugby player who doesn't imagine at some time or another how he might fare at it. I certainly did. So when I had an approach from Eastern Suburbs Rugby League Club I went along to the licensed club and had a talk with Ron Jones about the possibility of playing League. He made me an offer, in fact quite an outstanding one, of $75 000 a year.

Because I didn't have any money it was terribly tempting. I enlisted a solicitor to help with the contractual arrangements and after we worked those out it was up to me to make up my mind. So I went off and thought about it. I knew that the short-term cash would be fantastic, as would the challenge of playing League to satisfy my ego. But countering this was the fact that I'd made many great friends in Rugby, had seen many fabulous places and could still see much of all that still ahead of me. I really didn't want to cut myself off from it. Financially, the long-term view was that I was also in a business where the potential was there to make big bucks. I felt I was going places in stockbroking. So after much hard thought I declined Easts' offer. I did think very seriously about it, but the pluses of staying in Rugby simply outnumbered those of going to League.

I'm not sorry now that I stayed in Rugby. I love the game. It's the greatest game of all, although the realities and pressures of modern living, or even Rugby-starved South Africa, might eventually force it into becoming professional. If that occurs I could foresee a structure like cricket, where the representative players are paid and the club players compete for the enjoyment.

In that scenario Rugby League worldwide would be squeezed so much that it could disappear entirely. I simply don't see how League could survive in such direct competition with Rugby, which is now played by huge numbers everywhere in the world. Why would you want to play League here and maybe overseas in only England, France or New Zealand when you could play Rugby for the same money and go to literally hundreds of countries.

If these changes were ever to take place, it would be vital for the game that it always remained amateur at club level, because that is Rugby's greatest strength. I fantasise at times about not having any commitments and simply wandering the world and playing the game, walking into clubs in America, France, Italy, Canada, Germany, New Zealand, South America, Fiji, South Africa, Britain, Japan. Or even going to places like the Philippines, Sweden, the Ivory Coast, Bahrain, Israel. The list goes on and on. Rugby's all about friendships. It's a real brotherhood out there. Any club would immediately take you under its wing and you'd have a job, a home, buddies ... they'd take care of you simply because you're a Rugby player. It's a wonderful game and people don't get paid for playing it; they play it simply because they love it.

A really good game of Rugby is very hard to beat as a spectacle. It's a real thinking game. Another of its great appeals is that it caters for individuals of all shapes and sizes. You can get a game if you're built like Steve Cutler, who's two metres from end-to-end, or Tommy Lawton, who's like a slab of concrete at around 110 kg. Or else fly-by-nighters like Jeff Miller and me, halfbacks of varying shapes and sizes, or flighty speedsters like David Campese and Brendan Moon. It really caters for everyone and is the ultimate team game where everyone has a purpose.

So what's wrong with Australian Rugby, if anything? The 1989 season really brought home to me the extraordinary benefits of club Rugby, and made me realise that there's too much representative Rugby altogether. At times it's like playing weekly Test matches. That's bad because it puts unrealistic pressures on players, their work and their families, and often forces them out of the game far too early. Administrators often forget that players aren't getting paid. You obviously get terrific trips and create an image for yourself in the community when you're tied up with representative Rugby, but that most definitely doesn't pay the bills. In the immediate future the administrators must look to a more even balance of club and representative Rugby. We used to have all club and little representative Rugby, but now it's the other way round. We've got to get back to club Rugby being encouraged more than it is and less of the big-time stuff.

I also cannot believe how blinkered the International Rugby Board is to what seem to be necessary changes. Forget whether the game will eventually be forced into going professional, the time has already come when the top Rugby players should be paid to play Test matches. I don't mean direct payments. They should be paid indirectly, as in track and field. The money should be put into a trust account for them, a form of compulsory saving. They should be able to do advertising and endorsements, as long as the proceeds go into the trust. And when you retire you'd finish up with a lump sum. It could be as much as $100 000. It would be an added inducement for a player to stay in the game longer and would compensate him for all the time he had given to Rugby. Sure you get payment now through enjoyment. But it's a real world out there. You can't survive on love and emotion. Bills have to be paid.

In just the last decade we could also have kept some fantastic Australian players from going to League under the scheme I'm promoting ... Ray Price, Michael O'Connor, Mitchell Cox, Matthew Burke, Brett Papworth, James Grant, Ricky Stuart and Chris Roche. Maybe not all of them, but certainly some of them.

The IRB is being so pig-headed about the whole amateur situation that it's going to blow the game right out of the water if it's not careful, because what's happening now is that players are being openly paid to play in places like France and Italy. Good luck to them. I only wish I'd done it myself. Players in New Zealand are also being taken care of. The same in South Africa. Why do you think more of them don't switch to League? It makes it all very hard for true-blue Australian Rugby when you compare us with what's happening in those other places. In fact, it's outright amazing what Australia has achieved given our adherence to the laws of amateurism and our playing resources. Just imagine what we could do in this nation if every kid played only Rugby, as is largely the case in New Zealand and South Africa, and then stayed with the game. Australia would be absolutely unbeatable—there's no doubt in the wide world about that.

It is also a standing disgrace that Rugby is not an Olympic sport, and the IRB undoubtedly has to carry the can for this. It's shameful to see tennis and soccer in all their professional glory being part of the Olympics while Rugby, one of the world's truly amateur sports, remains ostracised. I can't understand why the IRB isn't making every effort to get Rugby back into the Olympics, which it hasn't been part of since 1924. Could you imagine the benefits to the game worldwide if countries such as the United States, the Soviet Union, West Germany, East Germany and China began putting into Rugby the resources they now allocate to other Olympic sports?

And where does Simon Poidevin go from here? I'll keep playing. I enjoyed the 1989 season more than ever and I'll at least play for the club next season, even though my stockbroking career is accelerating on a daily basis. I'd miss Rugby if I retired now. I often get ragged for being the most over-publicised player in Australian Rugby, and there's a standing joke in the stock market that when my publicity machine gets rolling it's almost unstoppable. I guess the reason I've attracted so much publicity is that I've been around a long while, I've always been prepared to say what I feel, and there has been a lot of controversy on and off the field during my years at the top.

Of the countless benefits and awards I've had out of the game the most important thing to me is that this red-haired kid from the country has succeeded and that my parents have got so much enjoyment from what I've done. It has made Mum and Dad very proud. They've gone through some troubled times financially, and several droughts, and yet they've gained inspiration by being able to walk down the main street of Goulburn and have people being complimentary about my Rugby. That in itself has meant a lot to me. My old school, St Patrick's College, has also benefited. And Goulburn itself, because in 1989 two local kids did pretty well in both Rugby codes, with Gavin Miller winning the Rothmans Medal in League and me winning the same medal in Rugby.

It has been a great journey and I've kicked lots of goals (figuratively speaking in my case). But you don't do what I've done by yourself. I've had great support from my family, especially my brother Andy, and girlfriends, whose love and support was a great source of encouragement during the many highs and lows of playing international Rugby. Because I've always been hard and uncompromising in the way I've played the game, and because I've come through several different regimes, it could have been easy to make enemies, but I'm glad to say I've come through it fairly well. I've made many, many good friends and very few enemies out of it.

As a youngster growing up in Goulburn I didn't want to live the stereotyped life I saw many of my schoolfriends drifting into. There were big challenges and great experiences out there and ten years of international Rugby became my vehicle for discovering them. During that time I've played in New Zealand, Fiji, Hong Kong, Japan, America, Canada, Argentina, Paraguay, Italy, France, England, Ireland, Scotland, Wales and Monaco.

In what other game could you play for Monaco representing its Royal Family at a seven-a-side tournament in Monte Carlo, be guest of Queen Elizabeth and the Duke of Edinburgh at Buckingham Palace and attend a dinner in Tokyo with a Japanese princess as the patron of that country's national team?

As someone who has seen a fair slice of the world—even if it was

The incredible Jeff Sayle after his hip replacement, 1989

from the bottom of a ruck much of the time—there's little doubt that Australia is the lucky country. But the tragedy is that many Australians don't appreciate its beauty, wealth and democratic freedom. It's potentially one of the truly great countries of the world, but unfortunately its future is being undermined by laziness and attacks on those Australians striving to achieve.

I think it wouldn't be such a bad idea if this country reintroduced National Service. This view is not based on military objectives, but I see it as a means of providing discipline and direction for an increasing number of aimless young Australians. Sweden is a prime example of a country that has used National Service as a means of improving the national character.

Any type of sport, especially a team sport, would do the same job. If you want to be in a team and succeed than you must have enough discipline to train, take care of yourself and work in unison with others who may come from radically different backgrounds. I become very angry when I read of schools abandoning sporting activity in favour of total freedom for their students. Sport has a great capacity to bring people together, to make them care for one another and provide tremendous satisfaction merely from participating. These ideals are most strongly nurtured at the highest levels of international Rugby.

Above all else, education with a decent emphasis on the basics must be a priority if Australia is to keep pace with the rest of the world. To travel to Japan or the United States and to witness the technological progress in those countries is very sobering, and a rewarding experience. Undoubtedly it illustrates comprehensively the view that knowledge is power.

THE MOST DIFFICULT QUESTION

I've left until last the most difficult and sensitive subject of all. As a consistent member of our Test and touring teams since 1980, I've been through the most successful, controversial, progressive and radical (yes, they all apply) times in Australian Rugby history.

There never has been a decade in our game quite like the eighties and I was there every inch of the way. I've helped Australia thrash the best of the world's Rugby nations and in turn have copped a fairly decent hiding or two. I've seen the slow emergence of some enlightened thinking regarding Rugby's amateurism in this highly commercial world, although much of it sadly remains thought and not action. I've endured all the off-field argument and turmoil that came about through the long-standing NSW v Queensland rivalry, the issue of South Africa, the controversial Concord Oval redevelopment, loony team selections, strange coaching attitudes, captaincy puzzles and so on. I've spilled plenty of my own blood along the way and just a little of some rivals. And I've also been proud to have played alongside some of the greatest names and nicest people this game of ours has ever produced.

Finally, I've played under three national coaches, Bob Templeton, Bob Dwyer and Alan Jones, and of all the questions I'm hounded with concerning Rugby, the one that recurs most is: which of them is the best coach? I've always ducked the issue, but now's as good a time as any to answer the question as best I can. Whether they are considered successful or not, the time, dedication and energy Templeton, Dwyer and Jones have put into Australian Rugby should not be underestimated. Many people would assume the coach of the Australian Rugby team is a full-time, professional position. Nothing could be further from the truth. It is an honorary position and the national coach has to make huge sacrifices at both the business and family level to meet the demands of the job.

Rather than blithely listing them first, second and third, as if they'd just finished a horse race, and leaving it at that, it's better that I discuss what I regard as the main qualities in coaching and how they compare in each area. At the end I'll give my overall assessment.

Allow me to preface my comparisons by stating that while all three coaches have had great victories and terrible disappointments, there's no doubt that Jones was the most successful in purely statistical terms. His teams also won arguably the two most historic victories for Australian

Bob Dwyer with Tom Hafey. Dwyer was always the innovator, often bringing in outside help

Rugby ever (the 1984 Grand Slam and 1986 Bledisloe Cup win over New Zealand).

Although Dwyer doesn't have as consistent a record, his periods as coach have seen some of the most brilliant victories Australia has achieved: the second Test against Scotland at the SCG in 1982; the second Test in New Zealand the same year; and also the Scotland Test at Murrayfield in 1988. His stunning first Test victory over France in November 1989 also represents one of the greatest single triumphs Australian Rugby has had. But again the inconsistencies of Dwyer's coaching hit home in the second Test of that tour when the Australian team, as hot favourites, succumbed to a die-for-their-country French team. All credit to Dwyer and the team despite that particular Test defeat because, as someone who has made that long and painful French trip, I can appreciate the difficulty of winning consistently in such an enormously strong Rugby nation.

Tempo also had his glorious moments as Australian coach, and I couldn't have asked for a better start to my international career than to have won the Bledisloe Cup series with him in 1980.

In all the other areas, here's what I thought of them:

Knowledge
Tempo was my first Australian coach. You could describe him much more than the other two as being 'one of the boys'. He had many years of experience with club, Queensland and Australian teams long before I ever came along and was very close to his players. Whatever else, he will always be associated first and foremost with the Queensland team, which he pulled from near obscurity to being one of the best provincial teams in the world. He had far more practical experience than either Jonesy or Dwyer, but in many ways his vast knowledge hamstrung any creativity. Tempo, and consequently Queensland, concentrated on a percentage game at times bordering on 10-man Rugby. Occasionally they could be very expansive, but generally Tempo's thinking was dictated by what he had picked up through years of Queensland playing against all the New Zealand provincial teams. (His initiative of organising regular clashes with the tough New Zealand teams should not be underestimated. Queensland and Australian Rugby dramatically improved as a result.) Then again, in 1980 and 1981 against the All Blacks and France, Tempo threw away the shackles and allowed free rein to the explosive Australian backline.

Dwyer played 347 games for Randwick, had immense success as the club's coach and was totally committed to Randwick's flashing style of back play, which has been so successful over the years. But the biggest problem he had was trying to get the Australian team to function like Randwick in the few days' training before a domestic Test match. It takes time to develop that particular style, and that's why Dwyer has always been better on an overseas tour than coaching Australia at home. If he had a failing, then, it was trying to implant all his ideas into the Australian team before home Tests when a more conservative approach would have achieved better results. One of his main qualities was his readiness to seek outside assistance, and at times he has arranged for Tom Hafey (Australian football) and Eddie Thomson (soccer) to give advice to his club and Australian teams. Dwyer's coaching ability doesn't purely revolve around intricate backline play. He is a superb forward coach and much of Randwick's success under his guidance revolved around an unheralded pack of thoroughly drilled forwards.

Because of Jonesy's own inexperience as a Rugby player and his diversified lifestyle it was impossible for him to know as much about the game as Tempo and Dwyer. But it was his ability to hone in on the most significant aspects of the game that gave him the appearance of having coached for years, when in reality his involvement in Rugby was far less than the other two. Jonesy also had a far broader sporting knowledge than the others. In his coaching he used what he had learnt from his early tennis days—when he came under the influence of the legendary Harry Hopman—and as an athletics coach. And those lessons were that discipline, hard work and a strong grasp of the basics are much more important than anything else. Natural ability will take you only so far and then the other qualities are needed to push you to the top. He felt very strongly about this, almost to the point of obsession, and forced the notion onto his Rugby players ahead of everything else.

In fact, Jonesy pursued his three coaching philosophies with such fervour that he could have been successful in almost any coaching field he chose, because they really are necessary for any sporting success. I've no doubt, for example, that if he had ever wanted to train racehorses he would have become another T J Smith or Bart Cummings. By applying discipline and hard work to a racehorse as strenuously as he did he could have prepared one of them magnificently for a campaign. That really was his greatest strength: his ability to thoroughly prepare any person or team for a campaign. Then, when it was needed to strike, or perform, it would.

So while Tempo had all the worldly experience and Bob Dwyer a specialised knowledge of playing an expansive game, they did not have anywhere near the breadth of Jonesy's knowledge on coaching sport in the wider sense.

Dedication

While all were tremendously dedicated, it was Jonesy who had the hunger and ambition to devote his whole life to the Australian team and its success while he was coach, particularly on tour. Every international Rugby coach knows that his own success is ultimately linked to the success or failure of the team, but he went to extremes to achieve it.

On tour Jonesy would train his team for several hours each morning and then dismiss us. Then he'd return to the hotel and for the rest of the day would do detailed analysis of videos, or else homework on the team we were about to play. He'd also talk at length to individual players.

Bob Dwyer and Bob Templeton provide an interesting contrast to the intensity displayed by Jones. Both have contributed and will continue to contribute a large part of their lives to Rugby. They are in there for the long haul and as such don't follow the mad dog, 24-hours-a-day attitude, which characterised Alan Jones's coaching.

Both could relax and enjoy the pleasures of travelling much more than Jonesy. On and off the training paddock, however, Bob Dwyer is certainly not far behind in the volume of work he can get through in preparing an Australian team for a Test.

Toughness
You've got to be very tough to be a successful international coach. Tempo could be an extremely hard trainer, but he has a soft spot and sometimes worried unduly when things went wrong. Dwyer could also be a hard trainer, but at times tended to listen too much to the players and often allowed some of them far too much freedom. Conversely, he could sometimes apply the screws as hard as any coach I've known and not shift ground at all. On the other hand, Jonesy was like a Sherman tank. Not many people could get through him. Even when the team was under the most sustained attack off the field for some reason he could always find the arrogance, the confidence and the cutting word to support us.

Respect
Tempo was a great friend of everybody, particularly the senior players. But his friendliness towards them often made newer players in the team feel as if they weren't getting a fair go, which eroded their respect for him. I might add that Tempo was in charge during a very difficult period when Paul McLean and Mark Ella were challenging each other. I've got all the time in the world for McLean. He's a fantastic Australian, a great five-eighth and a gutsy player. Yet Mark Ella remains the most talented Rugby player I've ever seen. As for their playing styles, McLean was very disciplined while Ella at times lacked discipline, and Tempo often found himself in the no-win situation of having to choose between the two.

In contrast with Tempo being a favourite of the senior players, the newer players had more respect for Dwyer. He almost had a rebellion on his hands from the senior players in the series here against Scotland in 1982 when he dropped Roger Gould and Paul McLean from the first Test team. The established players virtually took control. So while Dwyer was a very personable and intelligent coach he also didn't enjoy the complete respect that he should have.

During Jones's golden years from 1984 to 1986, all the players respected him although they didn't necessarily like him. They didn't like how hard he trained them, or the pressure he could apply to a team. But in 1987 that respect started to wane. Many of the players felt alienated by the collapse of the South African tour, and there was less respect for him on that year's tour of Argentina than at any other time. It was like a mighty empire starting to crumble.

Confidence
All coaches need this. Tempo and Dwyer could become fragile in this area if things started to go wrong. They were great worriers and this was transmitted to the players. But Jonesy had undying confidence in his own ability and that of the team. The only time it weakened was in

1987 during the lead-up to the World Cup. We started to run into trouble and his confidence was momentarily shot to pieces. But he recovered remarkably well.

Stamina

Coaches must have at least as much stamina as the players. Tempo enjoyed life immensely and at times hit the training paddock in the morning doing it a bit hard. Dwyer was consistently well-prepared. He had a great amount of stamina, and could survive any adversity and continue to run the team hard. Jonesy's stamina was almost superhuman. He'd never stop. If any part of the team's preparation had to be taken care of, he'd do it. If anything concerning team management had to be attended to, he'd do it. If anything had to be organised, he'd do it. He'd just keep going and going. Mind you, he's virtually an insomniac. Like Rupert Murdoch and Margaret Thatcher, he needs hardly any sleep. He exists on only two or three hours shut-eye every night, which means he immediately has five or six more daily working hours than the rest of us.

Man management

Tempo and Dwyer could both get on with all and sundry, more so than Jonesy. He easily put noses out of joint, but would argue that noses had to be put out of joint to gain the successes we had. But Jonesy's demands on people can border on arrogance, and he needs to be far more considerate of others' weaknesses. While nobody is perfect, he forgets that some people are less perfect than others, and should think a lot more before opening up on them verbally. In this area, he comes a bad last to the other two.

Yet Jonesy was a great communicator with the players. He'd never stop talking with them. Dwyer would too. Tempo not so much. But Jonesy would spend hour upon hour discussing their football, their careers, their private lives, listening to their problems, pepping them up, getting them into the right frame of mind. One player in particular he spent hours talking to was Michael Lynagh, who responded more than anyone to this form of communication. Jonesy also had the ability to pick (or at least influence the selection of) the right people around him. Charles (Chilla) Wilson was the perfect team manager as far as Jonesy was concerned and he constantly supported his appointment. Chilla would do his job in his laid-back style and, if there were any problems, then Jonesy would generally sort them out. They were like the Odd Couple in many ways. Chilla was an disorganised as Jonesy was organised, but Chilla never got in Jonesy's way, which suited him down to the ground. Together they made a magnificent manager-coach combination.

Organisation

Jonesy excelled in this area. Under him, everything ran like clockwork and to a pattern. Every part of the machine fell into a rhythm and rarely got out of it. On tour he'd train the 30 players together, but differently. Leading up to a Wednesday game, that particular team would take things easy. But on Friday, Saturday and Sunday ... nightmare. Similarly, with Saturday's team coming into Saturday's game, training would finish on Thursday. Friday nothing. But Monday, Tuesday, Wednesday ... nightmare. Jonesy also felt right from the outset as national coach that he needed a helping hand, so he arranged for Alex Evans to be his assistant. It had never been done before in Australian Rugby. Before that, a national coach on tour had done all the coaching himself, which meant working with one side and sending the other off on a road run or doing sprints or whatever. With two coaches working in tandem, Jones could supervise the two teams simultaneously, work more on individual skills and fitness and, at any one time, either team could have gone out and done the job for Australia. Jones's practice of having two coaches has now been accepted by almost every other national team for domestic matches as well as on tour. Certainly Dwyer would acknowledge that Jones did every subsequent Australian coach a favour by introducing this. I haven't been on a recent tour with Dwyer, but I'm sure the training patterns Jones used with Alex Evans as his assistant have now been duplicated by Dwyer with Bob Templeton.

Jonesy's attention to detail was also far superior to the others. On tour you always encounter problems with scrummaging practice. Often you'll have props injured (and it's the one position where you can't throw in just anybody as a substitute), and sometimes even tension arising from selections to the point where we've had punch-ups between our props at training. It's rare you can get two packs from within your team to scrum against one another. So when we arrived in the United Kingdom in 1984, Jonesy made contact with a fellow he knew who had built a revolutionary new scrum machine and asked him to have one at every training session. His friend was only too happy to oblige, given the publicity it would generate, and thereafter the team worked relentlessly on that machine throughout the tour. Leading up to the Welsh Test, I remember one session where we put down hundreds of scrums against the machine. We were absolutely buggered, but when Tommy Lawton called quits Topo Rodriguez turned to us and said sternly: 'We do more!' So we did more. And a few days later when Wales put a mighty shove on against us in the scrum at Cardiff Arms Park they hit steel, and then we turned around and crushed their pack like no other team has done before or since, as epitomised by our now-famous pushover try. Two years later in New Zealand, Jones arranged for another of these machines to be flown over from Australia at his own expense and organised for two brothers to cart it around New Zealand for us. As a result, we never gave an inch against the best the All Blacks had to offer. But in Argentina in 1987 the only scrum machine we could find was in Buenos Aires. There were none in the country areas at all, so we found scrum practice hard going and it showed in our match results.

Generally, Jonesy would move mountains to provide us with the best. If the hotel wasn't good enough, then he'd simply walk out. I'm sure, for example, that Tempo and Dwyer would have remained in the hotel in New Zealand in 1986 that Jonesy ordered the Wallabies to walk out of. He was always prepared to take the flak and to make the tough decisions. He was certainly tough, but justifiably so when you look at his success.

Jonesy also had much easier access to the power-brokers of this world than either Tempo or Bob Dwyer. He was always prepared to use this network for the advancement of the team, which was consequently made to feel it was the most important team in the world.

Training

Again there's no doubt that Jonesy had the best training skills of the three. He'd work for hours devising new skills to suit different playing surfaces. For example, we had sloppy grounds on the early part of our 1986 New Zealand tour. So for hour upon hour at training we did skills designed for slop. He'd also apply skills bearing in mind the particular team we were playing against. He put a huge amount of thought into what we did at training, and the team really enjoyed the different challenges he came up with.

Tempo's training was the most conservative of the three, while Dwyer could be very innovative and entertaining in devising training programs. But consistency is the name of the game and Jonesy had that. He also worked us at breakneck pace at training, to the point where blokes were ready to tell him to get nicked and hop on the next plane home. But as their fitness improved, so did he wind down the training intensity. As he would tell us, 'Long after you've paid the price the quality remains'—the Gucci factor.

My judgment of training techniques is coloured by the fact that Alan Jones, in the period he coached the Australian team, had an assistant coach of immense ability in Alex Evans.

The players who returned from the 1989 French tour with Bob Dwyer as coach and Bob Templeton as assistant coach raved about the excellent training programs devised by the two Bobs on what is traditionally one of the hardest Rugby tours on offer.

There is little doubt that Bob Dwyer is now lifting the preparation of the Australian team to a level equal to anywhere in the world. His biggest hurdle is the rapidly changing face of the team, due in great part to the poaching by Rugby League clubs of Rugby players.

Strategy

Tempo would have specific instructions for us to follow before a match. So would Dwyer. On the other hand, Jonesy had more of a broad pattern and not really any specific game plan. Rather, the team was given his overall ideas and approach to playing Rugby at every training session. He drilled into us what each of us had to do, and his philosophy was that we simply keep firing away, wearing down the opposition all the while, and then victory would follow.

Personalities

Tempo. A great bloke. Very personable. He could be tough if he wanted to, but could also be hurt. Dwyer had a great deal of confidence and ambition. He could also be tough, but at the same time was vulnerable to criticism.

Jonesy was one of the most intelligent people I've ever met and the most articulate. His pre-game talks should have been recorded. I regret I didn't sneak a tape recorder into the dressing-room at times because I'd have been able to sell his talks as motivational speeches. Even in his last year as coach, players who had been around as long as me were still inspired by many of the same words. His experience in politics also enabled him to use people for the team's benefit to a much greater extent than the other two. Jonesy would deliberately leak statements to the media leading up to a Test. For example, he'd want the referees to read his statement that Steve Cutler was going to be targeted by the opposition in the lineouts, so that when the time came you could bet that's what the ref would watch. The media loved him for the way he fed them stories like this—and simply because he couldn't shut up on any subject. Ask him anything and he'd leap in with an answer. Some just liked the challenge of mixing it with him intellectually, but few won. Tempo was much more likely to stand back where the media was concerned and let the manager take on the spokesman's role. But Dwyer and Jonesy were never slow in asserting themselves, particularly Jonesy. He was always the up-front man.

It's shameful for Australian Rugby that more collective use could not have been made of the talents of the three coaches, especially Jones and Dwyer. Just imagine if those two had pooled their resources, instead of standing off and harbouring suspicions of each other as they have always done.

I've always been alarmed at the vicious, high-powered attacks launched by Dwyer or Jones upon each other on the return of the Wallabies from a statistically unsuccessful trip away. Neither coach does himself any good whatsoever with these public attacks, which are very detrimental to Australian Rugby. I well remember wincing when I saw the Daily Telegraph report in which Jones called Dwyer's record 'abysmal' on the return of the Wallabies from France in 1989. There's no doubt Jonesy would have done himself a far greater service by simply keeping his peace, despite having suffered previous attacks along the same lines by Dwyer.

In many, many ways they're very similar people. Both are well-spoken, Jonesy more so. Both are intelligent. Both have huge amounts of confidence. And both love a challenge. The one thing that has prevented them from working together is their monstrously large egos and, while ego is not a dirty word, rarely would either have conceded that the other was right about anything.

While Tempo and Dwyer were leaders in their field in specific areas, Jonesy was undoubtedly the master coach and the best I've ever played under. He was a freak. Australian Rugby was very fortunate to have had a person with his extraordinary ability to coach our national team. New Zealand's Fred Allen and the British Lions' Carwyn James are probably the other most remarkable coaches of modern times. But given Alan Jones's skills in so many areas, and his record, probably no other Rugby nation in the world has had anyone quite like him, and perhaps none ever will.

It is particularly sad to contemplate the energy and devotion that Bob Templeton, Bob Dwyer and Alan Jones have channelled into the game when Australian Rugby may be soon destroyed unless the administrators quickly realise that the world of sport has changed dramatically while Rugby has in many ways stood still, leaving it very vulnerable to attack from the professional sports.

I don't want to see this great game become professional but no game will grow and prosper when its players, coaches and officials are financially disadvantaged by their involvement in it. The world has changed and unfortunately, to play the game, one can't live on love alone.

Addendum

The world stops for no-one and, since the second edition of *For Love Not Money* was published, Rugby has marched on at a hectic pace.

Just as coalition forces opposed to Saddam Hussein were brilliantly victorious against Iraq in early 1991, so, too, the coalition forces leading Australian Rugby were gloriously successful in 1991.

When I speak of the coalition forces of Australian Rugby I refer to Bob Dwyer, the head coach, and his two forwards generals in Bob Templeton and Jake Howard. The support team working directly with the coaches included team manager John Breen, Greg Craig (physiotherapist), John Moulton (team doctor), Brian Hopley (trainer), Steve Goddard (baggage man), Holly Frail (dietician) and an army of other professionals working closely and intensely with them.

Dwyer and his elite support team guided the Wallabies to the most successful and exhilarating year in the history of Australian Rugby. Their status as world champions was not achieved without the most intense and thorough preparation ever undertaken by an Australian Rugby team. Few stones were left unturned by the administrators and coaches in seeking the best for the team.

Whereas Alan Jones took a small step down the path to setting up a team of professionals around the players, Dwyer hurtled down the path, setting up a machine that would take us to number one in the world. The mistakes of the past were analysed and rectified. He drew on the immense experience of Templeton and Howard to guide the Australian forwards through the most demanding year experienced by any Australian team. This left Dwyer with time to constantly indoctrinate the backs with his straight running, close passing theory of backline play. Theory became practice and Australian Rugby in 1991 featured the most exhilarating display of running Rugby seen on the world stage.

In 1991, the Wallabies' defensive record was by far the most successful and lethal of any team in the world. Again, this was no accident, but a product of team fitness, strength, concentration and meticulous defensive patterns. Dwyer was at the forefront.

Much of the day-to-day responsibility of coaching the forwards was in the hands of Templeton and Howard. Throughout the year their guidance was first rate and outstanding prior to the All Black semi-final in Dublin. Both contributed significantly to the pre-game mental preparation of the team.

But the architect of Australia's outstanding success in 1991 was Dwyer. He planned, pushed, schemed and coordinated for years to nurture the Rugby talent in Australia into the most powerful team in the world. His was a master team effort, utilising the talent and skills of many to achieve success. Alan Jones, on the other hand, chose to carry much of the workload on his own shoulders, with the exception of the huge contribution from assistant coach Alex Evans.

It seems ironic that Templeton and Dwyer, coaches on either side of the Jones era, pooled their talents to achieve the ultimate coaching honour—a World Cup. In so doing, they have attained the highest status in the history of Australian Rugby, a status they fully deserve.

CHANGING TIMES

The issue of universal interest which has happened recently has been the alteration to the Rules of Amateurism by the International Rugby Board. The IRB gave the sport's top players the right to cash in on their name and fame from last December. We are now able to receive money for personal appearances, speaking at dinners, writing books like this, broadcasting, advertising and endorsing any products for cash provided that they are acceptable to our individual unions.

Each Union is required to set up a watchdog to police the rules and be prepared to investigate reports of malpractice and impose sanctions on clubs and players if necessary. As has been the case so often in the past, most of the changes were either proposed or supported by Australia, which can rightly claim to have been the dominant force in the most important changes which have occurred in Rugby in the last two decades. New Zealand became a much more vocal supporter of these latest changes after their first major defections to Rugby League. All Blacks John Gallagher, Matthew Ridge and Frano Bottica switched codes and suddenly New Zealand Rugby had a taste of what Australia has been experiencing for years. With New Zealand's economy in such a depressed state it's understandable that these players wouldn't turn down the huge money being offered to turn professional.

In a related story with a bizarre twist the Argentinian Rugby Union has banned any player for a period of three years who leaves Argentina and plays for a Rugby club in another country. The authorities interpret such a move as professionalism. With 53 of Argentina's top Rugby players now playing in Italy, the widespread bans have had a devastating effect on the fortunes of Argentina's national Rugby team, the Pumas. Certainly things are bad economically in Australia and New Zealand at the present time but in Argentina the economy is 1000 times worse. As such it's easy to understand the decision of the Argentinian players to spend a season or two with an Italian club which gives them a well-paid job, accommodation and a nice car among other things.

Although the changes made by the IRB are very positive for Rugby players, they still don't go far enough to stem the flow of players to Rugby League. I've voiced my views on payments for Test matches being paid into trust funds and the great necessity to reintroduce Rugby as an Olympic sport. These two initiatives would further revolutionise the game in a very positive fashion.

I've got to laugh though. Last year I was in New Zealand playing an invitation game for a Murray Mexted XV in Wellington. At one stage during the weekend Mex said to me 'Poido, we were born a decade too soon. Rugby is going to be financially very rewarding for players in the near future.' But I'll be honest and say many of us have never wanted to play the game on a professional basis. We love being amateur and playing for our country. That was one of the very reasons for our wanting to play Rugby in the first place. Yet in this day and age nobody could sensibly be expected to forfeit as much time and salary as international players do without getting some recompense. After all, honour and glory don't pay the water rates.

It's just a shame that these historic changes have come at the end of my career; that only now can international players be compensated in some small way for the devotion and dedication they have given the game. The pity is that these changes have taken so long. Still, allow me to congratulate Rugby for finally starting to move with the times.

*O*n the field, Australia provided a mixed bag of performances in 1990, which has become fairly normal these past four years. At home against France, we won the first Test 21-9 in Sydney and then wrapped up the series with a breathtaking 48-31 victory in the second Test at Ballymore, which will go down in history as one of the finest ever played. It really had everything. The match contained ten tries and produced one short of 80 points. The 48 points scored by Australia is the most it has scored against an International Rugby Board member country. The try count of six, which included a penalty try, was also the highest number of tries scored against a fellow IRB country. Michael Lynagh also broke his own record for the most points by an Australian in a Test, scoring 24 points to break his previous best of 23.

But for my money, the one memory which stands out is the amazing try scored by Serge Blanco. Taking the ball on his own line, the French captain sliced between Carozza and Little on the quarter line before swerving past Campese at halfway. Then Blanco beat Williams, Carozza and Campese in the run to the line to score one of the greatest individual tries of all time. When Serge Blanco gathers his game to its mightiest pitch, there's simply no-one better.

The third and final Test in Sydney was a totally courageous performance by the French and a lost opportunity by Australia. I wouldn't criticise the Australians too much for their 28-19 defeat. The French were on a mission. Defeat would have spelt the ultimate disaster. Victory would save playing careers and restore battered Gallic pride. Down a man, a front-rower at that, the French lived to fight another day. It was emotional stuff.

The win was a wonderful tonic for the French. Too much so it tragically turned out. On the way home, the team stopped off in Noumea for a little relaxation in this French paradise in the South Pacific and undoubtedly celebrated in rousing fashion. Their loose-head prop Dominique Bouet, a 26-year-old from Dax with only a handful of Tests behind him and a long career ahead of him, apparently vomited in his sleep and choked to death. It devastated not only his teammates, but the entire world of Rugby.

His body was flown home to France and at the same time I received a telephone call from the Australian Rugby Football Union asking if I was available to fly to the funeral as Australia's representative. I agreed and within twenty-four hours was on my way.

It was one of the most emotional occasions I have ever witnessed, with Rugby players and officials from all over France gathered in the beautiful cathedral in Dax to pay homage to Dominique Bouet who, only weeks before, had been so full of life, fitness and competitiveness as he scrummed in the front-fow of his national Rugby side.

The United States then came for a short tour and copped another hiding as Australia ran riot at Ballymore. One day they'll get their act together and when they do ... look out!

The Wallabies then headed off to New Zealand in their quest to regain the Bledisloe Cup. I'd made this journey on long tours in 1982 and 1986 and had no desire to undertake 'one of the life's great pleasures' once again. Unfortunately the tour was a near-disaster with Australia losing the first two Tests and a number of provincial games. The players, coach and management, understanding the gravity of the situation, knew there was only one way to short-fuse disaster—to win the third and final Test. I was lucky enough to be a spectator at Athletic Park in Wellington on that cold, windy day when Australia returned from the dead and ended New Zealand's 1373-day unbeaten reign as world champions with an historic 21-9 victory. Australia became the first team to beat the All Blacks since November 15, 1986, including 23 undefeated Test matches.

Most Australians will remember it for the animation shown by my Randwick teammate Phil Kearns when he grabbed a ricochet ball from Gary Whetton's hand at the front of a lineout before diving over for the try which provided Australia with the lead. Then he turned and screamed what looked like obscenities at the All Blacks on the ground who'd tried to stop him scoring. Many Rugby clubs have since arranged guessing competitions with prizes for the best attempt at picking (a) what he yelled at them, and (b) what he told his mother he yelled at them ...

Back in the cauldron of the Sydney club premiership, Supercoach

Jeff Sayle again guided Randwick to an awesome grand final performance against Eastern Suburbs. We won 32-9 for our fourth straight premiership and tenth since 1978. There was much talk beforehand about how Easts' nippy threequarters might do this-and-that, but after only five minutes we felt the game was well within our control. Even that early, their scrum was starting to give. You could feel them fighting to keep their footing under our power and, once we were dominant there, they lost purpose and we took over. In the finish it turned out to be probably the most convincing and authoritative grand final victory of my career.

Incidentally, a rather important point which might have escaped many is that there wasn't an Ella on the field that day. While they had an immense influence on the club, there has been a misconception that Randwick's unrivalled success through the eighties was totally reliant on them; that without their waltz routine we'd become a mob of plodders. Well, that was proved well off-beam and we showed in that grand final against Easts that we could still be a highly successful outfit without Mark, Glen and Gary. Randwick's success stems from its strength right through the grades and our future, minus the Ellas, still looks as bright as ever.

Speaking of the Ellas, 1990 will also be remembered as the year Mark Ella played his last game for Randwick, for he left us before the season was over. In a sensational end to a glorious career, Mark scored under the posts with seconds remaining to seal a 20-3 win for Randwick against the champion English club Bath. It was no ordinary try and spectators at Coogee Oval sensed divine intervention as Mark swung the ball wide in Randwick's own 22-metre area, positioned himself behind the attack and took the final pass to spring to the line just as the final bell rang.

For someone who has done so much for Rugby and sport in Australia, it is truly ironic that a testimonial year similar to that launched for Wally Lewis was not arranged for Mark. There's little doubt that his name is a household word throughout the Rugby world and this produced substantial benefits for Australian Rugby and Australia in general. Why a testimonial wasn't arranged I don't know, but certainly one factor is the sad ability of Australians to forget their champions.

Financially, Mark made very little out of Rugby in Australia, not that this was a big priority for him anyway. But a windfall may be in the offing with the success of the Ella-coached Milan side in Italy. An extremely wealthy Milan industrialist has taken a very close interest in the team's success and his generosity may be greater than that forthcoming in Australia.

Finally, I've managed to get myself in the Australian squad for the Rugby World Cup in the United Kingdom at the end of this year. I've been

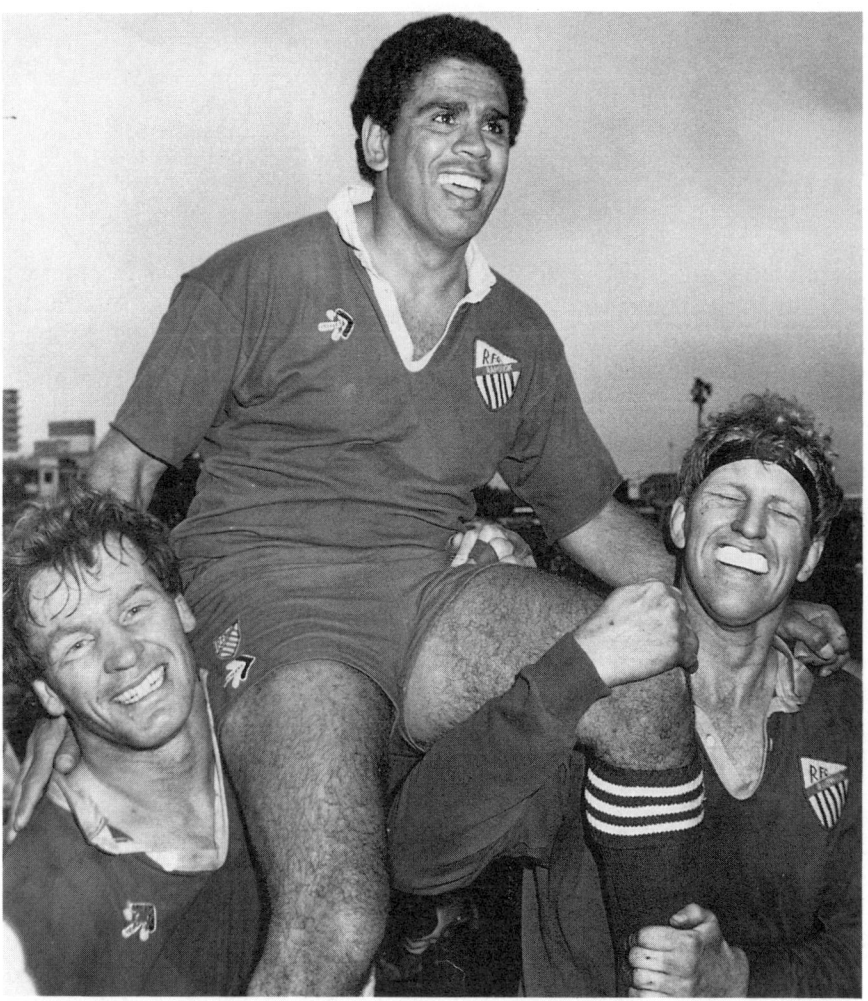

Mark Ella after his last game for Randwick. He is carried off by myself and Gavin Boneham.

through one World Cup and, before I finally retire, would like to think I can round off my career by being on the winning side. We've got some enormously talented young players like Daly, Kearns, McKenzie, Horan and Little and, with some old hard-heads like Farr-Jones, Lynagh, Miller and myself thrown in, I think we've got the mix which could really give the All Blacks and whoever else a real run for their money. And believe me, if I can help the other Australian players hold aloft the silverware at Twickenham on November 2 then I will retire once and for all. And there will definitely be no coming back this time.

AUSTRALIA COMES OF AGE

I ended the introduction to the previous edition of *For Love Not Money* with the statement: 'And believe me, if I can help the other Australian players hold aloft the silverware at Twickenham on November 2 then I will retire once and for all. And there will definitely be no coming back this time.' (see p. 209 this edition)

Am I a man of my word? Well ... we'll come back to that later.

Let's start the 1991 Rugby season at the very beginning and, for me at least, it got under way in early January when the fax machine in my office churned out a most welcome invitation to a sevens tournament in, of all places, Uruguay. Tucked like a doorstop between its vast neighbours Brazil and Argentina on South America's eastern coastline, it might seem an unlikely place for Rugby to be prospering. But the national body there was formed in 1951 and at last count had more than 1300 players spread among fourteen clubs. The national team, which wears sky blue jerseys, gives its neighbours Brazil, Chile, Paraguay and Peru fairly regular hidings, but in turn is often on the receiving end of hefty defeats from the more famous Pumas of Argentina.

I'd been to Uruguay for the same tournament the previous year and, knowing the hospitality, couldn't get my acceptance off quickly enough. The others invited from our neck of the woods and forming an Anzac team (with the help of a lone Uruguayan) were Darren Junee and All Blacks Zinzan Brooke, Walter Little, Craig Innes and John Timu. The organisers were so delighted with our participation that they wanted Australia and New Zealand to send separate national teams in future, but we snuffed out the idea before it got started. We belt each other regularly enough on the Rugby paddocks back home without wanting to do it on the other side of the world. Just occasionally it's enjoyable being on the same team as the All Blacks. No, we told them, keep it an Anzac team and we'd love to keep coming back.

Uruguay's an incredible place. The tournament's played at Punta del Este, which is very much the Riviera of that part of the world. All the beautiful people from Uruguay, Argentina and Brazil flock there at holiday time. None of the All Blacks had been there before and just couldn't believe it. We were put up in the very best hotel-casino the town had to offer and the people simply couldn't do enough for us.

We played in the three-day tournament as an entry from our hosts, the British Schools Old Boys' Rugby Club of Montevideo. The tournament's most unusual. If you win all your matches on the first night you jump straight through to the third night. That was incentive enough for us, because it meant we could win ourselves a day off. The only problem was the games didn't start until eight o'clock at night and finished in the early hours of the morning.

Sure enough, we won all our games on the opening night, went back to the hotel, changed, then headed for the casino to try to win enough money for us to drink through what was left of the night. By the time we turned in it was around seven or eight o'clock in the morning. We slept until early afternoon, had a few hours at the beach and went through the whole cycle again, minus the Rugby. On the third night, we were back to business.

Despite the high life, we won both our quarter-final and semi-final in extra time (although our quarter-final opponents only needed to kick a penalty to beat us) and then had a much easier win over an Argentinean club team in the final. The organisers had heartaches over the closeness of those qualifying games, especially the local president Pedro Bordaberry, because without the Anzacs in the final the tournament would have flopped.

There was no need to worry. Not only did we beat everybody in the tournament, we also won the beer-drinking races and finally I managed to beat the local arm-wrestling champion. So, all told, it was a wonderful time and everybody went away happy.

Next came the long haul home. I lobbed in Sydney on the Friday night, made a hurried taxi ride to my house, grabbed some fresh gear, took another taxi back to the airport and flew straight to Brisbane for the Australian squad's first training camp. All I managed on arriving at the Queensland University college where we were staying was a few brief words before hitting the sack.

At six o'clock the next morning someone was banging on my door. Get your butt out of bed and be ready for a 3000-metre time trial in one hour! Gawd. I needed that like a hole in the head. It was also hellishly warm, yet given the keen competition between various team members everything we did had a very sharp, competitive edge to it. We were put through a lot of fitness and physiological testing and the support staff also had us running on treadmills, where we were filmed with a video camera and any faults highlighted. Even the type of football boots each of us favoured were examined and changes recommended if they weren't thought suitable for our individual build and style! It was a very comprehensive assessment of the team as a whole and made it abundantly clear that no stone was going to be left unturned en route to the World Cup.

The testing showed I was lacking in the strength area. I hadn't done nearly as much weight-training as the Queensland players and so I needed to get stuck into the weights between then and the second camp in February.

Before that camp, however, another was held at Narrabeen Fitness Centre in Sydney for the NSW squad members. This was the introduction for many players to new coach Rod Macqueen and his backline guru Peter Carson and even old-timers like myself who knew him were still keen to see how he'd turn out. I'd played against Macca when he was with Warringah. He was a tough, uncompromising character in those days, who wouldn't take a backward step. He'd also been a member of Collaroy's surfboat crew and had won a few national titles with them. So he was a coach who knew a lot about both Rugby and fitness.

It turned out he was also brilliantly organised, for that camp was equally as impressive as the national camp. Initially, each of us was asked to analyse past failures by NSW against Queensland and offer ways and means to reverse those defeats. Everything we said was documented, discussed and the plan hatched for sweet revenge.

Conditions that weekend were pretty spartan, but Macca's support team devised a lot of fun training methods which kidded you into believing it was enjoyable, but in fact it was very tough work.

The following weekend we had the second Australian camp at Sydney University and again it was terrifically hard. The same deal as before. Bang, bang, bang first thing Saturday. Another 3000-metre time trial at seven o'clock! Our times were compared with those we'd run in Brisbane and fortunately there wasn't much difference in mine. On each occasion I ran with Nick Farr-Jones, who had been a top-line distance runner at Newington College and he dragged me along until I just couldn't keep up. I really thrashed myself in those runs. I hadn't played for Australia since 1989 and, with so many keen contenders pushing for Test selection, I had to make every post a winner to prove how much I really wanted to get back into the side. Except I went harder at the Sydney camp than I should have. Even though my time was well ahead of the other backrowers I finished bent over, dry-retching, wobbly and feeling very, very crook indeed. But my strength level had picked up noticeably by that time and so I left the camp feeling pretty content with myself. Yet it was obvious there were some exceptional players around and throughout the team there was going to be some ultra-intense competition for Test positions, which was great for Australia.

The State team's first matches were drawing near and Rod Macqueen had us training regularly at North Sydney Oval No 2. Training? That doesn't adequately describe it. Commandos would baulk at it. It was the toughest training I've done in my life. It was intensive and competitive. We busted our guts night after night with our conditioner Brendan Mockford grinning with delight. Brian Hopley also introduced us to his beneficial, but extremely hard, plyometric routines which added significantly to our fitness.

When the World Cup came around later in the year I often thought that the work which the NSW players had done had a lot to do with the extreme fitness levels of the Wallabies.

Before the domestic matches, NSW was making a short tour of Argentina. I didn't know if I could afford the time off work, but after intense discussions with the NSW Rugby Union executive committee and coach Macqueen I reconsidered. The bottom line was that I couldn't have gone without the selfless support of my employers, Prudential Bache Securities. So I made myself available and it was the best thing I ever did. The spirit in the NSW team was fabulous, we played with a lot of confidence, there were a lot of laughs with a great bunch of blokes and, yes, on tour we continued to train extremely hard.

The fact the players had to raise about $20 000 beforehand to assist with the trip brought us even closer together. It wasn't exactly the old chook raffle or blanket collection at halftime, but we did have to participate in several fund-raising functions and at one trivia night the players acted as food and drink waiters for the guests and worked their insides out.

What was nice was that the tour didn't take us to places like Buenos Aires, but rather to some of the small provinces, where we were so much appreciated. We beat Rosario 36–12 in the opening game, had a close squeak against Tucuman before drawing 15-all and finished the tour with a 13–10 triumph over Mendoza.

On the field one memory stands out: the match against Tucuman, who had been Argentinean champions for four years. The atmosphere that evening was incredible. I've experienced Lang Park during Rugby League State of Origin matches and, take it from me, this was that same steamy, pulsating, thunderous atmosphere all over again. There was the constant feeling that the whole place was set to erupt either on or off the field—or both. We played at nine o'clock at night and had to walk from our dressing-room up a long tunnel onto the ground. Coming out into the lights and all the noise had my nerve-ends stretched like a violin string. The whole place was chanting 'Tuc-u-man ... Tuc-u-man ... Tuc-u-man', fireworks were going off, bands were playing.

The opposition wasn't all that big, but they had the biggest hearts of any team I've played against. From the opening whistle they ripped into us like you wouldn't believe and kept catching our backs behind the advantage line. Before we knew it we were trailing 15–3. Clearly we were in deep trouble, so I told Nick Farr-Jones to forget the backs and we'd take it to them through the forwards. We had some good, hard runners in Tim Gavin, Michael Miller, Phil Kearns, Tim Kava, Tony Daly, Ewen McKenzie, Warwick Waugh and myself and so we started driving the ball smack up the middle just as hard as we could and only let the ball out to the backs close to their line. Somehow it worked and we squeezed out a draw with only minutes to spare.

On the way home from South America we diverted to New Zealand and played Wayne Shelford's North Harbour team. I hadn't faced my old All Black rival for a while and our clash generated considerable media interest. Again our forwards carried the day. Early on we absolutely smashed the North Harbour pack, although they came back at us and it finished up fairly close with us winning 19–12. Nevertheless, we had completed the tour undefeated in our four games.

Then we hit the NSW domestic season. We whipped Waikato (20–12), then Otago (28–17) and soon it was time for the first interstate game at Ballymore. We went north for that with more confidence and fitness than I'd ever experienced from the sky blues and consequently were able to beat them 24–18. In the leadup games, Queensland's backline had been going like a house on fire. But we put their forwards under extreme pressure, their backs couldn't get started and when they did our backs just kept bowling them over like ninepins. The no-names NSW backline was suddenly starting to unearth some stars.

A fortnight later a highly-determined Queensland came to Waratah Rugby Park at Concord looking for revenge and yet we beat them again, this time by 21–12. Playing at Concord these days provides us with a decided hometown advantage. The NSW players really enjoy it and we defend our goal-line more stoutly there than anywhere else. That double whammy over Queensland, incidentally, was only the second time in 16 years we'd managed two wins over them in the same season.

We were ready then for anything. I've often heard the comment that Rugby players aren't as fit as Rugby League players, simply because they're professionals and we're not. Well, let me tell you that right then we were the fittest NSW team I'd ever played with and were at least as fit as any League players could hope to be. We were jumping out of our skins. Still, we'd had to make a lot of sacrifices getting into that shape. It was very demanding on your time, with State training three nights a week, two other sessions on your own doing weights and with club training thrown in if you had any spare nights. It was fulltime Rugby.

The next challenges for NSW were against England and then a week later against Wales. We weren't too concerned with the fact that England were Grand Slam champions. More important to us was protecting our unbeaten record and we weren't about to surrender it to anyone, Grand Slam champions or not.

AUSTRALIA COMES OF AGE

We defeated England 21–19 on a day when we probably didn't play as well as we could have. Then we absolutely massacred Wales by 71–8. It wasn't a day any Welshman or woman could feel proud of. It was surely the worst performance ever by a major Rugby nation at that level. Certainly it was the worst defeat ever for Wales, eclipsing their 52–3 thrashing by New Zealand in Christchurch in 1988. We all know how intensely they love their Rugby in the valleys and this represented abject humiliation. They just caught us on the wrong day, with NSW on fire and scoring twelve tries (five of them by David Campese) to two, with Marty Roebuck kicking nine goals. Wales had a fair amount of spirit but they just didn't have the skills to counter us. And they wouldn't tackle.

Was I disappointed at seeing the once proud Welsh so dreadfully humiliated? No damned fear. I remembered being in Australian teams which lost to them at Cardiff in 1981 and again at Rotorua in the playoff for third and fourth places in the 1987 World Cup and dearly wanted them to pay for those losses. And that afternoon we got our reward ... with just a little bit of interest. A major casualty from the clash was that Warwick Waugh broke his leg. At the time he was pushing for Australian selection, with some devastating performances for NSW. But he's young and his time will come. Potentially Waugh's as good as any second-rower who has ever pulled on the green and gold.

That glorious victory was the last of NSW's matches for the season. We'd won nine games and drawn only one. No losses. It's a record of which I'm very proud and Macqueen and Carson can take most of the credit. Take it from me, Macca will coach Australia before long. He has the knack of being able to get very close to his players, but at the same time get what he wants from them, which is hard. And tactically he's superb. Virtually all the backrow moves which Australia used in the domestic Tests and in the World Cup which people raved about were devised by him for the NSW team.

The night of our win over Wales they announced the Australian team for the Test against them the following weekend. Naturally I was pretty hopeful after what NSW had achieved. But when the names were read out mine was missing. Jeff Miller's was there instead. I was devastated. I quickly exited the scene with my girlfriend Robin, Steve Cutler and his wife Carolyn. Like Cuts, whose hopes had also vanished, I had to get away from everybody. I thought I'd outpointed 'Ginger' Miller in the interstate matches, but obviously the selectors thought otherwise. What was particularly disappointing was the NSW backrow of Willie Ofahengaue, Tim Gavin and myself being split up after all those weeks together. We'd blended into a very effective unit and had virtually become a team within the State team. More importantly, we'd built up a fantastic friendship.

So I played for Randwick the following Saturday, then drove home dejectedly to the family farm in Goulburn. The next afternoon I watched Australia on television pulverise the Welsh by another mountainous score (63–6). Afterwards their tour really reached the pits when several of them scuffled amongst themselves at the after-match function. Later I went for a walk on my own in the paddocks and thought there was no way I could ever possibly make the team for the Test against England the next weekend. Jeff Miller had rightfully been singled out as man-of-the-match, which made my chances even more remote.

That night I drove back to Sydney and no sooner had I walked in the front door than the phone rang. It was a friend, Jeff James. 'Heard the news?' he asked. 'You're in the team to play England!' Sure enough, they'd dropped 'Ginger' and brought me in. I was stunned. Queenslanders were pretty unhappy about the change and had every reason to be. Dwyer explained: 'England pose a great threat close to the scrum and we need to combat that. For that reason, we need Poidevin ahead of Miller, just for his strength.'

Before the Test the Australian team headed down the New South Wales coastline to a new training venue at Wollongong and I found the change tremendous. The Northbeach Parkroyal where we stayed is right on the beach and you're well away from Sydney, the media and all the distractions you normally get before a Test match.

I was deeply moved and excited about playing a Test at the Sydney Football Stadium, because I'd never done so before. During the game against England I found some problems playing open-side breakaway, which I'd only played once before, and at fulltime I was absolutely knackered. I also pinched a nerve in my neck which took some of the gloss off my return to the Test team. Despite the fact that England played very well, we won 40–15 before 39 681 people, scoring five tries to one, with Michael Lynagh knocking over eight goals.

Despite the big win, we kept our feet well and truly on the ground. There was still a long way to go before we started thinking about winning the World Cup. Initially, there was the small hurdle of the All Blacks. We had two Tests against them in August, one at home, the other in Auckland.

Again the Test against the All Blacks at the Sydney Football Stadium was one we were all very excited about, because of our tremendous confidence that we could beat them. We trained particularly well down at Wollongong beforehand and on the day of the Test I vividly remember the silence on the long bus haul from the south coast. I sensed a certain resolve which told me that we were going to make life extremely tough for our old enemy. You can never underestimate the All Blacks, but we were determined that instead of waiting to see what they had to offer we were going to take the initiative for a change. From my point of view, it was going to be a big test playing against Auckland's Michael Jones, who has incredible skills, pace and fitness and was regarded by many as the best flanker in the world.

When we ran out in front of those 41 565 spectators I really felt fantastic. Compared with the England Test, I got into a much better rhythm, which was helped by the fact we were going forward all afternoon and everybody played extremely well. The atmosphere at the Sydney Football Stadium was also colossal. With the crowd so close and peering down on top of you—more so than at most international grounds—it really gets the adrenalin pumping and if you can't play well in that atmosphere then you can't play well anywhere. We were tied 9–9 at halftime, but then we pulled away in the second half and there was no sweeter moment in the whole Test than when our apprentice fullback-turned-winger Rob Egerton pinched the ball clean out of the hands of his opposite number John Kirwan and went for line like a startled rabbit. It was a case of the new kid on the block embarrassing the old hard head and I know Kirwan wouldn't have liked it one little bit. The final scoreline was 21–12 and that was undoubtedly the high moment of my domestic season. At the end of the day, too, Michael Jones hadn't shown any marked dominance in the loose and so this old bloke felt pretty good about life right at that moment.

Referees never get many accolades but let me add that the superb way the Test flowed was due in no small part to the man with the whistle, Ray Megson. He spent most of his childhood in Sydney until, when he was twelve, his family returned to Scotland. Now an Edinburgh solicitor, he showed great understanding of how to allow a game to flow which belied the fact that this was only his fourth major international. He's destined to become one of the world's best referees.

Before the return Test match, Australia received a tragic blow when Tim Gavin, who was undoubtedly the best number eight in the world, suffered a serious knee injury which put him out for the remainder of the season. It was tough news for Tim, the team and the backrow unit in particular. Not only was he playing extremely good Rugby, but he has a great soul and lends a lot of character and humour to the team. The big Queenslander Troy Coker was signalled as his replacement.

So we headed off across the Tasman and, while our Wollongong preparations and the Sydney Football Stadium were genuinely worth points to the Australian team, all those extraneous factors worked in reverse in Auckland. We stayed smack in the middle of the city and couldn't get the same quiet, rested preparation as we'd had back home. The team knew that would count against us.

Because of their Sydney defeat the All Blacks had been carved up unmercifully by their own media and public and I warned our players that they'd come onto Eden Park in Auckland ready to go beserk. A strong anti-

Auckland feeling runs through New Zealand Rugby and by that stage John Hart had joined Alex (Griz) Wyllie in coaching the New Zealanders. And there was still much feeling locally about Zinzan Brooke being at number eight instead of everybody's hero, Wayne Shelford.

So the All Blacks had all the motivation they needed playing in front of the Auckland crowd. It also rained cats and dogs in the days prior to the Test and so overall it shaped up as a really tough assignment for us.

As it was, New Zealand just scraped home 6–3 in a tryless Test. We gave a remarkable defensive performance, because they threw absolutely everything at us in the first 30 minutes. Although eventually we started to gain control it was not enough to win. We weren't helped by Michael Lynagh having an atrocious day with the boot and missing six of his seven penalty shots. His counterpart Grant Fox didn't fare much better.

Afterwards it surprised some of our players when I told them I wasn't really disappointed and history might show it as being the best loss Australia ever had. Sounds crazy? Had New Zealand lost, there would have been total turmoil, radical changes and they'd have lifted their whole tempo going into the World Cup. As it was, they thought 'we've got them, Australia has peaked'. They kept virtually the same side and didn't have nearly the same hunger which two losses to Australia would have given them.

Having given the previous referee a pat on the back, let me give the pedantic Scottish whistle-blower Ken McCartney a swift kick in the rump for effectively destroying the Test as a spectacle. If it was dreadful watching it, then rest assured it was even worse playing! He almost blew the pea out of his whistle. There were no fewer than 33 penalties and too few (none, in fact, that come to mind) advantages played. In short, McCartney was a disgrace. He tried to referee as though he had charge of a third-grade game on the Scottish Borders, instead of two international teams wanting to play to the death. He was much too inexperienced, outdated in his interpretations of the Laws and probably intimidated by the intense atmosphere out in the middle. The All Blacks didn't help him with the way they played the game. Boots were flying everywhere in attempts to disrupt us and Graeme Bachop at halfback was screaming at his forwards 'they don't like it ... give it to them ... give it to them ... use the feet ...' The atmosphere was certainly very volatile, but the players were kept in check because the referee just went beserk with the whistle and kept awarding penalties, which kept the teams apart.

Back from New Zealand, I still had the premiership finals to worry about. Randwick ran into Eastern Suburbs in the major semi-final at North Sydney Oval and copped a decent walloping by 25–12. We deserved it too. Our number eight Michael Cheika took the field in one piece but virtually came off in two, when his head was sliced open in one of the worst injuries you're likely to see. Although nobody seemed to spot the culprit, Easts prop Geoff Bucknell was subsequently cited to appear before the Sydney Rugby Union judiciary committee not once, but twice, the latter occasion on the night before the grand final. Both times he was exonerated. It was tough on Bucknell and the whole incident could have been handled much better by the Sydney Rugby Union. For the grand final, Easts also insisted on using Bucknell at loosehead instead of Test representative Tony Daly, which was a huge mistake. They didn't help either themselves or Australia, because being dropped by his club knocked Daly's confidence around enormously.

Coach Jeff Sayle was deeply stung by our semi-final defeat and we worked night and day to reverse the result. Randwick wiped Parramatta 50–10 in the final and so lined up against Easts again in the grand final. Many were expecting a bloodbath after the Cheika episode, but that was never going to happen. Instead there was just a great resolve and a cold-blooded feeling among the Randwick players and with Daly not in the frontrow we knew their scrum was always going to be under pressure. Sure enough, on the day we carved them up well and truly, winning 28–9 for our fifth straight premiership and eleventh in 14 years. Easts were a little over-confident, probably expecting Randwick to play as they had in the major semi-final. That was a bad miscalculation, because that loss only meant we lifted our determination to a much higher pitch.

I can't see Randwick surrendering its pre-eminent place in Australian Rugby for a long while yet. The club doesn't recruit all the good players who flock there. They come to us. Success attracts success. It's a fact of life. We also have a major assset in Supercoach Sayle. He's an extraordinary person, with a great understanding of players' needs, a devoted team man and loved by one and all in the club.

Is Randwick's dominance good for Australian Rugby, which many suggest it isn't? A quarter of our World Cup squad were from Randwick. Surely there's nothing wrong with one club providing so many talented players for the national team if, in turn, it's also playing exceptionally well. Even if there weren't these good effects there's nothing anyone can do about it. You can't have a draft system, because we're amateurs and can roam to and from clubs as we please. And Randwick certainly don't pay players under the lap for going there. Many gossips think we do, but I'll swear on a stack of Bibles that's not the case.

After a few days' celebration following the grand final, Randwick's World Cup players had to quickly get our minds back on the track. Shortly we faced a much bigger assignment on the other side of the globe.

The outfitting for the Wallabies at the Airport Parkroyal in Sydney was another sign of the Australian Rugby Football Union's changing attitude, for we were given more gear than you could imagine. If you wanted to, you needed only take your own toothbrush and Speedos. Virtually all the rest was supplied.

Each player also had his own room at the hotel. No need to suffer any more from the loud snoring of someone like Stan Pilecki. It meant you had space to spread all this gear around and your wife or girlfriend could stay a few nights before departure. Things had certainly changed since I started my international career.

The team trained like Trojans before leaving and at one of these final sessions some officials from the Australian Sports Drug Agency arrived unannounced. Ten players were randomly selected for drug-testing, including me. My attempt to provide a sample didn't quite work as planned. I was doing fine until urine started spraying everywhere and only then did I discover that the beaker was cracked. The sample was disappearing quicker than I could provide it.

We had a succession of farewell lunches and dinners in Sydney, with several of the largest and best-attended organised by Alan King, managing director of A.S.K. Solutions, a company which services the computer industry. He's a Rugby nut who employed at the time both coach Bob Dwyer and hooker Phil Kearns and put on these functions simply because of his enormous love for the game.

Girlfriend Robin Fahlstromm farewelling me on the way to the 1991 World Cup
(Mirror Australian Telegraph Publications)

On boarding the Northwest flight to London via Los Angeles we received a nice surprise. No longer did we head way down the back. For the first time in my experience the Australian team was travelling business class. The second-rowers in particular thought it Heaven being able to stretch out and not have to curl up in the foetal position for hour after hour. It's a disgrace that the World Cup organising committee would only provide economy class travel for teams attending the tournament and the ARFU intelligently struck a deal with Northwest to fly business class. At the end of the day, we're the entertainers and without us there would be no World Cup or the huge profits which go with it.

I had never been more thankful than when the door of the big jet finally slammed closed. There was no turning back. I'd really made it and felt like going around and shaking each teammate by the hand just to convince myself I was off to my second World Cup. I'd had doubts at times that I'd make it. But no more.

For our stopover in LA all our luggage had to be offloaded and this provided not only a lot of work for Northwest staff, but plenty of laughs. Our gear was all stamped with the logo of XXXX, the sponsor of the Wallabies. Yet in America the same logo belongs to one of the largest manufacturers of condoms! The airport staff couldn't believe it. 'Hey, whadda you guys from Down Under doing carting trunks and suitcases full of XXXX around the place? Wherever ya going, you're sure going to have a hell of a time ...'

We travelled down to the University of Southern California, trained in very hot conditions and then had a night on the town provided for us by the Legends Bar at Long Beach. It was our last chance for a decent drink before the World Cup. Except a few of us lingered too long, then found ourselves without transport and had a $50 cab ride back to the Airport Sheraton. We weren't amused.

Nothing had changed when we walked off the plane at Heathrow Airport. It was drizzling and overcast. A fairly normal London day. Seems it's been like that every time I've arrived there. The Wallabies stayed at the Lensbury Club, which is owned by the Shell Company. The training facilities were excellent, although the accommodation was fairly spartan; very small rooms with two players in each. We trained extremely hard morning and afternoon. Dwyer and his offsiders, Bob Templeton and Jake Howard (alias Jake and the Fatman), drove us unmercifully and soon we were counting the days until the first match, so that the volume of training would ease. This idea of training like mad dogs when the team arrived at its destination had worked successfully for Alan Jones back in 1984 and so Dwyer had adopted a similar pattern with his teams.

The World Cup welcome dinner at the Lancaster Gate Hotel was colourful and interesting, for it was the first opportunity to see what the

*Australia's Philip Kearns powers through to score a try. 1991 Rugby World Cup—Australia v Argentina (**Bob Thomas, Fotopacific**)*

opposing teams looked like. The Canadians were monstrous. We couldn't get over their size, but as luck would have it we wouldn't see them again at close quarters. At dinners like this, the Wallabies always run a sweep on how many heavies (officials) there might be at the main table. Nobody got anywhere near the number this time, because the main table was so long and contained so many heavies that you could barely see the end of it. The second World Cup seemed to have spawned more officials than I'd seen in my entire playing career.

The next day we headed for Swansea to prepare for our opening game on October 4 against Argentina at Llanelli. We thought the media coverage in London had been considerable, but it really overflowed down there in Wales. It was nonstop.

Argentina's Pumas were always going to be a problem. Coming up against opponents as strong as them with some of our team not having played for six weeks made it tough.

The Pumas played extremely well. They exuded confidence and as always their scrum proved very strong and dangerous. We took a while finding some combination and in the end got home 32–19 through some very slick backline play from David Campese and Tim Horan. Normally such a scoreline would be considered an easy day's work, but it wasn't, because most of our points came late in the game. Still, it was a gutsy effort by Australia because panic can often set in when you're under the pressure we were and it didn't. It was a further indication of the team's ability to remain composed when things weren't going right. After the match, Dwyer was critical of the forwards' effort and indicated he wasn't nearly satisified with the secondrow and backrow, where John Eales hadn't been all that successful at number eight. The players too knew that they could do much better than that.

As we were leaving the field, sidestepping people and at the same time trying to sign autographs, the referee Keith Lawrence came across to me and said: 'You've been chosen for random drug-testing ... follow me.' So off I went to the testing room, but being so dehydrated I couldn't pass water for the life of me. The two Welsh medical officers were giving me cans of Diet Coke to help the process when it suddenly dawned. 'Isn't caffeine one of the drugs you're testing for?' They agreed it was and I pointed out in no uncertain terms that Diet Coke contains caffeine! You've only got to read the label on the bottle to know that. They were understandably shocked—though not half as much as me—and, suitably embarrassed, went searching for some other drinks to help me urinate. The medical commission of the International Olympic Committee would have died laughing—or crying—at Rugby's primitive drug-testing methods. And the result? Negative.

Our next game was five days later against Western Samoa at Pontypool. In the meantime, we watched the Samoans say the last rites over Welsh Rugby by beating this once proud nation by 16–13 at Cardiff Arms Park. At times I actually covered my face at their ferocious tackles because I thought they were going to maim themselves, the Welsh, or both. It was like ducks being picked off in the shooting gallery at sideshow alley. The Samoan team management and reserves were seated right in front of us and started going berserk when it became obvious they were creating Rugby history. We were cheering them too. We hail from the same part of the world and the Samoans had also bobbed up at one of our training sessions in New Zealand back in August and been across and played a friendly game against the Barbarians in Sydney. So there was a good deal of dialogue and friendship between the two teams. And plenty of respect, because something like a dozen of them were good enough to have played provincial Rugby in New Zealand, including five who had represented the All Blacks. So we knew that when it was our turn to face them it wasn't going to be all that easy.

It wasn't. Pontypool was a most unappealing venue, with rain pelting down and the ground covered in rolling fog. I was on the reserves' bench, not altogether a bad spot to be. Jeff Miller and Brendan Nasser were the breakaways, Eales was again number eight and Steve Cutler in the secondrow. Before kickoff, I was outside the ground with Ewen McKenzie doing the customary thing of selling spare tickets from the Wallabies' allotment to raise money for some team drinks. It's an age-old practice. We were offering undercover seats for ten quid. As kickoff approached we discounted the price to five quid because we needed to get rid of them. It was enormous value. People had difficulty believing they were genuine and someone must have said something because the next thing there was a policeman alongside us. He thought we were flogging fake tickets. Then suddenly he recognised us and we explained what we were up to. He was understanding, wished us luck and wandered off.

Watching the game, Australia were always in control, but it felt like the Samoans might score an intercept try or do something outrageous at any moment. Many other teams would have been intimidated by them and fallen away, but Australia kept their minds on the task, played for position and waited for the penalties. They came and Michael Lynagh potted three in our 9–3 win. His leadership after Nick Farr-Jones left the field with an injured knee was also exceptional. Despite the win, Dwyer was still concerned about the forwards and the fact they weren't harmonising as they should. Of more concern though was Farr-Jones' injury, although we had a very able replacement in Peter Slattery.

While on the Samoans, they were undoubtedly the team which really caught the public's imagination in the World Cup. The IRB owes a great deal to these little fish from the South Pacific.

During this period it was enormous fun each night watching the other pool matches on television. It helped make the whole occasion so special. What disappointed us more than anything was Fiji's poor showing. I couldn't believe they didn't win a game. I thought they'd do extremely well, but obviously they found it hard playing in France and had much worse weather than us. I'd also like to think that in future when the pool matches are finished teams such as this which miss the quarter-finals have repercharge matches instead of being abruptly shunted off home as they now are.

Leading up to the next game against Wales, there was a real frustration among the team because we knew we weren't playing as well as we could. We were getting a fair amount of deserved criticism and the Rugby world was calling us pretenders. So we determined to lift ourselves another level and the training became even harder.

The Welsh were hoping for a shock victory and some parts of the media were tipping an upset. Alan Davies, the Welsh coach, stoked the fires nicely and brought our motivation to just the right pitch by stating that the Australians had no spine.

Dwyer's address to the team in our Cardiff hotel just before we went to dinner on the eve of the game was his most impassioned of the whole World Cup campaign. After explaining what he wanted his forwards and backs to do, Dwyer finished with the words: 'Now we've got to take the opportunity. I do not want to die an unhappy man.' His voice began to break: 'I do not want to look back at 1991 thinking we were good enough to do it, to win the World Cup, but did not do it.' He challenged us not to go home losers.

We went to the Arms Park that day intent on totally destroying Wales. And we did. But beforehand the teams lined up on the pitch to be introduced to Princess Diana. That was fine, I shook her hand and then watched mesmerised as this beautifully radiant young woman drifted on to the next player. Suddenly I sensed another presence. I looked down and realised I'd forgotten little Prince Harry, who was trailing along behind mum. He had his hand out and wanted to shake hands too. Like me, most of the players forgot about him and he had a real problem attracting the attention of some of our tallest forwards, who towered over him.

The Wallabies set what must be something of a world record by winning virtually every lineout against Wales. They tried to distract us by putting on a bit of stick, but it wasn't very effective. With Willie Ofahengaue playing number eight this time and the Ginger Bees of myself and Jeff Miller on the side, the forwards started to function much more smoothly. As the game continued Australia were obviously far superior, the threequarters played some fantastic running Rugby and we finished up inflicting on Wales their heaviest ever Test defeat (38–3) on home soil. That was the last of our pool matches and we had confirmed a World Cup quarter-final date with Ireland at Lansdowne Road in Dublin. On the strength of that we allowed ourselves a few quiet drinks that evening.

Then it was onto a charter plane to Dublin. It was nice getting away from Wales, where the pressure because of the country's love for Rugby can become quite overpowering. On our arrival at Dublin Airport, we were loaded on a bus and our two police motorcycle escorts took off like the starting gun had been fired for a 100-metre sprint. They screamed through red lights, waved pedestrians out of the way and then cleared the whole area in front of the grand Westbury Hotel ready for our arrival. We weren't sure of the reason for all the haste. Apparently there was none. They were just trying to show us how efficient they were.

The people of Dublin seemed genuinely delighted to see us and we fostered this warmth by regularly going to the local mall and signing Australian team booklets for passers-by. We won many friends doing that and everywhere we were treated with great warmth and kindness. The players all fell in love with the place. There's a special feel about Ireland and you could scarcely believe that we were about to play them in a sudden-death encounter.

One day a few of us, including manager John Breen, Tim Horan, Steve

Cutler and radio commentator Ray Hadley, accepted an invitation to visit the renowned Coolmore Stud to check some of its famous thoroughbreds. The bus driver told us that it should take two hours to get there but, in typical Irish fashion, that came and went and he said we still had another hour's drive. Despite the long haul, it was one of the most amusing bus trips ever with Hadley entertaining all and sundry. The stud is partly owned by Vincent O'Brien, one of the world's greatest thoroughbred trainers, and in his absence his Australian wife Jacqueline treated us like family. We were fascinated at seeing the stallion Sadliers Wells and could scarcely believe that he's worth something like 27 million pounds!

Before the quarter-final, I warned the players that the Irish would give us an incredibly hard time. Forget their track record. They would lift themselves enormously and the noise from the crowd at Lansdowne Road would be so deafening as to be distracting. As it turned out, the game was just as I expected. From the outset the Irish began pouring through our lineout, which meant our inside backs were under extreme pressure. In the 16th minute Nick Farr-Jones hurt his knee again and Slats had to come on just as the Irish forwards were gaining some control. Nevertheless, we didn't get rattled, turned on some good Rugby and towards the end had a three-point margin. Then in the 74th minute the Irish flanker Gordon Hamilton broke away and charged for the line. I couldn't believe it when he went over for the try. In that split second it seemed the world had come to an end. What followed was absolute pandemonium. People jumped the fence to congratulate their heroes and the noise was so loud it was like a plague of locusts buzzing around in your head. My stomach turned inside out. As we headed back behind the goal-line I thought, God, what a waste of a year, because defeat here meant we were on the plane home the next morning. When Ralph Keyes kicked the goal to make the score 18–15 it seemed almost impossible for us to win. Yet given the circumstances, everyone recovered their composure very quickly. Lynagh, the acting captain, told us there were only four minutes left. Only four minutes to catch up. But there was no panic, only encouraging talk along the lines that 'We can do it ... we can do it ... let's get ourselves down the other end on their line.'

On the resumption we immediately responded by pushing the ball upfield towards the Irish line where the Irish halfback Rob Kennedy made the fateful mistake of not finding touch. Marty Roebuck replied with a magnificent 'bomb' that left the Irish number eight with only one option—to kick out three metres from the Irish line. We won the lineout, worked a move bringing Campese in off a scissors' movement and set up a scrum-feed for Australia. Lynagh then masterminded a backline move through the opposing centres. There was never any thought of a dropped goal, only a try. And when Lynagh himself went over in the other corner and up went the referee's arm it was the most relieved I've ever been. Only seconds remained. Surely at that moment God had to be an Australian. Everyone felt as though they'd been born again. The Irish players and fans were devastated. For a few minutes they had glory and suddenly it had been cruelly ripped from them. But the moment the whistle finally sounded for fulltime at 19–18 all those Irish fans immediately transferred their loyalty and support from their own team to us.

This one got away against Ireland **(Fotopacific)**

That extraordinary escape meant that we stayed in Dublin a while longer. No-one was more delighted than our reserve five-eighth David Knox, who had become something of an expert on Dublin's pubs and its nightlife. For most of us though, it meant something else again. Assistant coach Templeton, who mainly looked after the forwards, was livid at the way we played against Ireland and promised us even more work between then and the semi-final against New Zealand.

When the team was announced for that do-or-die semi-final against the All Blacks, everyone's jaw dropped when Jeff Miller's name wasn't there. He'd been dumped, with Troy Coker coming in at number eight and

Willie O joining me on the side of the scrum. Nobody could believe the change, because Miller had a great game against Wales and another excellent game against Ireland. He was very put out by the decision, but nothing could be done about it. Miller's dignity in accepting the selectors' decision again illustrated the breadth of his character.

We then buckled down to beating New Zealand in what was considered the most important match to that point in the whole tournament. Whoever won the semi-final was seen as ultimately becoming world champions. England were up against Scotland in the other semi-final.

From then on the level of intensity, preparation and aggression in the team as we prepared at Trinity College in Dublin was incredible; unsurpassed by anything I'd ever encountered. At one stage Rod McCall even accused our reserve forwards of eye-gouging! Dan Crowley (the shadow Test prop) piped up that if he was going to gouge anyone it would be Ewen McKenzie. Spectators watching couldn't believe just how hard we trained. We were priming ourselves for the mother of all battles.

We sensed some weaknesses in the All Blacks team, given the changes they made to their lineup. Michael Jones was both unavailable (his religious beliefs prevent him playing on Sundays) and irreplaceable, with Auckland flanker Mark Carter called up in preference to Paul Henderson to fill the gap. Kieran Crowley, who had quit the game only weeks before when his provincial side Taranaki was relegated to second division, also came in at fullback for John Timu. We were also certain that Coker's height would negate their strength at the back of the lineout.

When the All Blacks hit Dublin they adopted a cloak-and-dagger attitude, while we continued our high profile, going out of our way to sign anything, be photographed with anyone and generally show ourselves off as much as we could. Our popularity reached even new heights when a number of us appeared on the front page of the local newspaper drinking pints of Guinness.

Again, we had another impassioned plea from Bob Dwyer before the game. Some of us also turned elsewhere for inspiration. The Roman Catholics amongst us had a priest come into the hotel to say Mass. It was very moving and there was a little of the crusades in this, remembering how the knights would have their last mass at the chapel before going into battle. The next morning Willie O, a very keen churchgoer, took a few of the non-Catholics to church too.

On the day of the game, October 27, I went out in the morning for some Sunday papers and found the streets teeming with All Black supporters. A few brash ones were sitting in the gutter and began hurling abuse at me. I said nothing because I knew we'd take care of their lot later in the day.

We hit Lansdowne Road more motivated and physically prepared than any Australian team I'd ever played in. For the first twenty minutes, the All Blacks were obviously in a state of shock at the pace and physical presence of the Wallabies. They hadn't expected anything like it, given we'd only beaten Ireland by a single point.

Campo really left a huge imprint on that semi-final. In the sixth minute he scored the most exhilarating solo try of the tournament, and later created an even better team try, to show he was the best attacking player in the world and definitely the star performer in the World Cup. The memory of Campo angling across field and bamboozling Mark Carter, Sean Fitzpatrick and John Kirwan will remain forever. This was then topped in the 34th minute by his incredible one-handed pickup from a clever Lynagh kick, a wiggle to offset John Timu and then an inspired flick over his right shoulder to the brilliant Horan to give us a decisive edge. Our defence was also staggering. So hard and efficient was it that the All Blacks started running out of attacking options. Normally they are most dangerous in the ten minutes either side of halftime and when they didn't score just before the break, I began feeling confident. And in the spell just after halftime they got only three points. We had the smell of victory in our nostrils by then and were climbing over one another to make tackles. In the last ten minutes the All Blacks really panicked when they couldn't make any impression on the 16-6 scoreline. The ball was being thrown everywhere in a desperate gamble to score. But the horse had well and truly bolted.

When the final whistle went—and we were into the final—I couldn't believe what gracious losers they were. Humility hasn't always been the All Blacks' greatest attribute, but they were very humble that day. Later in the dressing-room, just as Dwyer was saying there was only one team in it, All Black coach Griz Wyllie walked in behind him and acknowledged that was so.

To say we were delighted with our win and celebrated accordingly totally understates the position. Indeed if anyone had bombed the Westbury Hotel in Dublin at five o'clock the next morning they wouldn't have collected too many Wallabies.

Later that day at the airport, we bumped into the defending champs as they prepared to fly to Cardiff and the playoff for third and fourth placings (they beat the Scots 13-6). We were headed for Twickenham and the final against England. Their heads were down and they were obviously hurting. I genuinely felt sorry for them and went over and joined Zinzan Brooke, Michael Jones, Alan Whetton and a few others in the ball game they were playing. They might have been All Blacks, but they were also friends. (Later in the tournament their assistant coach John Hart told me how much he appreciated my action.) When their boarding call came, many of them walked over, shook hands and wished us luck. It was a unique moment for us—and them.

Where's All Black Rugby headed? I don't know. Hart went to the World Cup as something of a Messiah and the logical successor to Wyllie, but didn't have the effect that had been expected. He paid for this by missing out on his burning ambition when Laurie Mains was appointed as the new All Black coach last December. From our point of view, we've discovered in the last four Tests the real key to playing the All Blacks and that's shown by the fact they've scored only one try against us in that time. We certainly don't hold them in nearly the same awe as we used to. But you can bet they'll be out to reverse that attitude as New Zealand Rugby is just too strong to be satisfied with second place to Australia.

The Wallabies' arrival at Heathrow Airport that Monday afternoon before the final was remarkable. There were reporters, TV crews and photographers everywhere. Suddenly we realised what we were in for. Luckily we were put up in the lovely, spacious Oatlands Park Hotel in the Surrey countryside. Despite that, the media bombardment was something else and we couldn't believe the scene at our public training run on the Wednesday. There must have been ten television crews and there were dozens of photographers. It was a job getting around them all and afterwards every man and his dog was wanting to shove a microphone, TV camera or loaded question down our throats. We were severely restricted in what we could do. So from Thursday onwards the team management imposed a media blackout so we could get some peace and quiet and do some work. We also had to psyche up again, after the enormous mental buildup we'd had for the All Blacks game.

We were all confident we could beat England but at times like that it often helps if some critic comes along and sharpens your motivation. This time it was British Lions' captain Finlay Calder who labelled the Australian forwards immature and said they wouldn't be able to handle the English. His view was blurred by what had happened when he led the Lions to Australia in 1989. We were a much different team this time around. There was also a photograph in one of the newspapers of England captain Will Carling on a Harley-Davidson motorbike in a leather jacket and dark glasses, with the headline declaring 'WILL: EASY RIDE TO VICTORY.' There was also much talk about how much money the England team was going to make out of its World Cup victory. I told the forwards 'we've worked too hard to hand victory to someone else ...'

In those last few days before the final we were also besieged by well-wishers ringing us up and sending us faxes of encouragement ... a whole 50 000 of them! It gave us great determination, knowing so many thousands of Aussies from all over the country, not just from the game's heartland on the eastern seaboard, were behind us. Everyone was obviously willing us to win just so much. And in the last 48 hours we managed to find two most important ingredients to our success—sleep and silence.

On the big day in the bus going to Twickenham one particular drunk stood on the footpath screaming at us 'UNLUCKY ... UNLUCKY ... AUSSIES UNLUCKY ...' It took a lot to restrain some of the boys from jumping out and belting this loudmouth. I've never seen as many people as there were in the Twickenham car park that day and it was a huge relief just to get into the sanctuary of the dressing-room.

Just before we ran out for the game of our lives, Templeton quietly recited the four-verse poem, 'Spirit of the Wallabies', written some years ago by former Sydney coach Peter Fenton, which begins:

There's a spirit in the Wallabies
Mere words cannot describe,
It's as if they descended
From some legendary tribe.
As in days so long since past,
Of crusades, of knights in armour,
And of men before the mast.

We promised ourselves that we weren't going to return to the dressing-room as losers. Then out we went. For the next twenty minutes we had to absorb the incredible atmosphere while meeting the Queen. At that time it was very important to concentrate amid all the action, the chanting and the singing. We noticed, though, that some of the England players waved back to the crowd and were even laughing. We weren't. Aussie blood was boiling.

The game was a mirror image of the All Black game. We went ahead early and they had to catch us. England departed from their previous negative 10-man approach which they had followed religiously throughout the tournament and attempted a higher risk game by running the ball much more. Yet they failed because of the overwhelming steel of our defence, although it was only an amazing effort by second-rower John Eales to come from nowhere and plough England five-eighth Rob Andrew into the turf late in the second half which saved a try. Our defence throughout the tournament had been amazing, but that day it was superhuman, shown by the fact that Andrew handled the ball 41 times compared with Lynagh's 17. And yet still they couldn't get past us. Willie Ofahengaue's performance in the final also left many in awe.

Australia only rarely came near England's line, but when we did we took full advantage of it. Our only try in the 26th minute could not have come at a better time, particularly with England looking dangerous. It resulted from some great solo work by Horan. He took a bomb near his own line, spun out of the defence and sprinted 60m before kicking ahead and seeing fullback Webb run the ball into touch near the corner flag. From the lineout, Willie O took a two-handed catch, the two props Daly and McKenzie enveloped him as part of a rolling maul and dived over the line together, both holding the ball. Two points apiece. The try and conversion gave Australia a nine-point comfort zone and we managed to keep England at bay for the next 54 minutes.

One of England's best opportunities came in the 69th minute when their breakaway Peter Winterbottom tried to send the unmarked Rory Underwood away just outside the Wallaby quarter. But Campo knocked down the pass with one hand, conceding a penalty which Jonathan Webb booted. English critics claimed later that a penalty try should have been awarded, but there was no certainty Underwood would have scored with our defence converging on him as fast as they were.

Among the many moments I remember from the final was the hit on me early in the game by rival flanker Mickey Skinner, without doubt the best English player on the day. I spotted him only a fraction of a second before he collected me with his shoulder and he caught me a beauty. He waited for a reaction and got it. 'Do your bloody best, pal!' and I laughed at him. I wasn't about to let him know that it was a great hit and my head was still spinning.

The end of the game seemed forever coming. Twickenham doesn't have a game-clock, so you don't know how long there is to go and in the frantic atmosphere there didn't seem time to ask the referee. Finally when the whistle sounded with us winning 12–6 there was more a huge surge of relief than anything. Dreams do come true. The William Webb Ellis Trophy was ours. The names of the 15 who did it—Roebuck, Egerton, Little, Horan, Campese, Lynagh, Farr-Jones, Coker, Ofahengaue, Poidevin, McCall, Eales, McKenzie, Kearns and Daly—will never be forgotten, because they had provided Australian Rugby with its greatest moment. But it was not just us. Every member of our World Cup squad was responsible for Australian Rugby's grandest achievement: the players, coaches, conditioners, doctors, physiotherapists and baggage-men all played their part.

As soon as we got into the dressing-room we burst into Advance Australia Fair. Then the smart oldies like myself jumped into one of the much-sought-after baths for a warm soak and a few beers. We were all singing and shouting. Then in walked the British Prime Minister John Major. He headed straight for the naked Nick Farr-Jones, who stood there chatting with nothing on but a delighted, if embarrassed, smile. Next he came across to me and I shook his hand while wallowing around in the tub. I didn't bother standing up!

That night before going off to the official closing dinner at the luxurious Lancaster Gate Hotel in London the team talked about being humble in victory. Not that anyone needed to be told, but we didn't want any boasting. The dinner before nearly 1200 people was superb, but rather stuffy as English dinners always are. There was also the usual agitation within the team that our wives and girlfriends weren't invited to such black tie extravaganzas. Then we headed back for our Surrey hideaway and what turned out to be rather subdued celebrations. There was not the rollicking good fun you might expect, because there was the realisation that it was all about to finish. It was an unbelievable achievement, but now it was all over.

At 9.30 the next morning Dwyer, Templeton and I farewelled 16 team members heading immediately back to Australia from Gatwick Airport. After the waves, handshakes and special parting words, the three of us got back on the bus and headed for Oatlands. I was staying behind to do a few days work in London. It was a very lonely time; among the loneliest of my life.

It was a good time to reflect. Campo had been our undoubted star. From the very outset of the season he was clearly on a mission. Given the way he prepared himself, it was obvious he wanted to play the best he'd ever played. And he did just that. Once he got to the United Kingdom the media went absolutely beserk over him, which I might add caused some ill-feeling among the team. I just wish the media had better appreciated the team as a whole, especially players like Eales, Horan, Little and Ofahengaue, more than they did. The impression at times was that Campo was the whole Australian team. He undoubtedly was the leading light in the whole tournament, but he would be the first one to agree that it was a team performance, and not one individual, which won Australia the World Cup.

Eventually when I left London I flew to America and had a couple of days fantastic skiing with a friend Bill Anderson and his family in Aspen, Colorado. I couldn't believe that smack in the middle of Aspen is a Rugby ground, worth $US40 million in real estate value. A Rugby nut deeded it to the local club and determined that it could only ever be used for Rugby. The bush telegraph got the message to the Gentlemen of Aspen Rugby Club that I was heading their way and I was lucky to get out of town alive, let alone reasonably sober. They adore the game up there in John Denver country and wanted me to come back next summer (that's when they have their Rugby matches) and play for them. I was certainly tempted.

When at last I arrived home in Sydney everyone was agog with the Wallabies' achievement and was talking about the ticker-tape parade through the city streets on November 20 which had been triggered by the Premier, Nick Greiner. I didn't fear like some players that no-one would

FOR LOVE NOT MONEY

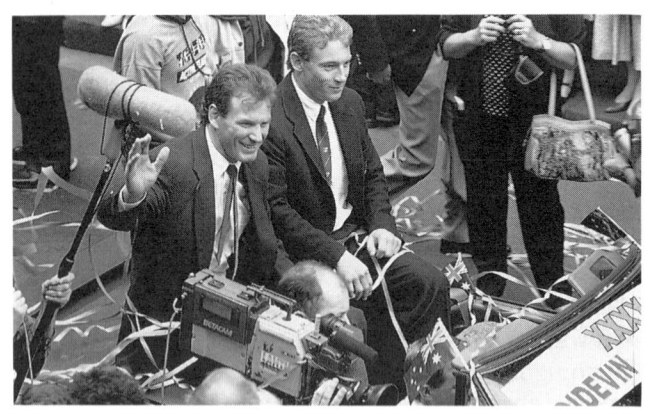

John Flett and I in the tickertape parade in Sydney after the World Cup (Jayne Russell)

turn up, but when the parade took place it was an incredible experience. We just couldn't believe the wholehearted support and happiness. George Street was chock-a-block with thousands of people ... office-workers, pensioners wanting to kiss your cheek, young kids wanting to shake your hand and a smattering of migrants whose backgrounds were obviously far removed from the game of Rugby. But they all simply wanted to help celebrate the greatest team achievement ever by Australia in a truly international sport and be part of Rugby's finest hour in this country.

The year 1991 was a golden one for Australian Rugby: ten Test matches, nine wins. One loss to New Zealand, 6–3 in the Eden Park slop. This team's momentum will undoubtedly continue. It has a spirit, a commitment and friendship which will carry it to even more success. Given that players like Warwick Waugh and Tim Gavin will come back into the lineup and few, if any, will go to League or retire then it's going to be an extremely strong Australian side for some time to come.

A lot now falls in the lap of the Australian Rugby Football Union, which is already one of the world's most progressive unions and genuinely takes the interest of players to heart. It has to ride on this tidal wave of success and market Rugby here like never before. All those television viewers who saw the World Cup (more than two billion of them in 70 countries) now realise that this game of ours absolutely kills international Rugby League. Once you understand the game it's just so enjoyable to watch and now it's up to the ARFU to get that across to the massive number of potential converts.

Our current Wallabies are also very special people, they present a wonderful image and deserve everything they get, financially or otherwise. Australia's reputation overseas in recent years, given what has happened to some corporate leaders, has been severely tarnished and now suddenly there's this hurricane of fresh air in the shape of the Wallabies. During the World Cup the team was continually complimented for its high standards and accessibility. There were no scandals and no cover-ups. We were the people's team, the entertainers, the media favourites, the athletes and—without dispute—world champions. Golden opportunities exist for the ARFU. We've had our turn. Now it's their turn to run with the ball.

The 1991 World Cup tournament is expected to gross 25 million pounds ($79 million). By the time the 1995 World Cup arrives the players themselves will want to share in such revenues. I know the ARFU does not want players being financially disadvantaged by their huge commitment to representative Rugby and will push for changes to more generously compensate them. The International Rugby Board has already opened the door for us to earn money outside the game, but very soon—in fact, sooner than later—Rugby must at least become professional at the highest level even if it remains amateur at club level (as in cricket). This will also keep players from going to Rugby League.

So will I be part of the Australian team in 1992 or will I retire?

Frankly, I don't know. In my heart I'd like to keep going forever, but I know that can't be. I'd very much like to play against Scotland and the All Blacks here in 1992, but the end-of-season tour of nine weeks to Wales and Ireland with a possible one-off Test on the way against the Springboks would make it very hard for me at work. My employers Prudential Bache Securities gave me over two months off last year and without that generosity I couldn't have played for Australia.

I'm also not sure that I'll have the same hunger in the future. I'd miss the camaraderie, but at some stage you've got to make a final decision and it's probably a very convenient time to call it quits. After all, you can't do any more than be a part of an unbeaten State team, win another Sydney club premiership, have 59 Test caps and then triumph in the World Cup. As well, I was honoured by being named Yardley Footballer of the Year and was inducted into the Confederation of Australian Sport's Hall of Fame.

I also had more niggling injuries last year than ever before. I'm now 33, but despite my age and these injuries I feel I'm playing as well as ever. It's more a question of whether this is the correct time to stop serious football. However, I've got a very strong allegiance towards NSW and wouldn't mind playing for them and Randwick for just one more season and that's the way I'm leaning at this moment.

So I'll think it over during the summer, have a few beers, catch some waves at Coogee and then decide exactly what the future holds.

If there are any words of advice for young players reading this book they are that there's no greater honour in Australian sport than to play for the Wallabies. It's a very special team which, year in and year out, takes on the best in the world and plays with a spirit admired by all. Any amount of hard work will be repaid many times over if you're ever fortunate enough to play for them and I sincerely hope you do.

SIMON POIDEVIN'S TEST CAREER
1980–1991

1980
Australia 22 v Fiji 9   Suva
Australia 13 v New Zealand 9   Sydney Cricket Ground *(1st Test)*
Australia 9 v New Zealand 12   Ballymore *(2nd Test)*
Australia 26 v New Zealand 10   Sydney Cricket Ground *(3rd Test)*

1981
Australia 17 v France 15   Ballymore *(1st Test)*
Australia 24 v France 14   Sydney Cricket Ground *(2nd Test)*
Australia 16 v Ireland 12   Lansdowne Road, Dublin
Australia 13 v Wales 18   Cardiff Arms Park
Australia 15 v Scotland 24   Murrayfield, Edinburgh
Australia 11 v England 15   Twickenham

1982
Australia 16 v New Zealand 23   Christchurch *(1st Test)*
Australia 19 v New Zealand 16   Wellington *(2nd Test)*
Australia 18 v New Zealand 33   Auckland *(3rd Test)*

1983
Australia 49 v USA 3   Sydney Cricket Ground
Australia 3 v Argentina 18   Ballymore *(1st Test)*
Australia 29 v Argentina 13   Sydney Cricket Ground *(2nd Test)*
Australia 8 v New Zealand 18   Sydney Cricket Ground
Australia 29 v Italy 7   Padova
Australia 15 v France 15   Clermount Ferrand *(1st Test)*
Australia 6 v France 15   Paris *(2nd Test)*

1984
Australia 16 v Fiji 3   Government Stadium, Fiji
Australia 16 v New Zealand 9   Sydney Cricket Ground *(1st Test)*
Australia 15 v New Zealand 19   Ballymore *(2nd Test)*
Australia 24 v New Zealand 25   Sydney Cricket Ground *(3rd Test)*
Australia 19 v England 3   Twickenham
Australia 16 v Ireland 9   Landsdowne Road
Australia 28 v Wales 9   Cardiff Arms Park
Australia 37 v Scotland 12   Murrayfield

1985
Australia 59 v Canada 3   Sydney Cricket Ground *(1st Test)*
Australia 43 v Canada 15   Ballymore *(2nd Test)*
Australia 9 v New Zealand 10   Auckland
Australia 52 v Fiji 28   Ballymore *(1st Test)*
Australia 31 v Fiji 9   Sydney Cricket Ground *(2nd Test)*

1986
Australia 39 v Italy 18   Ballymore
Australia 27 v France 14   Sydney Cricket Ground
Australia 39 v Argentina 19   Ballymore *(1st Test)*
Australia 26 v Argentina 0   Sydney Cricket Ground *(2nd Test)*
Australia 13 v New Zealand 12   Wellington *(1st Test)*
Australia 12 v New Zealand 13   Dunedin *(2nd Test)*
Australia 22 v New Zealand 9   Auckland *(3rd Test)*

1987
Australia 65 v Korea 18   Ballymore
Australia 19 v England 6   Concord
Australia 42 v Japan 23   Concord
Australia 23 v Ireland 15   Concord
Australia 24 v France 30   Concord
Australia 21 v Wales 22   Rotorua
Australia 19 v Argentina 19   Buenos Aires

1988
Australia 7 v New Zealand 32   Concord *(1st Test)*
Australia 19 v New Zealand 19   Ballymore *(2nd Test)*
Australia 9 v New Zealand 30   Concord *(3rd Test)*

1989
Australia 12 v New Zealand 24   Eden Park

1991
Australia 40 v England 15   Sydney Football Stadium
Australia 21 v New Zealand 12   Sydney Football Stadium
Australia 3 v New Zealand 6   Auckland
Australia 32 v Argentina 19   Llanelli, Wales—1991 World Cup
Australia 38 v Wales 3   Cardiff Arms Park—1991 World Cup
Australia 19 v Ireland 18   Lansdowne Road—1991 World Cup
Australia 16 v New Zealand 6   Lansdowne Road—1991 World Cup
Australia 12 v England 6   Twickenham—1991 World Cup Final